ORGANIZATION⟷COMMUNICATION

EMERGING PERSPECTIVES IV

Organization⟨⟶⟩Communication
Emerging Perspectives IV

Lee Thayer, Editor
University of Wisconsin, Parkside

George A. Barnett, Editor
State University of New York at Buffalo

 ABLEX PUBLISHING CORPORATION
NORWOOD, NEW JERSEY

Library of Congress Cataloging-in-Publication Data
(Revised for volume 4)

Organization--communication.
  (People, communication, organization)
  Includes bibliographies and indexes.
  1. Organization.   2. Communication in organizations.
I. Thayer, Lee O.   II. Barnett, George A.
HD31.0727   1986   302.3'5   85-6159
ISBN 0-89391-274-3 (v. 1)
ISBN 0-89391-995-0 (v. 4)

Ablex Publishing Corporation
355 Chestnut Street
Norwood, New Jersey 07648

Contents

SE 09 '94

The Contributors

Margaret Hilton Bahniuk (EdD, University of Tennessee) is Professor of General Administration in the College of Business Administration at Cleveland State University. She is a co-author of two books.

George A. Barnett is Professor of Communication at the State University of New York at Buffalo. He is co-editor of the *Handbook of Organizational Communication* and the editor of *Process in Communication Science*. His research interests include the mathematical modeling of communication processes including organizational culture and communication networks.

Ernest G. Bormann (PhD, University of Iowa) is Professor of Speech Communication at the University of Minnesota, Minneapolis. He received the Woolbert Award for research projects that have stood the test of time and the distinguished service award from the Speech Communication Association.

Roger L. Cude is Assistant Professor in the Department of Communication at the University of Tulsa. His research interests focus on communication processes associated with organizational assimilation, including the manner in which newcomers become competent organizational communicators and how they adapt to various kinds of transitions, such as retirement from work.

James A. Danowski is Associate Professor of Communication at the University of Illinois-Chicago. His research activities include studying how organizational communication management, media, and messages affect people's meanings of corporate symbols and information, both among members of the organization and among external publics. He has developed computerized content analysis methods for quantifying qualitative information in messages and perceptions.

Jean Dobos (PhD, Ohio State University) is Associate Professor of Communication at Cleveland State University. She has published extensively in the fields of Communication and Urban Affairs.

Cornelia Freeman is a doctoral student at the State University of New York at Buffalo. She works as an internal organizational and management development consultant for Memorial Medical Center in Springfield, Il. Her research interests include organizational climate and culture, newcomer socialization, and corporate rhetoric.

Susan E. Kogler Hill (PhD, University of Denver) is Associate Professor of Communication and Director of Evening/Weekend Studies at

Cleveland State University. She is author of *Improving Interpersonal Competency: A Laboratory Approach*.

Ann House is Assistant Professor in the Department of Communication Arts and Sciences at Western Illinois University. Her research interests focus on language use and language perceptions in interpersonal interaction.

Frederic M. Jablin holds a dual appointment as Professor of Speech Communication and Management at the University of Texas at Austin. He is co-editor of the *Handbook of Organizational Communication: An Interdisciplinary Perspective*. His research examines various facets of leader-member communication, group problem solving, and organizational entry, assimilation and exit processes.

Susan H. Komsky is Director of Academic Technology and User Services at Western Washington University. She earned her PhD at the Annenberg School of Communication at the University of Southern California and was an Associate Professor of Speech Communication at California State University Northridge before assuming her present position.

Jaesub Lee is Assistant Professor in the Department of Communication Arts at the University of Alabama, Huntsville. He is interested in comparative organizational research, and in particular similarities and differences between organizational communication processes in Asian cultures (particularly Korea) and those in other parts of the world.

Steve May is at the Department of Speech Communication, University of North Carolina at Chapel Hill. His research interests include poststructuralism, cultural studies, and the relationships between private and public life, work and family, and labor and leisure.

Marshall Scott Poole is Professor of Speech Communication at the University of Minnesota, Minneapolis and Adjunct Professor in the Hubert H. Humphrey Institute for Public Policy. He has conducted research and published extensively on the topics of group communication, computer-mediated communication systems, conflict management, and organizational innovation. Scott is a principal co-investigator with the Minnesota Group Decision Support Systems Project.

Nancy L. Roth is Assistant Professor in the Department of Communication at Rutgers University. Her research interests center on qualitative approaches to organizational communication, and in particular how organizations communicate to their members about health-related issues.

John F. Stone (PhD, University of Minnesota) is Assistant Professor of organizational communication in the Department of Communication at the University of Wisconsin—Whitewater. When not teaching or pursing research interests, he works as an organizational development consultant.

Lee Thayer is Adjunct Professor of Communication at Clemson University, South Carolina.

Introduction

George A. Barnett
Lee Thayer

Over the last decade two intertwined perspectives have emerged as central in the study of organizational communication. They include the study of organizational culture (Barnett, 1988; Putnam & Pacanowsky, 1983), typically using the cultural studies approach for the analysis of organizational activities (Pacanowsky & O'Donnell-Trujillo, 1982, 1983), and the study of language in the context of formal organizations (Eisenberg & Riley, 1988). The essays and research reported in this volume represent the continued thrust of this foci.

Generally, *culture* is defined as a "historically created system of explicit and implicit designs for living, which tends to be shared by all or specially designated members of a group at specific point in time" (Kluckhohn & Kelly, 1945, p. 98). Culture consists of the habits and tendencies to act in certain ways. However, it is not the actions or products or these behaviors themselves that constitute culture. Culture exists at the cognitive level. It is the "forms of things that people have in their minds, their models for perceiving, relating and otherwise interpreting them" (Goodenough, 1964, p. 36). Typically, the values, feelings, and meanings are expressed in a society's language. Thus, culture may be treated as an ordered system of meanings, expressed through symbols during the process of social interaction. As Geertz (1973, p. 89) wrote:

> [Culture is] an historically transmitted pattern of meanings embodied in symbols, a system of inherited conceptions expressed in symbolic form by means of which men communicate, perpetuate and develop their knowledge about the attitudes toward life.

Culture is not a property of the individual. Rather, it is a socially shared expression and therefore a property of social groups (such as organizations) rather than individuals. Culture is normative and may best be represented by a measure of a central tendency of the group mind (Durkheim, 1938). These collective representations are formed during the process of social interaction. As members of social groups communicate, they negotiate the shared meanings of symbols. As such, culture is an emergent property of the communication of the members of a group. Communication as a shared symbolic process creates, gives rise to, and sustains the collective group consciousness (Bormann, 1983).

On the other hand, culture determines how group members communicate. The meanings that are attributed to verbal symbols and nonverbal behavior are determined by the social group as a whole. Culture may be thought of as a consensus about the meaning of symbols held by the members of the populace. This consensus is necessary for encoding and decoding messages. Without general agreement about the meaning of symbols and other communication rules, social interaction and the coordination of goal-seeking activities would be impossible.

As new members are socialized into a collectivity, they acquire its culture. The process of socialization is made possible by individuals expressing and interpreting symbols—stimuli that are culturally defined with generally recognized conventions of meaning (Becker, 1961, 1970; Glaser, 1968; Strauss & Rainwater, 1962). Individuals are transformed into group members during the process of social interaction with other members of the group. It is through common social activities that new members learn the meanings of the groups symbols and the generalized set of attitudes, values, and beliefs common to members of a social organization (Barnett & Carson, 1983). These make it possible to coordinate their activities.

The circular causal relationship between communication, the exchange of symbols, and culture has led scholars to define culture as a communication phenomenon. Gudykunst and Kim (1984, p. 11), for example, defined culture as "that relatively unified set of shared symbolic ideas associated with societal patterns of cultural ordering." One such cultural ordering is society's formal organizations. Pacanowsky and O'Donnell-Trujillo (1982) defined organizational culture in terms of the communication activities of social groups.

Organizational culture may be defined as "the system of such publicly and collectively accepted meanings operating for a given group at a given time" (Pettigrew, 1979, p. 574). This includes the amalgam of beliefs, ideology, language, ritual, and myth. It also includes the members' attitudes and values, the management style, and problem-solving and decision-making behaviors of an organization. Yet, it is not the overt behavior or artifacts of the company. "Rather, it is the assumptions that underlie the values and determine not only behavior patterns, but also such visible artifacts as architecture, office layout, dress codes, and so on" (Schein, 1983, p. 14).

According to Bormann (1983), the important components of organizational culture include the shared norms, reminiscences, stories, rites, and rituals that provide the members with a unique symbolic common foundation. An organization's culture includes its self-definition, consisting of the unique constraints, for identifying the collectivity, as well as the members' particular beliefs and goals that make up their self-image (Harris & Cronen, 1979). Organizational culture is influenced by the culture of the environment, society as a whole, but it is more narrowly defined (Chikudate, Barnett, & McFarland, 1990). There is less variance in the range of acceptable attitudes, values, and behaviors, and less tolerance for deviance. In part, it is this restricted range that sets an organization's culture apart from society's.

The chapters in this volume all contribute to our understanding of the role of language and culture in organizational life. The first essay (Chapter 1), "The Modernist Monologue in Organizational Communication Research: The Text, The Subject, and the Audience," by Steve May, describes the current state of organizational communication theory and research and suggests that the field should be more self-reflexive in the future. He argues that if the study of communication in the context of formal organizations is to move beyond the modernist perspective and its logical positivist paradigm, we must examine three topics—text, subject, and audience. In doing so we can avoid management bias, the emphasis on prediction and control, and the metaphor of the organization as a purposive goal-seeking machine in which communication is viewed as a tool for the privileged to manipulate.

May views *text* as the object of study: It is that to be interpreted by an audience. The study of text focuses on the meanings that are fixated in the text. They are representative of a unified symbolic structure within a specific context—the social organization. The *subject* is a cultural construction with social, political, economic, and ideological components. Representational practices specify meanings and produce subjects. The subject can only be constructed, represented, and understood in language and discourse. Like culture, subject is independent of the individual. Traditionally, organizational communication has focused on individuals. May suggests that it should focus instead on subjects (cultural or symbolic entities) that are historically constituted, socially situated representations that change over time. The third area of focus is the *audience*, the consumers of the text. May suggests that we should study their interpretations (responses) to the cultural constructions—the subjects of the text.

Semiotics is the science of equating "signs" or "system of signs" with the social production of meaning. At the center of semiotics is the concept of the *sign* or *expression*. An expression must have a physical form and must refer to something other than itself. Also, it must be recognized as a sign by those who use it. Signification occurs as a sign begins to carry a *content*, or *particular meaning*, for the communities (organizations) that share the sign. Semiotics is rarely concerned with the single expression. Rather, it focuses on series of expressions and contents that together compose a particular *code* or *language*. Ultimately, codes make systems of meaning possible within a given community.

When applied to the study of organizations it has afforded communication scholars great flexibility and precision in identifying and interpreting codes of meaning shared among organizational members. John Stone ("Examining the Praxis, Assessing the Pitfalls, and Enhancing the Potential of Semiotics in Interpretative Organizational Research"— Chapter 2) focuses on the use of semiotic theory to examine research in four areas of organizational research: cultural studies, information-processing studies, rhetorical studies, and political studies. From this analysis emerges a discussion of the specific shortcomings of semiotic research, a number of proposed changes to the current semiotic frame, and speculation regarding what such changes might tell us about symbol use in organizations.

Ernest G. Bormann's "The Symbolic Convergence Theory of Communication and Organizational Culture" (Chapter 3) focuses on organizational culture—the sum total of ways of living, organizing, and communicating built up in a group of human beings and transmitted to newcomers by means of verbal and nonverbal communication. Bormann, however, goes beyond this limited notion of organizational culture and departs from current thinking by using a different locus of investigation. Rather than viewing organizational culture as a homogeneous monolith, he suggests that organizations exhibit complex symbolic geographies composed of smaller "conglomerates of consciousness." These generally arise out of the interactions of small task groups that come together to complete some organizational function. Through the process of communicating on the job, the members of task groups create a sense of history and cohesiveness leading to separate small group cultures. An organization's small group cultures may exist in a state of greater or lesser harmony with others throughout the organization. The symbolic geographies provide the basis of an explanation of communication practices and organizational successes and failures, as well as a tool for consultants to engage in organizational development practices.

Bormann's essay suggests an underlying structural or network model of organizational communication (Farace, Monge, & Russell, 1977; Monge & Eisenberg, 1988; Rogers & Agarwala-Rogers, 1976; Wigand, 1988). Individuals intercommunicate and small groups emerge out of these regular patterns of interactions. These groups tend to have uniform attitudes, values, and beliefs (Danowski, 1980) and even use language in the same way. Communication links among the small groups develop due to the formal and informal relations within the organization. Typically, the structural relations are examined through network analysis (Richards & Barnett, 1993). In an attempt to merge the symbolic and structural perspectives, an approach to network analysis has emerged which differentiates the members of a network based on their common use of symbols (Monge & Eisenberg, 1988). An example of its application is provided in this volume by Danowski (Chapter 7).

Cornelia Freeman and George Barnett (Chapter 4) propose the use of network analysis for the examination of organizational messages. They provide an alternative approach to the interpretive method for the examination of content of the texts produced by organizations. Institutional theory (Scott, 1987) suggests that it is the meaning of these texts that constitutes organizational culture. Freeman and Barnett propose using computer-based content analysis to examine organizational texts, although the method may be extended to all verbal data, including everyday language in the workplace and informant interviews that have been traditionally analyzed with interpretive methods. By objectifying the examination of culture they hope to avoid the problems of radical subjectivity that leads to problems of evidence and a variety of idiosyncratic methodologies, which result in value judgments and all sorts of observer bias (Wuthnow, 1987), the outcome of that is vague theory.

Freeman and Barnett provide an empirical example in which a sample of organizational text is content analyzed. The first step in the process is simply a frequency count of the occurrence of individual words or symbols. Next, the text is network analyzed using the same procedures as organizational scholars currently use to examine information flows.

After noise words (conjunctions and prepositions) have been removed, a co-occurrence matrix of words is created. Words are considered to co-occur (to be linked) if they appear in the same grammatical units (sentence or paragraph) or if they occur within a predetermined number of words in the text. The co-occurence matrix is then analyzed using graph theory, spatial modeling, or cluster analysis. The software required to perform these procedures includes Joseph Woelfel's CAT-PAC (Woelfel & Jacobson, 1992) and James Danowski's NETIMAGE (Danowski, 1986, 1990).

One component of an organization's culture is its climate. Specifically, according to Marshall Scott Poole;

> [Climate is] a relatively enduring quality of the environment that is experienced and perceived by individuals; influences individual interpretations and actions; and can be described in terms of a particular set of characteristics which describe system practices, procedures, and tendencies.

In "The Structuring of Organizational Climate" (Chapter 5), Poole indicates that neither objective nor subjective interpretations of organizational climate is adequate. Rather, climate as an aspect of culture is an intersubjective social construction that can only be understood in terms of the processes that create and reproduce shared perspectives. To examine these processes, Poole proposes a model of the structuration of organizational climates.

Structuration refers to the production and reproduction of social systems via actors' application of generative rules and resources. Systems are taken to be observable "regularized relations of interdependence of individuals and groups" (Giddens, 1979, p. 66), such as formal organizations. Structures are rules and resources used in the production and reproduction of systems, including language, organizational norms, money, and knowledge. The central assumption of the theory of structuration is that structures have dual natures. They are both the media and outcomes of action.

Poole suggests that climate is a structure underlying organizational systems. As a set of generalized beliefs and expectations about system practices, procedures, and tendencies, climate can be construed as a structure of rules and knowledge resources. And as generalized knowledge structures, climates serve as common frames of reference for member activities. They enable members to create order in the workplace, to adopt to novel situations, to understand others, and to organize and coordinate their activities.

Fred Jablin, Roger Cude, Ann House, Jaesub Lee, and Nancy Roth examine the concept of communication competence in organizations in Chapter 6. Typically, the concept of communication competence in organizational research has focused on the communication skills of individuals within the organization. They suggest that this research is problematic because it does not take into account a variety of unique attributes of the organizational context. In particular, communication competence within organizations must consider an individual's understanding of the organization's culture.

It is the culture or the system's shared knowledge that serves as the standard by which communication competence is evaluated (Schein, 1985). After all, organizations develop idiosyncratic languages (Barnett, 1988) that are shared by the members of the organization and learned in the socialization process. These unique code systems are used to share common task and social experiences. As communication produces more shared assumptions and multiple layers of meaning, a group may then develop more interaction flexibility and adaptiveness, which would enhance its communication competence. In other words, organizations may develop high-context cultures in which most communication is implied by the setting or organizational context (Hall, 1977).

Jablin and colleagues also point out that existing research has considered the notion of communication competence only at the individual level and has not explored competence at the group and organizational levels. They suggest that future research in this area considers higher levels of analysis—the group and organizational levels.

In "An Emerging Macrolevel Theory of Organizational Communication: Organizations as Virtual Reality Management Systems" (Chapter 7), James Danowski takes off where Jablin, et al. leave off. He discusses the relative success or competence of organizations by how they develop and manage their cultures through the process of signification. Signification is the process of creating signs and symbols. Organizations seek to control their internal and external environment uncertainties by the management of meaning. Differences in these meanings have social, and perhaps more importantly, economic consequences for organizations. This chapter is significant because it describes the process that organizations engage in to facilitate intersubjectivity of its members and publics. It provides an additional theoretical justification for the examination of organization-produced messages suggested by Freeman and Barnett in Chapter 4. Also, it represents an initial attempt to integrate contemporary media technology theory with the emerging perspective in organizational communication theory.

Because of organizational size, diversification, and spatial dispersion, control of the signification process may be accomplished through the use of a variety of time- and space-shifted media. Danowski discusses the differences in media richness between time-shifted and space-shifted media. He argues that asynchronous communication technologies (time-shifted media) are more effective in decontextualizing the communication process. This facilitates an organization in signifying more abstract meanings and thus creating stronger, more uniform, less ambiguous organizational cultures in which individuals have a greater sense of system identity.

Danowski then goes on to relate semantic networks—the meaning structures that emerge from the signification process—to the communication (information flows) structure, suggesting that an individual's interpretations are dependent on their positon in the communication structure. He concludes that signification and meaning by themselves are not sufficient to understand mediation. One must also know the source and medium of the messages.

Susan Komsky, in "Electronic Mail and Democratization of Organizational Communication" (Chapter 8), discusses the potential changes in organizational culture that might occur as a function of altering a system's channels of communication. Theoretically, new organizational media such as electronic mail, will change interaction patterns, resulting in the dissolution of traditional hierarchical structures. This will occur because these media facilitate entry into the communication process while reducing the social and contextual (cultural) cues that convey and reinforce the existing social structure and act as barriers to communication.

To gain some perspective on the future, Komsky conducted open-ended interviews with 43 regular users of electronic mail at a western university and found that perceptions of democratization differ according to their positions in the organization hierarchy. Only the lowest status group thought that electronic mail facilitated democracy in the organization. Further, she found that the organization's traditional cultural norms and the political and status rules constrain opportunities to communicate, dictating who can interact with whom, and about what topics they can communicate, even when communicating via electronic mail.

The final chapter (Chapter 9) in this volume is by Susan Kogler Hill, Margaret Hilton Bahniuk, and Jean Dobos. In "A Model of Mentoring and Other Power-Gaining Communication Strategies and Career Success," they develop a model that focuses on one aspect of organizational culture—power in the organization and the role of communication. Communication strategies are proposed that will enhance an individual's work and career achievements. The model includes two sets of predisposing components that might influence career success: individual factors, including gender, education, career length, and power orientation; and organizational factors, such as life-cycle stage. In addition to these predisposing factors, the model includes two sets of communication strategies: (a) those concerned with connections (structural relations), and (b) those that emphasize the possession of information. In the model, the predisposing factors interact with the communication strategies to determine an individual's level of career success. They suggest that if communication strategies facilitate a person's success and these strategies can be learned, then people can take more control of their jobs and careers and attain organizational power, thus altering organizational culture.

In summary, all of the chapters in this volume provide differing perspectives which add to our understanding of the emerging cultural perspective of organizational communication. Some are methodological, suggesting different ways of coming to understand organizational processes and cultural manifestations (e.g., May, Stone, Bormann, and Freeman and Barnett). Others provide abstract theoretical prospective that facilitate the intergration of structural information and knowledge from other subdisciplines of communication (Poole, Danowski, and Jablin, et al.). Finally, others focus on specific changing taking place in organizations today and how these changes impact on organizational cultural (Komsky, and Dobos, et al.).

REFERENCES

Barnett, G.A. (1988). Communication and organizational culture. In G.M. Goldhaber & G.A. Barnett (Eds.), *Handbook of organizational communication*. Norwood, NJ: Ablex.

Barnett, G.A., & Carson, D.L. (1983, May). *The role of communication in the professional socialization process*. Paper presented at the annual meeting of the International Communication Association, Dallas.

Becker, H.S. (1961). *Boys in white*. Chicago: University of Chicago.

Becker, H.S. (1970). *Sociological work: Methods and substance*. Chicago: Aldine.

Bormann, E.G. (1983). Symbolic convergence: Organizational communication and culture. In L. Putnam & M. Pacanowsky (Eds.), *Communication and organizations: An interpretive approach*. Beverly Hills, CA: Sage.

Chikudate, N., Barnett, G.A., & McFarland, S.D. (1990, June). *A cross-cultural examination of organizational culture: A comparison of Japan and the United States*. Paper presented to the International Communication Association, Dublin, Ireland.

Danowski, J.A. (1980). Group attitude-belief uniformity and connectivity of organizational communication networks for production, innovation and maintenance content. *Human Communication Research, 6*, 299–308.

Danowski, J. (1986, May). *Linking who-to-whom communication networks and message content networks in electronic mail: An automated word-network analysis over time*. Paper presented at the annual meetings of the International Communication Association, Chicago.

Danowski, J. (1990, June). *Semantic networks, message value, and optimal message creation*. Paper presented at the annual meetings of the International Communication Association, Dublin, Ireland.

Durkheim, E. (1938). *The rules of sociological method* (2nd ed.) (S.A. Sulovay & J.H. Mueller, Trans.; G.C. Catlin, Ed.). Glencoe, IL: Free Press.

Eisenberg, E.M., & Riley P. (1988). Organizational symbols and sense-making. In G.M. Goldhaber & G.A. Barnett (Eds.), *Handbook of organizational communication*. Norwood, NJ: Ablex.

Farace, R.V., Monge, P.R., & Russell, H. (1977). *Communicating and organizing*. Reading, MA: Addison-Westley.

Geertz, C. (1973). *The interpretation of cultures*. New York: Basic Books.

Giddens, A. (1979). *Central problems in social theory*. Berkeley: University of California Press.

Glaser, B.G. (1968). *Organizational careers: A sourcebook for theory*. Chicago: Aldine.

Goodenough, W.H. (1964). Cultural anthropology and linguistics. In D. Hymes (Ed.), *Language in culture and society*. New York: Harper and Row.

Gudykunst, W.B., & Kim, Y.Y. (1984). *Communication with strangers: An approach to intercultural communication*. Reading, MA: Addison-Wesley.

Hall, E.T. (1977). *Beyond culture*. Garden City, NY: Anchor.

Harris, L., & Cronen, V.E. (1979). A rules-based model for the analysis and evaluation of organizational communication. *Communication Quarterly, 27*, 12–28.

Kluckhohn, C., & Kelly, W.H. (1945). The concept of culture. In R. Linton (Ed.), *The science of man in the world crisis*. New York: Columbia University Press.

Monge, P.R., & Eisenberg, E.M. (1988). Emergent communication networks. In F. Jablin, L. Putnam, K. Roberts, & L. Porter (Eds.), *Handbook of organizational and management communication*. Newbury Park, CA: Sage.

Pacanowsky, M. E., & O'Donnell-Trujillo, N. (1982). Communication and organizational cultures. *Western Journal of Speech Communication, 46*, 115–130.

Pacanowsky, M.E., & O'Donnell-Trujillo, N. (1983). Organizational communication as cultural performances. *Communication Monographs, 50*, 26–147.

Pettigrew, P.M. (1979). On studying organizational culture. *Administrative Science Quarterly*, *24*, 570–581.

Putnam, L., & Pacanowsky, M.E. (Eds.). (1983). *Communication and organizations: An interpretive approach*. Beverly Hills, CA: Sage.

Richards, W.D., & Barnett, G.A. (1993). *Progress in communication science* (vol. 12). Norwood, NJ: Ablex.

Rogers, E.M., & Agarwala-Rogers, R. (1976). *Communication in organizations*. New York: Free Press.

Schein, E.H. (1983). The role of the founder in creating organizational culture. *Organizational Dynamics, 12*, 13–28.

Schein, E.H. (1985). *Organizational culture and leadership*. San Francisco: Jossey-Bass.

Scott, W.R. (1987). The adolescence of institutional theory. *Administrative Science Quarterly*, *32*, 493–511.

Strauss, A.L., & Rainwater, L. (1962). *The professional scientist: A study of American chemists*. Chicago: Aldine.

Wigand, R.T. (1988). Communication network analysis: History and overview. In G.M. Goldhaber & G.A. Barnett (Eds.), *Handbook of organizational communication*. Norwood, NJ: Ablex.

Woelfel, J., & Jacobson, T.L. (1992, February). *CATPAC: An artificial neural network for the analysis of text*. Paper at the annual meetings of the Sunbelt Social Networks Conference, San Diego.

Wuthnow, R. (1987). *Meaning and moral order: Explorations in cultural analysis*. Berkeley: University of California Press.

1

The Modernist Monologue in Organizational Communication Research: The Text, the Subject, and the Audience*

Steve May

> The stupidity of people comes from having an answer for everything.
> The wisdom of the novel comes from having a question for everything. . . .
> The novelist teaches the reader to comprehend the world as a question.
> There is wisdom and tolerance in that attitude.
> —Milan Kundera

As an émigré from Czechoslovakia who endured the February 1948 takeover of Prague and later saw all his books removed from public libraries in the Russian invasion of 1968, Kundera aptly summarizes his concern with modernist culture. For him, both personally and politically, a world built on sacrosanct certainties—totalitarianism—is a world of answers rather than questions. The cultural strategy which produced such totalitarianism is what Kundea refers to as "organized forgetting," in which Czech literature has not been published for 20 years, 200 Czech writers have been proscribed (including the death of Franz Kafka), 145 Czech historians have been dismissed from their positions, and culture has been restructured and represented (Kundera, 1981). In Kundera's terms, "this is the great private problem of man: death as a loss of the self. But what is this self? It is the sum of everything we remember. Thus, what terrifies us about death is not the loss of the future, but the loss of the past. Forgetting is a form of death ever present within life" (p. 234).

---

* Paper presented at the International Communication Association Annual Conference, San Francisco, CA., May 1989.

It is a similar strategy of "organized forgetting" which presently pervades the area of organizational communication. While some authors argue that "modernism is dominant but dead" and, consequently, postmodernism in organizational communication has arrived (Smirchich & Calas, 1986; Tompkins, 1986), I suggest that such statements neglect the strength of modernist assumptions in the discipline. To state, at a theoretical level, that postmoderism is alive and well among us does not preclude the daily practices and conditions—the traces—inherent in modernism which are powerfully present. To transcend modernism conceptually (although significant) does not necessarily indicate that we have transcended modernism either materially or practically. As Jameson (1983) notes, radical breaks within periods "do not generally involve complete changes of content but rather the *restructuration* of a certain number of elements already given: features that in an earlier period or system were subordinate now become dominant, and features that had been dominant again become secondary" (p. 123).

In order to recognize this restructuring process, Redding and Tompkins (1988) outline the basic conceptual assumptions of modernist organizational communication research as follows:

- Goal—prediction and control
- Ontology—objective reality as given
- Epistemology—logical positivism
- Form of knowledge claim—nomothetic
- Perspective—management
- Rationality—privileged
- Causality—manipulative
- Levels/boundaries—differentiated
- Root metaphor—machine
- Organizations—purposive, goal-seeking
- Communication—tool

From this conceptualization, "organizational research can only provide us with *what-is*, but seldom *what-might-be*" (Tompkins, 1986, p. 4) The project of modernity, then, is to institutionalize the "what-is" so that "each domain of culture could be made to correspond to cultural professions in which problems could be dealt with as the concern of special experts" (Habermas, 1983, p. 9). As a result, a burgeoning gap develops and separates the culture of institutionalized experts from the culture of the general public; a public, ironically, institutionalized to accept the logic of reifying the "knowledge of truth." Such a "politics of truth" (Grossberg, 1983) conceals the potential "insurrection of subjugated knowledges" (Foucault, 1980, p. 81). These subjugated knowledges are

The historical contents that have been buried and disguised in a functionalist coherence or formal systemization. . .as well as a whole set of knowledges that have been disqualified as inadequate: naïve knowledges, located low down on the hierarchy, beneath the required level of cognition or scientificity. (Foucault, 1980, p. 81)

It is in the area of this popular knowledge that organizational communication research should begin to perform its task.

To do so, however, requires researchers to ask themselves the "what-might-be" questions, not only conceptually, but at the level of concrete research practices as well. In this sense, organizational communication, in response to other areas in the discipline, has begun to suffer from a "modern moment." It is a moment of crisis in which it becomes self-conscious as a period (Foster, 1983). Postmodernism in organizational communication, then, presents itself as anti-modernity. It is, for Jameson (1983), "a periodizing concept whose function is to correlate the emergence of a new type of social life and a new economic order" (p. 113). But since postmodernism is a reaction against various forms of modernity, there are likely to be as many forms of postmodernisms as there were modernisms.

Presently, at least two forms of postmodernism have developed support: "a postmodernism which seeks to deconstruct modernism and resist the status quo and a postmodernism which repudiates the former to celebrate the latter; a postmodernism of resistance and a postmodernism of reaction" (Foster, 1983, p. xii). While a postmodernism of reaction critiques the practices of modernism, the result is a return to the economic and political status quo. An "affirmative" culture is proposed which appears surprisingly similar to the old culture. Reactionary postmodernism most clearly resemble authors in organizational communication whose "organized forgetting" of past difficulties is clouded within discussions of the future (see Smirchich & Calas, 1986). Discussions of the future direction of organizational communication, absent of critical reflection of the past, paradoxically return us to the practices we initially strove to transcend.

A postmodern strategy of resistance, on the other hand, intends to "deconstruct modernism not in order to seal it in its own image but in order to open it, to rewrite it" (Foster, 1983, p. xi). As Kundera summarizes in his novel *The Book of Laughter and Forgetting* (1981), there is both wisdom and tolerance in resisting answers in exchange for addressing questions. As a form of resistance, or "interference" (Said, 1983), this essay attempts to question rather than answer the claim that organizational communication has reached a state of postmodernism. So rather than argue that organizational communication is presently "postmodern" and leave it at that, I prefer to pose the following question: To what extent is organizational communication postmodern and what might postmodern practices look like? The former approaches relies on hope, absent of critical assessment, while the latter combines both hope and reflexivity. More specifically, this essay addresses three issues crucial to the future of organizational communication: textuality, the subject, and the audience. Given these three areas of concern, I initiate the following question:

- What is the text?
- What is the subject of study?
- For whom are the texts written?

THE TEXT

> If you want to understand what a science is, you should look in the first instance not at its theories or its findings, and certainly not at what its apologists say about it; you should look at what the practitioners of it do.
> —Clifford Geertz

The notion of what constitutes a text, the representation of the object of study, has emerged as a significant issue in the realm of aesthetics, literary criticism, mass communication, and, presently, organizational communication. For Geertz (1983), the metaphor of text, although a "dangerously unfocused term," holds much promise for the study of social phenomena:

> The great virtue of the extension of the notion of text beyond things written on paper or carved into stone is that it trains attention on precisely this phenomena: on how the inscription of action is brought about, what its vehicles are, and how they work, and on what the fixation of meaning from the flow of events-behavior-implies for sociological interpretation. (p. 31)

For Cheney and Tompkins (1988) in "On the Facts of 'Text' as the Basis for Human Communication Research," the concept of text becomes more focused when viewed with five "identifiable but interrelated meanings" (see also Belsey, 1980): life-as-text, text-to-be-interpreted, text-to-be-read, text-to-be-comprehended, and text-to-be-constructed (p. 8).

The first meaning, life-as-text, is the reemergence and reinterpretation of Nietzsche's view of being as text. "Being is similar to a text that requires our exegesis, as task complicated by the fact that the text is obscure, often full of gaps, by the fact that several 'readings' are possible and that certain fragments even remain undeciphered" (Granier, 1985, p. 192). The second view, text-to-be-interpreted, develops out of the hermeneutic tradition, advocated most strongly by Ricoeur (1979; see also Schrag, 1980). Directed toward multiple "readings" of social praxis, Ricouer is most concerned about "the process of inscription by which meanings become 'fixated' in writing" (Cheney & Tompkins, 1988, p. 4). Ricouer (1979) states that

> Meaningful action is an object for science only under the condition of a kind of objectification which is equivalent to the fixation of a discourse of writing. . . In the same way that interlocution is overcome in writing, interaction is overcome in numerous situations in which we treat action as a fixed text. (p. 80)

The text-to-be-read approach, advocated by Mauss, suggests that "reading" is the primary task of the social researcher, with direct attention towards a goal of interpretation of social phenomena.

> When we speak of *reading* a text, instead of *observing*, this reflects and implicit understanding that it is not the words as physical entities that is important but their meanings. . . .The social fact is no longer an obdurate, concrete reality; instead it has become explicitly symbolic; it is a web, or language, of symbols with its own particular grammar and syntax, morphemes, and phonemes. (Brown, 1978, p. 150)

The fourth perspective, text-to-be-comprehended, is consistent with views of behavior as "scripted," as seen in discourse-processing studies in psychology (Schank & Abelson, 1977) and later in interpersonal communication. Here, the text is an object to be comprehended in the routinized, patterned responses to communicative contexts. "A 'script' is then a 'standard event sequence,' a key structure through which the 'text' is understood" (Cheney & Tompkins, 1988, p. 7).

In response to these notions of text and textuality, Cheney and Tompkins argue for Burkean indexing as an alternative perspective for the interpretation and analysis of texts. But for Cheney and Tompkins the process of constructing a research text itself is not a significant issue, and their argument "rests soundly on a positivistic understanding of what facts and texts are" (Strine, 1988, p. 381). Cheney and Tompkins suggest that the communication research text is a "unified symbolic structure" which can be regarded as a motive. Therefore, the presupposition of a final product, the research report, communicated to colleagues in the discipline constrains the creation of the text. "To imagine the end-point of research as a text is to constrain or force one to *conduct* research in such a way, and only that way, so as to reduce all facts, inferences, and proofs to the product of a research report" (Cheney & Tompkins, 1988, p. 12). Unfortunately, such distancing from the process of inquiry further contributes to the modernist emphasis upon answering or responding to the "facts" before the important questions have been raised. For Cheney and Tompkins, the process of inquiry is "fixed" or "located" (answered) by its product:

> To contribute to science one must publish a text qua journal article. There is no other way; there is nothing outside of such a text. . . .Nothing can be studied, no manipulations performed, no results can be gathered, no conclusions can be reached, without the possibility of transcendence into a text. To put it another way, the need to realize a text is a limiting factor *prior* to the conduct of research. (p. 12).

In order to reconsider the potential for how social praxis is represented in texts, such a positivistic and unreciprocal manner of research interpretation should be called to account. The authority of the researcher in such cases is called into question since

> neither the experience nor the activity of the scientific researcher can be considered innocent. It becomes necessary to conceive [research], not as the experience and interpretation of a circumscribed 'other' reality, but rather as a constructive negotiation of involving at least two, and usually more, conscious, politically significant subjects. (Clifford, 1983, p. 133)

According the Ulmer (1983), the strategies of Western philosophy to "try to pin down a specific signified to a given signifier violates. . .the nature of language, which functions not in terms of matched pairs (signifier/signified) but of *couplers* or *couplings*" (p. 89).

Contrary to the notion of a priori and fixed texts, Derrida (1977), for instance, prefers to discuss the "iterability" of texts. Every text has the

> possibility of disengagement and citational graft. . .the possibility of its own functioning being cut off, at a certain point, from its 'original' desire-to-say-what-one-means and from its participation in a saturable and constraining context. Every sign, linguistic or otherwise, spoken or unwritten (in the current sense of this opposition), in a small or large unit, can be *cited*, put between quotation marks; in doing so it can break with every given context, engendering an infinity of new contexts in a manner which is absolutely illimitable. (p. 185)

The text, in this sense, is a "procession" both through space and time, which produces the breakdown of the relationship between signifiers. Jameson (1983) states that as meaning is lost in the breakdown of signifiers (as characterized by schizophrenia), "the materiality of words becomes obsessive" (p. 120). Not surprisingly, then, we see the paradox of Tompkins (1986) applauding the future of postmodernism in organizational communication research, while later construing the text as "a factual territory" (Cheney & Tompkins, 1988, p. 18). As Hall (1980) importantly notes, such a practice represents ideology at work; it is the power of a particular system to represent its own representations as a direct reflection of the real and to produce its own meanings as experience. It is a question of signifying *practice* and *representation* (Grossberg, 1984). In short, the organizational texts we produce "represent" the discursive space of our modernity.

To rethink the means of textualizing the object of study in organizational communication requires a critical reflexivity of institutionalized forms of representation and explanation (Clifford, 1986); a "politics of textuality" for Grossberg (1984). For the purposes of this essay, it is beneficial to utilize the fifth category of textuality proposed by Cheney and Tompkins, the text-to-be-constructed and, more specifically, Barthes's "From Work to Text" (1979). According to Barthes, developments in the conception of language in linguistics, anthropology, Marxism, and psychoanalysis have necessitated an opposition to the notion of work (as typified by Cheney & Tompkins). Barthes's (1979) propositions are enunciated by comparing and contrasting works and texts on seven dimensions: method, genre, sign, plural, filiation, reading, and pleasure.

1. *Method* (of construal): The work is concrete, is displayed, and may be held in the hand, while the text is "a methodological field" which is held as language. The text "exists only as discourse," and, as such, "is experienced only in an activity, a production" (p. 75).
2. *Genre*: The work is apprehended as part of a hierarchy or as a division of genres (i.e., the research report), while the text problematizes classification and is paradoxical; the "text is that which goes to the limit of the rules of enunciation" (p. 75).
3. *Sign*: The work closes its meaning as a signified, while the text is approached and understood in relation to the sign. "The work (in the best of cases) is moderately symbolic (its symbolism runs out, comes to a halt), but the text is *radically* symbolic. A work whose integrally symbolic nature one conceives, perceives, and receives is a text" (p. 76).
4. *Plural*: The work is monistic while the text is plural. The text achieves an irreducible plurality of meaning characterized by "an explosion, a dissemination." "The Text is not coexistence of meanings but passage, traversal." Consequently, every text being itself the intertext of another (i.e., within a research tradition), belongs to the intertextual, which must not be confused with the text's origins; "to search for the 'sources of' and 'influences upon' a work is to satisfy the myth of filiation" (p. 77).
5. *Filiation*: The work is situated in a process of filiation.

It is a *determination* by the outside world, it is a *consecution* of works among themselves, and it is allocation of the work to its author. The work grants authority (respect) to the author, as it is treated as the author's 'right' to his/her declared intentions. The Text, on the other hand, has no 'paternal father' and the respect for it can be broken; the I that writes the text is never, itself, anything more than a paper I. (p. 78)

Therefore, the author can return to the text only as a guest.

6. *Reading*: The work is an object of consumption, while the text is "play," production, and activity. Because the work reduces reading to consumption, boredom is inevitable as the reader "cannot produce the text, play it, open it out, make it go." The text, on the other hand, calls for the reader to actively collaborate. Here, the reader is a "coauthor of a score which he completes rather than 'interprets' " (p. 80).

7. *Pleasure*: The pleasure of the work is in the consumption of it, which means the reader cannot rewrite it and, thus, "separates one from the production of those works." The pleasure of the text, however, is linked to the enjoyment or pleasure of reading without separation form the "author." "It is the space in which no one language has hold over any other, in which all languages circulate freely" (p. 80).

Reconceptualizing the research report in terms of a text instead of a work reminds the researcher that systems of representation are "the codes of intelligibility, the formats for experiencing the material conditions of everyday life. These systems represent and mediate the immediate conditions of existence" (Hawes, 1988, p. 5). It is impossible to experience or "report" organizational life immediately; therefore, all practices of representation are ideological (but are nothing but ideology). Both representation and explanation by the researcher and the researched are implicated in this process. But with the researcher lies the ethical responsibility to recognize that "the specification of discourses is thus more than a matter of making carefully limited truth claims. It must be thoroughly historicist and self-reflexive" (Clifford & Marcus, 1986, p. 19). It is then contended that the research report is not the only form of "text" which can adequately display or represent organizational life; nor is it even the most useful in some instances. The area of organizational communication must begin to develop and grant authority to novel systems of representation which are responsive to the multiple voices of organizational members as well as the polysemic modes of interpretation used by readers. At present, the author of organizational texts is celebrated at the expense of those we purport to study. New forms of representation will allow responsibility to fall to the reader who functions as "an orchestrator of open dialogic interaction among multiple textual voices in concert" (Strine & Pacanowsky, 1985, p. 297). These representations will not be texts-to-be-read but, rather, will be texts-to-be-constructed.

THE SUBJECT

A postmodernism of resistance in organizational communication requires acknowledging not only the text-to-be-constructed as an ideological representation, but also recognizing the subject-to-be-constructed as a social and political configuration as well. The question here is: Who/what is the subject of study in organizational communication? By subject I do not mean topics or concepts (although we often examine these rather than humans), or even historical individuals. The subject in this case is, instead, a social, political, economic, and ideological construction constituted in and through systems of representation; in this instance, the research report. These representational practices close off meanings and produce subjects as their supports. "It is meaning, as closure, that delimits and fixes the individual as a subject of and for discourse" (Hawes, 1988, p. 5). In organizational research, as in all other forms of knowledge production, ideas (i.e., conceptualizing the research project) materialize in concrete *practices* which are themselves defined by ideological apparatuses (Althusser, 1971, p. 170). The creation of the subject in research, then, is inherently politicized; "the work of ideology is the production of the continuity of the unitary ego as subject, by closing off the inherent openness of discourse and its contradictions, ideology produces the experience of meaning and of the singularity of the subject" (Hawes, 1988, p. 5). The subject can only be constructed, represented, and understood in language and in discourse.

Consequently, the subject may appear very different in modern vs. postmodern discourses. For Jameson (1983), modernism is characterized by individualism "predicated on the invention of a personal, private style, as unmistakable as your fingerprint, as incomparable as your own body" (p. 114), while postmodernism is typified by the "death of the subject." The death of the subject suggests that "not only is the . . . individual a thing of the past, it is also a myth; it *never* really existed in the first place; there have never been autonomous subjects of that type" (Jameson, 1983, p. 115).

But how is it that the human subjects we study are myths (don't we record their conversations and tabulate their responses to questionnaires)? First, we must recognize that the self, the subject, is not a positive affirmation per se, but is instead constituted in and through a relationship. The subject comes to define himself/herself in a relationship of opposition to, and identification with, the "other." "Our identity is identity with the other, the image of perfection apparently denied us" (Nichols, 1981, p. 31); therefore, the development of the ego or the subject depends upon the paradoxical and often contradictory relationship between the self and the other. It is only in this sense that *we* can understand ourselves by studying the organizational subject who, in effect, becomes the object of reflection. And given that the organizational subject rarely acts autonomously, those behaviors are coded, rationalized, and represented in research, he/she may be considered not only as an object, but as a direct object as well. The organizational subject frequently consumes rather than produces action.

The subject, then, remains dependent upon the other for its identity. "The ego's articulation of desire always pivots around this moment of formation: the goal of desire is the recognition by the other, the very sense of an autonomous ego depends upon acknowledgement by the other. Only by being the object of another's desire can the ego be the subject of the self's desire" (Nichols, 1981, p. 31). According to Wilden (1980), the question of the desire of the other creates a paradox "because all desire—for 'objects' or for 'subjects'—is a desire for a relationship. All desire is fundamentally an expression of the analog relationship between human beings; it is therefore mediated by those relationships" (p. 92). However, the analog relationship between the self and the other is mediated more specifically in the digitalization of relationships which splits man from woman, man from nature, man from machine, and so on:

> The internalization of the digital—the efficient, the 'rational,' the 'technical'—as the agent of exploitation (rather than as the instrument of relationship) engenders a SPLITTING OF THE SUBJECT into mind and body, reason and emotion, self and other, male and female. The schizophrenia of modern society can be explained only in these terms: in the terms of the supervaluation of opposition and identity at the expense of the real and material differences upon which all communication depends. (Wilden, 1980, p. 92)

In this manner, the organizational researcher is able to "objectively" treat the subject as a discrete and privatized individual separate from himself/herself. It is, in fact, this objectification of the subject which characterizes the realm of professionalism in such diverse fields as medicine, psychology, law, journalism, communication, and so on. As Hawes (1987) notes, professionals (including ourselves) are legitimated "to the extent that [we] are subjects who experience practices objectively (that is, as impersonally and autonomously intended; 'If I did it for you, I'll have to do it for everybody') and that [we] experience those subjects on whom the practices work as subjects/objects (that is, as personally categorical; 'Don't take it personally, but you're fired'") (p. 8). The researcher, in short, must feign separation from the subject of study in order to grant authority to the project.

The objectification of the subject (object) in research, then, is not a naive, apolitical process from which the researcher is detached. Instead, the subject of organizational research must be understood as constituted in historical praxis and not as pure, rational, ahistorical "essences." The subject should be viewed as constantly constructed and reconstructed, produced and reproduced, by socially situated representations which, over time, develop a logic of their own. Although each subject is unique, "that an individual is always-already a subject, even before he is born, is nevertheless the plain reality, accessible to everyone and not paradoxical at all" (Althusser, 1971, p. 162).

We experience professional research practices as if they "emanate freely and spontaneously" from within us, as if we are "working by ourselves." "Actually, we are spoken by and spoken for, in the ideological discourses which await us even at our birth, into which we are born and find our place" (Hall, 1985, p. 109). Subjects, then, are "positioned" and "interpellated" by discursive formations of historical, political practices. So because "ideology has the role of constituting concrete individuals as subjects, because it is produced in the identification with the 'I' of discourse and is thus the condition of action, we cannot simply stay outside of it. To do so would be to refuse to act or speak, and even to make such a refusal, to say 'I refuse,' is to accept the condition of subjectivity" (Belsey, 1980, p. 62). Ironically, then, those persons who authorize and claim objectivity are, in reality, complying with their own subjectivity. To deny one's subjectivity to another is to deny one's humanness.

Importantly, however, the subject, though positioned, is never indeterminately fixed, because the discourses which hail subjects are constantly shifting and slipping. The subject is, thus, the site of contradiction and is constantly in the process of construction/reconstruction, thrown into crisis by alterations in language and in the social formation. The subject is, in the end, capable of change. "In the fact that the subject is a *process* lies the possibility of transformation" (Belsey, 1980, p. 65). Such transformation is not likely to occur, however, until we acknowledge that every use of "I" in research presupposes a "you" and every discourse is inherently linked to a relationship, a shared situation (Clifford, 1983).

The initial step in this understanding is to develop novel forms of research representations, beyond the research report, which do not silence the subject's voice at the outset. According to Dwyer (1979), the failure to do so leads to either a monologue or an antilogue in which the researcher and the subject may speak but never to one another. A discursive model of research practices, on the other hand, would bring to attention the intersubjectivity of all speech and its performative context. As Bakhtin (1981) suggests, "language lies on the borderline between oneself and the other. The word in language is half someone else's" (p. 293). Representing organizational subjects in writing should not be construed as monological, as the authoritative statements of a textualized reality since "there are no 'neutral' words and forms—words and forms that can belong to 'no one'; language has been shot through with intentions and accents" (Bakhtin, 1981, p. 276). So instead of listening to one metanarrative as in modernism, "the postmodern subject listens to a variety of voices, some contradicting one another, some directly competing, and some completely independent of one another" (Hawes, 1987, p. 18). As Bakhtin (1981) succinctly argues, "the ideological becoming of a human being, in this view, is the process of selectively assimilating the words of others" (p. 341). Hence, the subject of study "becomes" no less than the representational form "becomes."

THE AUDIENCE

> Consumption produces production. . .because a product becomes a real product only by being consumed. For example, a garment becomes a real garment only in the act of being worn; a house where no one lives is in fact not a real house; thus, the product, unlike a mere natural object, proves itself to be, *becomes*, a product only through consumption. Only by decomposing the product does consumption give the product the finishing touch. (Marx, 1973, p. 91)

Given that the research product is "complete" only when consumed, a postmodernism of resistance must finally ask: For whom do we write and under what circumstances? While Tompkins has already noted that the research report as a text anticipates the conduct of research, we must also consider the nature of the response to that text; every text anticipates an audience as well. As Barthes (1977) suggests, "a text is made of multiple writings, drawn from many cultures and entering into mutual relations of dialogue, parody, contestation, but there is one place where this multiplicity is focused and that place is the reader, not, as was hitherto said, the author. . . .A text's unity lies not in its origin but in its destination" (p. 148). As such, the "death of the author" instigates the birth of the reader in the reciprocal creation and consumption of texts.

Bakhtin (1981) notes that every word is directed toward an answer and, therefore. cannot escape from the effect of the response that it expects. The word, either in oral or written form, "is directly, blatantly, oriented toward a future answer-word: it provokes an answer, antici-pates it, and structures itself in the answer's direction" (p. 280). Within the constraints of words already spoken, "the word is at the same time determined by that which has not yet been said but which is needed and in fact anticipated by the answering word" (p. 280). For Bakhtin, this process of anticipating an answer is representative of a "living dialogue."

Reconceptualizing the production/consumption of the text in this fashion implies that production and consumption are inexorably inter-related in the research text. Here, the production of positivistic truth claims by the author does not grant a text authority in the same sense as does the "pleasure of a reading which guarantees its truth" (Barthes, 1985, p. 162). This latter pleasure is not so much a pleasure of recogniz-ing that which is familiar (for don't we find that some hypotheses were supported and others were not?), but rather the pleasure of actively collaborating in understanding. Unfortunately, most research to date assumes understanding for the audience to be most suitable as a passive process (actually, a process already complete before being "processed" or represented in the research text).

Primacy, then, should belong to the response as the activating princi-ple. "It creates the ground for understanding, it prepares the ground for an active and engaged understanding. Understanding comes to fruition only in the response. Understanding and response are dialec-tically merged and mutually condition one another; one is impossible without the other" (Bakhtin, 1981, p. 282). The text, from this point of view, should devise various forms and practices which employ the "sur-plus knowledge" inherent in all texts. Gadamer (1975) states that to recognize the surplus knowledge of a text, we must remain open to the meaning of the other person(s). Rather than merely interpreting the text, the reader is always in the process of reinterpreting. This is a logic of question and answer, in which the reader asks questions of the text, yet remains flexible to the preferred answers it provides to the questions (Gadamer, 1975, p. 326).

For the reader, then, the text is neither declarative nor imperative, but rather interrogative (Beneviste, 1971). The interrogative text dis-rupts any unity of understanding with the reader. "It refuses a single point of view, however complex and comprehensive, but brings point of view into unresolved collision or contradiction. . . .It refuses to point to a single position which is the place of the coherence of meaning" (Belsey, 1980, p. 92). The end goal of a research text, in this respect, is to make the reader a producer of the text rather than a mere consumer. Because there are always new and different readers, the text is constantly recre-ated and reproduced. Yet, these recreations of unique interpretations can only be understood within the institutionalized and historicized conditions of reading.

These institutional conditions are most forcefully confronted by Said (1983a, 1983b; see also Bauman, 1987; Brodkey, 1987). The difficulty is that while the postmodern strategy of the "interpreter" entails

> the abandonment of the universalistic ambitions of the intellectuals' own tradition, it does not abandon the universalistic ambitions of the intellectuals towards their own tradition; here, they retain their meta-professional authority, legislating about the procedural rules which allow them to arbitrate controversies of opinion and make statements intended as binding. (Bauman, 1987, p. 5)

At issue is where and how the boundaries get drawn around the interpretive community, to the exclusion of the outside world, in order to allow for truth claims to be made. Said's (1985) response to such collusion in the practices of "noninterference" is "that we argue in theory for what in practice we never do, and we do the same kind of thing with regard to what we oppose" (p. 158).

For Said (1983), texts are "worldly" and inherently situated within the world of politics:

> Criticism in short is always situated; it is skeptical, secular, reflectively open to its own failings. This is by no means to say that it is value-free. Quite the contrary, for the inevitable trajectory of critical consciousness is to arrive at some acute sense of what political, social, and human values are entailed in the reading, production, and transmission of every text. To stand between culture and system is to stand *close to*. . . a concrete reality about which political, moral, and social judgments have to be made and, if not only made, then exposed and demystified. (p. 26)

Although the researcher is inherently implicated as one who stands close to culture, the "cult of professional expertise" has produced intellectuals who are silent about the historical and social world which they perpetuate through noninterference. The culture of professionalism "works very effectively to make invisible and even 'impossible' the actual *affiliations* that exist between the world of ideas and scholarship on the one hand and the world of brute politics, corporate and state power, and military force, on the other" (Said, 1983b, p. 136). By affiliation in the academic community, scholars are taught that disciplines "exist in a relatively neutral political element, that they are to be appreciated and venerated, that they define the limits of what is acceptable, appropriate, and legitimate" (Said, 1983a, p. 21). Affiliation becomes a literal form of representation, as the interpretive community identifies and reifies concepts, to the exclusion of worldly audiences. This process of representation, by means of scholarly affiliation, reinforces the known at the expense of the knowable (and doable). The consequence is that there is oppositional debate without real opposition; that is, journals and conferences stimulate simulated opposition *within* the academic community, while the "real" opposition lies *outside* those artificial boundaries. For Said, research presented only to one's peers limits its potential "force" for "worldly audiences."

Because culture exists within an economy of space, each production of a text must not only earn a place for itself, but it must also win over and displace other potential texts (Gramsci, 1971). But "nearly everyone . . . makes no allowance for the truth that all intellectual or cultural work occurs somewhere, at some time, on some very precisely mapped-out and permissible terrain" (Said, 1983a, p. 169), as supported by the hegemonic structures of state and civil society. As Matthiesen (1952) notes in *The Responsibilities of the Critic*, research is likely to become a kind of closed garden unless we realize "that the land beyond the garden's wall is more fertile, and that the responsibility of the critic lies in making renewed contact with the soil." Because texts acquire power or force over the world of common sense through the process of consent, the present status of scholarly work typically acquires consent within professional walls. Scholarly work displaces other scholarly work which, in a sense, is not a displacement at all but rather a replacement, allowing more space for oppositional texts to broader-based communities. Unfortunately, very little of these circumstances which make interpretive activity possible are allowed into the interpretive circle itself for consideration (Said, 1983b, p. 151).

The audience, in these interpretive circles, generally represent "constituencies" and not actual "opponents." This constituency in organizational communication is, in most cases, either management or other scholars who will use research to further their own studies. A constituency, then, is a clientele of individuals who utilize scholarly expertise in exchange for a reified and safe haven for the intellectual. In Said's (1983b) words:

> To an alarming degree, the present continuation of the humanities depends, I think, on the sustained self-purification of humanists for whom the ethic of specialization has become equivalent to minimizing the content of their work and increasing the composite wall of guild consciousness, social authority, and exclusionary discipline around themselves. Opponents are therefore not people in disagreement with the constituency but people to be kept out, nonexperts, and nonspecialists, for the most part. (p. 152)

To intersect the reification of the academic community of constituents in organizational communication requires a politics of interference in which the researcher must remember that no one writes simply for oneself. Consequently, research always implies another and must be considered both a social and political activity. Not surprising, it is all too frequent that the objectified subject of our studies, the worker, is also excluded as a potential audience/reader. The worker, then, is not only *not* provided a *voice* to speak, but he/she is also not provided an "*I*" to read.

CONCLUSION

This chapter argues that the questions of the text, the subject, and the audience reflect significant issues which must be addressed if organizational communication research is to call itself postmodern, both theoretically and practically. While organizational communication has become more reflective of itself conceptually (see, for instance, Putnam & Pacanowsky, 1983), it has nevertheless neglected the practical questions: What do we write? Who is the subject of our study? For whom do we write and under what circumstances? So although some authors suggest that interpretive efforts in organizational communication stand in opposition to the dominance of the functionalist paradigm, I argue that the nonreflective practice of writing research texts (and what writing "means" within the academy) precludes true opposition to functionalism. Even within naturalistic and critical traditions, for instance, the subject is both spoken by and spoken for the voice of authority.

The subject in organizational communication research texts is, in this sense, an epic hero (a representation who is distanced yet fully finished and complete) who is objectified without contradiction, and who speaks the voice of reason on a one-dimensional plane. There can be no conversing with this representation of the subject. It is as if the leading character in the drama of organizational life, the worker, has been relegated to the status of an understudy. He/she observes and responds to those who surround him/her, yet is never allowed to speak in the play which, ironically, is *about* him/her. To dislocate the voice of the worker is to reproduce an economy of space in which only the voice of management is heard. This dislocation, whether conscious and self-reflexive or not, is, in the end, a political and ethical decision (or nondecision). As Bakhtin (1981) suggests,

> at any given moment of its historical existence, language is heteroglot from top to bottom: it represents the coexistence of socio-ideological contradic-

tions between the present and the past, between differing epochs of the past, between different socio-ideological groups in the present, between tendencies, schools, circles, and so forth, all given a bodily form. These 'languages' of heteroglossia intersect each other in a variety of ways, forming new socially typifying 'languages.' (p. 291)

Organizational communication research negates the heterglot nature of these voices by producing research texts which represent social reality as if it were a closed system, a "dead language," a world without struggle and contestation. The scholar, in effect, "transposes a symphonic (orchestrated) theme onto the piano keyboard" (Bakhtin, 1981, p. 263). Bakhtin refers to the result of this transposing act as the "authority of discourse." "The authoritative discourse demands that we acknowledge it, that we make it our own; it binds us, quite independent of any power it might have to persuade us internally; we encounter it with its authority fused to it" (p. 342). It is a prior discourse whose authority has already been acknowledged and commands our allegiance. It is transmitted but not collaboratively and, once deprived of its authority, it becomes a relic, a thing.

The alternative in the form of organizational communication research is the "internally persuasive discourse." This discourse is in procession and evolving because the internally persuasive word is half ours and half some else's.

Such a word awakens new and independent words and does not remain in an isolated and static condition. . . .It enters into an intense interaction, a *struggle* with other internally persuasive discourses. . . .The semantic structure of an internally persuasive discourse is *not finite*, it is open; in each of the new contexts that dialogize it, this discourse is able to reveal ever newer *ways to mean*. (Bakhtin, 1981, p. 346)

This, I believe, is the present and future challenge of organizational communication research as we attempt to resist our own "organized forgetting" of the worker/subject. The monologue must become a dialogue.

REFERENCES

Althusser, L. (1971). *Lenin and philosophy and other essays* (B. Brewster, Trans.). London: Newhaft. (Original work published in 1970)

Bakhtin, M. M. (1981). *The dialogic imagination: Four essays by M. M. Bakhtin* (M. Holquist, Ed.; C. Emerson & M. Holquist, Trans.). Austin, TX: University of Texas Press.

Barthes, R. (1977). The death of the author. *Image-music-text*. Glasgow: Fontana/Collins. (Original work published in 1968)

Barthes, R. (1979). From work to text. In J. V. Harari (Ed.), *Textual strategies: Perspectives in post-structuralist criticism*. Ithaca, NY: Cornell University Press.

Barthes, R. (1985). *The grain of the voice: Interviews 1962–1980* (L. Coverdale, Trans.). New York: Hill & Wang.

Bauman, Z. (1987). *Legislators and interpreters: On modernity, post-modernity, and intellectuals*. Ithaca, NY: Cornell University Press.

Belsey, C. (1980). *Critical practice*. London: Methuen.

Beneviste, E. (1971). *Problems in general linguistics*. Miami: University of Miami Press.

Brodkey, L. (1987). *Academic writing as social practice*. Philadelphia: Temple University Press.

Brown, R. H. (1978). *A poetic for sociology*. Cambridge: Cambridge University Press.

Cheney, G., & Tompkins, P. K. (1988). On the facts of the "text" as the basis for human communication research. In J. A. Anderson (Ed.), *Communication yearbook*. Beverly Hills, CA: Sage.

Clifford, J. (1983). On ethnographic authority. *Representations, 1*, 118–146.

Clifford, J., & Marcus, G. (Eds.). (1986). *Writing culture: The poetics and politics of ethnography*. Berkeley: University of California Press.

Derrida, J. (1984). *Of grammatology* (G. S. Spivak, Trans.). Baltimore: Johns Hopkins University Press.

Dwyer, K. (1979). The dialogic of anthropology. *Dialetical Anthropology, 4*, 205–224.

Foucault, M. (1980). *Power/knowledge: Selected interviews and other writings 1972–1977* (C. Gordon, Ed.; C. Gordon, L. Marshall, J. Mepham, & K. Soper, Trans.). New York: Pantheon Books.

Foster, H. (Ed.). (1983). *The anti-aesthetic: Essays on postmodern culture*. Port Townsend, WA: Bay Press.

Gadamer, H. G. (1975). *Truth and method*. New York: Continuum.

Geertz, C. (1983). *Local knowledge: Further essays interpretive anthropology*. New York: Basic.

Gramsci, A. (1971). *Selections from the prison notebooks* (Q. Hoare & G. F. Smith, Eds. and Trans.). New York: International Publishers.

Granier, J. (1985). Perspectivism and interpretation. In D. B. Allison (Ed.), *The new Nietzsche*. Cambridge, MA: Harvard University Press.

Grossberg, L. (1983). Cultural studies revised and revisited. In M. Mander (Ed.), *Communications in transitions*. New York: Praeger.

Grossberg, L. (1984). Strategies of Marxist cultural interpretation. *Critical Studies in Mass Communication, 1*, 392–421.

Habermas, J. (1983). Modernity—An incomplete project. In H. Foster (Ed.), *The anti-aesthetic: Essays on postmodern culture*. Port Townsend, WA: Bay Press.

Hall, S. (1980). Race, articulation, and societies structured in dominance. *Sociological theories: Race and colonialism*. Paris: UNESCO.

Hall, S. (1985). Signification, representation, and ideology: Althusser and the post-structuralist debates. *Critical Studies in Mass Communication, 2*, 91–114.

Hawes, L. (1987, Summer). *Post-industrialism and its subject: Fueling the culture of addiction*. Paper presented at the Conference on the Interpretive Study of Organizations, Alta, UT

Hawes, L. (1988). Power, discourse, and ideology: The micropractices of common sense. *Communication yearbook* (Vol. 12). Beverly Hills, CA: Sage.

Jameson, F. (1983). Postmodernism and consumer society. In H. Foster (Ed.), *The anti-aesthetic: Essays on postmodern culture*. Port Townsend, WA: Bay Press.

Kundera, M. (1981). *The book of laughter and forgetting* (M. H. Heim, Trans.). New York: Penguin Books.

Marx, K. (1973). *Grundrisse*. Harmondsworth: Penguin Books. (Original edition 1939)

Matthiesen, F. O. (1952). *The responsibilities of the critic: Essays and reviews by F. O. Matthiesen.* New York: Oxford University Press.

Nichols, B. (1981). *Ideology and the image.* Bloomington: Indiana University Press.

Putnam, L., & Pacanowsky, M. (Eds.). (1983). *Communication and organizations: An interpretive approach.* Beverly Hills, CA: Sage.

Redding, C., & Tompkins, P.K. (1988). Organizational communication: Past and present tenses. In G. Goldhaber (Ed.), *Handbook of organizational communication* (pp.5–33). Norwood, NJ: Ablex.

Ricoeur, P. (1979). The model of the text; Meaningful action considered as a text. In P. Rabinow & W. M. Sullivan (Eds.), *Interpretive social science: A reader.* Berkeley: University of California Press.

Said, E. (1981). *Covering Islam: How the media and the experts determine how we see the rest of the world.* New York; Pantheon.

Said, E. (1983a). *The world, the text, and the critic.* Cambridge, MA: Harvard University Press.

Said, E. (1983b). Opponents, audiences, constituencies, and community. In H. Foster (Ed.), *The anti-aesthetic: Essays on postmodern culture.* Port Townsend, WA: Bay Press.

Schank, R., & Abelson, R. (1977). *Scripts, plans, goals, and understanding: An inquiry into human knowledge structures.* Hillsdale, NJ: Erlbaum.

Schrag, C. (1980). *Radical reflection and the origin of human sciences.* West Lafayette, IN: Purdue University Press.

Smirchich, L., & Calas, M. (1986). Organizational culture: A critical assessment. In F. Jablin, L. Putnam, & K. Roberts (Eds.), *Handbook of organizational communication.* Beverly Hills, CA: Sage.

Strine, M. (1988). Constructing "texts" and making inferences: Some reflections on textual reality in human communication research. In J. A. Anderson (Ed.), *Communication yearbook.* Beverly Hills, CA: Sage.

Strine, M., & Pacanowsky, M. (1985). How to read accounts of organizational life: Narrative bases of textual authority. *The Southern Speech Communication Journal, 50,* 283–297.

Tompkins, P. (1986). *The future of organizational communication: An outline of postmodernism.* Paper presented at the Annual Conference of the Speech Communication Association, Chicago, IL.

Ulmer, G. (1983). Op writing: Derrida's solicitation of theoria. In M. Krupnick (Ed.), *Displacement: Derrida and after.* Bloomington: Indiana University Press.

Wilden, A. (1980). *System and structure: Essays and communication and exchange* (2nd ed.). New York: Tavistock Publications.

2

Examining the Praxis, Assessing the Pitfalls, and Enhancing the Potential of Semiotics in Interpretative Organizational Research*

John F. Stone

The interpretive approach to organizational communication has been ground in a simple but significant axiom: To uncover the inner workings of an organization, the investigator most wisely focuses on how human symbols subjectively, intersubjectively, and socially construct meanings for organizational actors. Ultimately, adherence to this dictum has lead investigators to focus on the role symbols play in constructing a social reality. A sizable group of investigators, for example, have examined how metaphors guide member interpretation of organizational activity. Clark (1972) and Meyer and Rowan (1977) observed that metaphors, at the very least, functioned strategically to coordinate members' perceptions of the organization. Still other investigators have turned to root metaphors as the key to understanding an organization's design priorities (see, for example, Keidel, 1984, 1985, 1987; Morgan, 1980, 1983, 1986; Ramsay, 1987; Smith & Eisenberg, 1987).

Efforts to enhance the specificity of this sort of analysis would seem to be driving a small corpus of organizational investigators to turn to semiotics. Semiotics, the science of equating "signs" or "systems of signs" with meanings, has afforded these investigators greater flexibility and precision in identifying and interpreting codes of meaning shared

* John Stone wishes to thank Marshal Scott Poole, Charles Bantz, and Jerry Pepper for their comments on an earlier version of this essay presented at the Thirty-ninth Annual International Communication Association Conference, San Francisco, CA, May 1989.

among organizational members. Capable of accessing a broader range of organizational transactions and, perhaps more significantly, the interpretive rules guiding such transactions, organizational semioticians have appeared on the verge of keying a richer understanding of how symbolic activity undergrids the construction of organizational reality. On the whole, however, organizational researchers have been slow to embrace semiotics as an interpretive method. Questions about both semiotic theory and its value as a tool for organizational research would still seem to inhibit its acceptance.

What follows is an attempt to answer some of these questions. After providing an overview of salient concepts and constructs endemic to semiotic theory, this chapter turns to a review of the contributions of semiotically inclined investigators and an exploration of the relationship between semiotics as an investigative framework and current trends in interpretive research. Specifically, the focus here is on how semiotics has aided investigators approaching organizations from cultural, rhetorical, information-processing, and political perspectives. The third section distinguishes specific shortcomings in semiotic research, proposes some potential amendments to the current semiotic frame, and discusses what such amendments might still tell researchers about symbol use in organizations. What results is not an indictment of previous semiotic research, but a call for more rigorous and imaginative applications of a full range of interpretive tools.

THE NATURE AND MERITS OF SEMIOTIC RESEARCH

Defined simply, semiotics is the study of the social production of meaning from sign. Marked by a variety of philosophic approaches to the notion of sharing signs, there exist many, sometimes crucial, sometimes hairsplitting distinctions over the definitions of key terms and their importance.[1] The discussion in this section represents a philosophic hybrid and is confined to a lexicon of key concepts that have, to date, provided the foundation for organizational analyses.

---

[1] The two predominant strains of semiotics might be labeled "Anglo-American Pragmatism," fathered by U.S. philosopher Charles S. Peirce, and "Continental Structural Linguistics," spawned by the writings of Swiss linguist Ferdinand De Saussure. In short, these two strains differ in what they consider to be both the focus of the semiotic enterprise and the limitations of such an analysis. (See Steiner, 1989, for an excellent synopsis of the competing perspectives.)

At the center of all semiotic philosophies is the concept of *sign* or *expression*. An expression must have a physical form, whether it be a word, a gesture, a picture, or a sound. A sign must also refer to something other than itself, and it must be recognized as a sign by those who use it. Signification is thought to occur as a sign begins to carry a *content*, or particular meaning for the communities that share the sign. Barthes (1967) hypothesized that with any expression, signification actually occurs within a given speech culture at two distinct levels or orders: *denotative* and *connotative*. Signification that occurs at a denotative level will traditionally have a simple or literal relationship between a sign and its content. The link between the expression and this content is quite objective and value-free. A picture of a rose, for instance, at a denotative level might lead to a content interpretation such as "a flower." On the other hand, signification that occurs at the connotative level is decidedly more complex, reflexive, and subjective. Contents here become loaded with inherent values. The same picture of a rose, for example, might at a connotative level carry a content of "romantic passion."

Semioticians, however, are rarely concerned with the single expression. The focus, understandably, falls on series of expressions and contents that mark a particular *code* or language. Ultimately, codes make systems of meanings possible within a given communicative culture. Eco (1976) has suggested that codes have four key components: (a) a set of expressions, (b) a set of requisite contents, (c) a set of rules that govern how the expressions are linked to the contents, and (d) alternative responses to the expressions. The concept of codes is particularly significant to the organizational investigator searching for the patterns of discourse that might coalesce a series of meanings into shared philosophies or perspectives portraying the key values of a given organizational culture.

Hence, the analysis at some point must turn to the interpretive systems or how the expressions come to be linked to their contents. Disagreement seems to be the norm among semioticians about how this is best achieved. For while there is little conflict over the utility of using Aristotle's rhetorical forms or tropes such as metaphor and metonymy in delineating systems of meanings, there is disagreement over which tropes are the most valid and/or useful for discerning how coding protocol is formed (see Schofer & Rice, 1977). In that vein, the tropes most evident in organizational research—metaphor, metonymy, and opposition—are significant for they not only function to explain how meaning is generated, but also affirm the persuasive function of interpretation.

Each of these tropes depends on the existence of a *domain*, or category of symbols that provide a context to aid interpretation. The semiotic frame in Figure 2.1 details a code of expressions typical to Keidel's

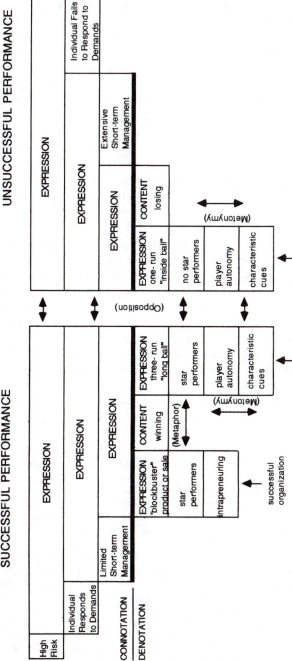

Figure 2.1. Diagram of Baseball Code

(1985) "baseball structured" organizations.[2] *Metaphoric* interpretations are characterized by a signifying process relying on resemblance and are made possible by the existence of common features. For instance, the denotative expressions "three-run long ball," "star performers," and "player autonomy" all operate metaphorically in linking themselves to the respective expressions of the successful organization, such as "blockbuster sale or product," "star performers," and "intrapreneuring." Those same expressions concomitantly signify by *metonymy* when they are associated with each other and suggest another concept. For example, as Figure 2.1 indicates, "three-run long ball," "star performers," and "player autonomy" are representative signs of a "winning team" just as "blockbuster sale or product," "star performers," and "intrapreneuring" are expressions signifying a "successful organization."

The expressions in Figure 2.1, at both the connotative and denotative levels, depend on the existence of bipolar domains—performing successfully (winning) and performing unsuccessfully (losing)—to suggest specific contents. That fact perhaps explains why *opposition* has been such a significant trope among organizational semioticians. Expressions signify by opposition by implicitly contrasting one sign in one domain with another sign in another domain, operating from the assumption that the members of a communicative culture know what something means by knowing what it does not mean. As Figure 2.1 suggests, for example, an organizational member would know that a successful baseball-structured organization relies on "Limited Short-Term Management" by recognizing that the unsuccessful organization uses "Extensive Short-Term Management."

Such concepts, and their requisite constructs, have provided the framework for semiotic investigators attempting to map out the various

---

[2] Keidel (1987) has proposed a triadic scheme of organizational strategies, structures, styles, and cultures based metaphorically on American team sports. Generally, baseball is a metaphor for organizations that stress the autonomy of organizational parts; football, for hierarchical control of organizational parts; and basketball, for voluntary cooperation among the parts. He argues that sports is "a fertile area for organizational experimentation not simply because it provides clear measures of performance and ample sources of data, but more importantly, because it offers archetypal organizational designs" (p. 608). Keidel's sports metaphors are instructive, particularly in the context of this chapter, because they identify the indispensable assumptions and expression that operate within sports structured organizations. These assumptions provide a point of departure for a semiotic analysis because they function as key expressions that are pivotal to understanding how members of these organizations cognitively structure their understanding of organizational strategies and activities. The semiotic frame shown in Figure 2.1 is an adaptation of a similar semiotic frame used by Barley (1983b) in chronicling the codes used by employees of a funeral home. Barley attributes this frame to the seminal work of Eco and his discussion of the four components of a semiotic code.

signs and signifying practices at work in contemporary organizations. Clearly, the preceding is not a complete review of semiotic theory. It does, however, provide a point of departure for a discussion of the interaction between semiotic practices and the various domains of interpretive research in organizational communication.

SEMIOTICS AND THE INTERPRETIVE RESEARCH PARADIGM

Like most any significant research paradigm, the interpretive approach to organizational communication has indicated that it encourages a plurality in foci, investigative assumptions, and methodologies. Variety in these elements have given rise to a new set of investigative perspectives. Attention here is directed only to the handful of significant perspectives identified by Putnam and Cheney (1985). Specifically, Putnam and Cheney posit that "information processing," "culture," "rhetorical," and "political" are unique perspectives that concurrently characterize the recent past and define the horizon of organizational research.

Developing an appreciation of the role that semiotics has played in the maturation of these four perspectives begins here with a closer look at the presuppositions behind these perspectives. Figure 2.2, for example, plots the four perspectives in relation to key variables that determine their approach to symbol sharing in organizations. The horizontal axis represents a continuum that reflects an investigator's unit of inter-

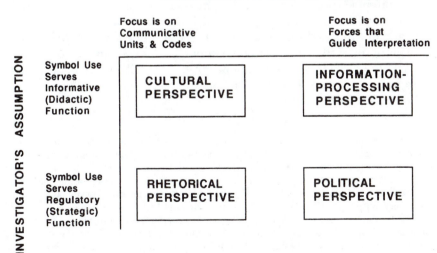

Figure 2.2. Four Perspectives of Interpretative Research

est. The left end of this continuum is a ground for research that focuses on specific communicative units and codes. The interest here is in identifiable symbols or series of symbols and what they mean to organizational members. At the far-right end of the continuum is ground for those investigations that focus on the forces that guide interpretations of specific symbols or series of symbols. The focus, more particularly, is on the unconscious rules and constraints that are not only taken for granted by members of the organization, but also function as directives for interpreting and responding to organizational situations.

The vertical axis in Figure 2.2 reflects differences in the central assumptions about how symbols are utilized in an organization. To the extent that "didactic" and "strategic" uses of symbols can truly be separated and bifurcated, the top end of the scale grounds research that turns on the assumption that symbols in organizations are essentially didactic, that is, they serve primarily an informative function. Symbol use in organizations under these auspices is thought to be an inevitable, if not an incidental occurrence that affects how members come to understand their organizational world. The bottom of this axis is home for the assumption that symbol use in organizations is either consciously or unconsciously regulated. The use of symbols or the forces that guide the interpretation of symbols are determined strategically by some segment of the organization.[3]

These vertical and horizontal continuums combine to provide a grid that frames the four perspectives in relation to one another. In the upper-left quartile of Figure 2.2, for example, are culture studies. Much of the emphasis in culture research centers on specific units or codes that are thought responsible for creating intersubjective understanding and common pursuits among organizational members. And if, as Pacanowsky and O'Donnell-Trujillo (1982) argue, the "underlying motive of the organizational culture approach is coming to understand how organizational life is accomplished communicatively" (p. 121), there is a concern also with the informative role symbols play in the sense-making activity of organizational members.

---

[3] The distinction between "use of symbols in organizations is informative" and "use of symbols in organizations is regulatory" is clearly arbitrary. For those who firmly believe that "rhetoric is epistemic" (see Scott, 1967, 1976), this distinction is, no doubt, particularly specious. One may note, for instance, that many culture studies—based in that end of a continuum that assumes symbol use is informative—have focused on how symbols are used (strategically) to guide interpretation of organizational life (see, most notably, Deal & Kennedy, 1982; Peters & Waterman, 1982). See Deetz (1982, pp. 133–135) for amplification of just such an argument. Nonetheless, it does seem clear that some investigations approach symbol use as an inescapable by-product of organizational life and others assume it is more purposeful and/or strategic; hence, the distinction that is forwarded here.

Such distinctions, particularly with culture research, are a bit stilted. A question such as, "What does a cultural analysis do?" would likely bring a variety of responses. Smircich (1983) has suggested, for instance, that there are five different types of culture research. And while the scope of this chapter prohibits a discussion of each, it is worth noting that semiotics research has played, arguably, a significant role in two of these schemata. Barley's (1983a, 1983b), for instance, detailed analysis of the occupational codes evident in funeral work suggested semiotics was a unique tool for tapping into what Smircich called a "corporate culture."

Like the cultural perspective, the rhetorical perspective is interested in readily identifiable units of communication. However, unlike the cultural perspective, the rhetorical perspective focuses on how the communicative units function strategically to bind the member to the organization and its objectives. Some examine communication within the organization at a "micro-level" with an eye towards how symbol sharing is endorsed and how it leads to "unobtrusive organizational control." Other rhetorical research examines how symbols are used to introduce change, reinforce public attitudes on assorted organizational issues, and establish arguments for business speakers. Significantly, semiotic research, to date, has focused primarily on the later of these to strains. Fiol (1989), for example, employed semiotics as a formal mode for analyzing external organizational communication (in the form of letters to shareholders) to discern how organization's defined the boundaries between themselves and their external environment and the boundaries between organizational subunits.

In the upper-left quartile of Figure 2.2 is the information-processing perspective; a perspective, according to Putnam and Cheney (1985), whose premise is that the essence of organizing is the collecting, transmitting, stocking, and using of information. Semiotics has seemingly had little to offer the information-processing perspective, perhaps because "most information-processing studies adopt a mechanistic view of communication emphasizing the amount, direction, structure, and type of information flow while ignoring the message reception and interpretation" (p. 145).

Finally, the political perspective is, like the rhetorical perspective, attuned to the persuasive power of organizational symbols, hence, its location on the bottom of the vertical axis. It assumes that "organizations are factions of subcultures who frequently compete for resources (Putnam & Cheney, 1985, pp. 149–150). Communication in this perspective refers to the overt and covert means that various coalitions use in manifesting power. As such, the investigative emphasis here isn't on the key symbols in the organization, but on the "deep structures. . .through which certain organizational realities come to hold sway over competing world views" (Mumby, 1987, p. 113). The political perspective recognizes a link between the structuring of sense data and the nature and center of power within an organization, holding that "deep structures of power are the limits that define and solidify a society or organization" (Conrad, 1983, p. 198). Semiotics has played, arguably, a nondiscernible role in advancing this perspective.

The distinctions between the four perspectives are not as clear or as simple as delineated in the preceding. The admittedly arbitrary distribution of the four perspectives on the two indices in Figure 2.2 are forwarded in an effort to bring the relative similarities and differences of the four perspectives into sharper relief. Nonetheless, to the extent that these perspectives provide an opportunity to accurately delineate key differences in investigative foci and research assumptions, they have provided a backdrop for assessing how semiotics has aided the interpretive research tradition. In that regard, semiotics has seemingly served admirably, if not exclusively, the culture perspective. Barley's (1983b) research in funeral homes has lead him to conclude that semiotics offered unique access to members' interpretations of their organizational and occupational worlds. Like any method, semiotics was incapable of portraying an entire culture. Semiotics did, however, allow an emphasis on the daily dialogue which, in turn, reduced dependence on the overtly symbolic phenomena—logos, stories, colorful terms, and arcane rituals—that had earmarked previous culture research. In this vein, should an organizational researcher fail to identify shared stories or handy terms, semiotics protects the investigator "from concluding that the unfortunate organization is bereft of culture" (p. 409). Manning (1988), also operating from an essentially culture perspective, employed semiotics as a tool to discern the factors that shaped, constrained, guided, or were associated with specific messages. In this capacity, semiotics served three related ends. First, it permitted the organizational investigator to work diagnostically to identify the "institutional codes" that acted on the messages circulating through the organization. These codes were significant because they provided information about how messages were to be interpreted. Second, semiotics offered an opportunity to explicate the very nature of the transformation of meaning that occurs when these codes function. Perhaps most significantly, semiotics affirmed the importance of context-bound logic and situated rationality that encompasses all organizational communication (pp. 264–266).

Ultimately, in the hands of these investigators, semiotics has proven to be an insightful, if not stimulating tool for conducting ethnographic research. More than simply forging a beachhead for semiotics in organizational studies, this corpus of research has provided a richer understanding of how members create intersubjective interpretations of the organization and its activities. It has allowed the investigator to become aware of a greater variety of organizational transactions and, in turn, to better determine which elements of a text are most representative of an organization. Perhaps more than simply responding to a multiplicity of texts, the organizational semiotician is better prepared to contend with the assumption that no text operates in a vacuum. In this vein, semiotics permits investigators to more directly account not only for the context of organizational discourse, but also explore how various bits of text interact and interrelate.

Only conjecture can reign in a discussion of why semiotics hasn't played a more significant role in the rhetorical, political, or information-processing perspectives. The apparent abstraction of the semiotic approach leads any investigator to run the risk of putting the emphasis on the means of analysis and not on the organizational discourse and, as such, may have prohibited all but a few researchers from embracing the method and its potential. Further, a case could be made that the "ends" of investigations in the political, information-processing, and rhetorical perspectives have not leant itself to the use of semiotics as a "means." Nonetheless, it is paradoxical that a postmodern method whose locus includes the deconstructing of symbolic constructions of reality erected by political elites, would be ignored when exploring the discourse within organizations generally or the nature of organizational power specifically.

Hence, inasmuch as investigators have demonstrated that relating the production of meaning to social relationships in organizations is a natural and profitable endeavor, the balance of this chapter seeks to substantiate the claim that the value of semiotic analysis in organizational research has yet to be fully realized. Specifically, my position is not that semiotic researchers have been myopic in their approach to semiotics as a research tool. Nor is it my position that semiotic investigators have inappropriately focused on culture studies. Rather, it is my position that semiotics, like any methodology, reveals certain elements of organizational life at the expense of concealing certain others. To the extent that the semiotic frame might be modified to tell investigators more about organizational life, it becomes a more useful research option—applicable to a greater variety of research perspectives.

EXTENDING THE SEMIOTIC FRAME AND ITS USE IN INTERPRETIVE RESEARCH

Barley's claim that semiotics arms the investigator with the potential to access a wider range of surface-level communicative phenomena, suggests there remains an impotence in discerning systems of meanings that fall outside the realm of the current semiotic frame. Decisions concern-

ing precisely what modifications should be made to the frame are probably best determined by the investigator and based on the dictates of the
investigation.

Such an observation should not, however, prohibit evaluation of the
current frame nor speculation about potential helpful amendments.
The current frame, for example, is devoid of a semiotic device capable
of identifying expressions that transcend simple signs evident at the
connotative and denotative level. These might be expressions that codify
tenets of strategic operation and planning—expressions that are not
significant to but a few members at the strategic apex of a centralized
decision-making organization, and are also expressions that, as such,
influence expressions emergent at the connotative and denotative level.
A sign such as "lean and mean" may be an expression that describes a
shared understanding of an organization's staffing principles, but may
not be an expression known to others outside strategic planning nor
evident in the daily interactions of organizational members outside staffing circles. However, the significance of such an expression shouldn't be
discounted. Such a sign may constrain other's expressions by directly
effecting the actual operation and, in turn, negotiated perceptions of the
organization. "Lean and mean," for instance, as a shared expression and
directive for organizational operation, might actually shape the emergence of other organization-wide expressions by limiting the number of
individuals participating in the social construction of reality. While current investigators don't lack the skills to identify such "subsuming"
expressions—the fieldwork of Manning (1989) is testimony to that—they
do lack an adequate method of explaining the significance of such
expressions.

Similarly, it was Manning's (1986, 1988) insightful work that not only
reaffirmed the significance of context in message decoding, but first
hinted at the semioticians' debilitating reliance on the oppositional
trope. The semiotic frames employed by both Barley and Manning were
ground in the existence of categories of meaning that were generated by
opposition. While the presence, if not the significance of the oppositional trope is not disputed here, caution is wise when relying so heavily on a
trope that purports binary interpretation. Communication is one of
those rare economies that operates without scarcity, particularly in terms
of potential schemes of interpretation (see Gellner, 1985, pp. 149–151).

Beyond it simply being presumptuous to assume that the only potential referent for an expression is determined by first deciding what the
referent is not, it simply seems logical to allow for a broader field of
referents—particularly in view of members' apparent penchant for creating expressions with indefinite meanings (see Eisenberg, 1984). That
is, as it becomes increasingly evident that many of the expressions

created in organizational settings exist because of their inherent referential uncertainty, adjustments must be made that account for a wider field of potential meanings. An expression from Figure 2.1, for example, such as "three run-long ball" may mean something other than the prescribed "don't play conservatively—don't work on the small sale." It may spawn unintended interpretations about the tensions affiliated with working in a high-risk environment. At the very least, semiotic frames must assign more significance to context—evident in the guise of recent events or experiences—that may exist to guide alternative interpretation to that presented through opposition.

Decisions regarding which rhetorical tropes or semiotic concepts to deploy in expanding the explanatory power of a semiotic model turn, potentially, on a number of issues. At one level, as noted earlier, the decision would stem from the results of the fieldwork. The investigator decides which tools to add to a semiotic scheme by first determining which expressions or systems of expressions were most significant in the organization under investigation.[4] The selection of explanatory tropes is contingent on what the investigator deems most important in his/her interpretations of the prevalent patterns of organizational discourse. The perspective taken here is a bit more generic in the sense that it focuses on *types* of expressions that currently elude the organizational semiotician. In this case, the strictures forwarded in the two preceding paragraphs direct the search for semiotic devices capable of elucidating categories of organizational discourse that are currently inaccessible.

Although *synecdoche* has been recognized as a master trope for deciphering the endocation and emplotment patterns of organizational discourse (see Manning, 1979, pp. 663–665), the function of synecdochal expressions in organizational contexts has yet to be fully explored. Synecdoche is characterized by a static relationship between or condition where two objects have entered into a stable and unalterable bond, and identifies something by naming a part of it or identifying a part of it by naming the whole thing. A "Corvette," for instance, may function as a synecdochical sign for the referent "sports car." When using a synecdochal expression, the communicator makes a claim that something deserves the attitudes and feelings evoked by the whole when only sharing a part.

As the "trope of representation" (Burke, 1962), synecdoche carries the potential to characterize the entire organization and even determine the nature or preference for expressions at the connotative and denota-

---

[4] Manning (1979) makes an interesting point when he claims just the reverse is true. He claims, in short, that the four master tropes (metaphor, metonymy, synecdoche, and irony) "have shaped the writing as well as the gathering of qualitative data" (p. 668).

tive level. A phrase such as "we try harder," may not only concurrently describe the operating philosophy of the organization and be functionally linked to the identity of the company itself, but may also play an essential role in directing the expressions emergent in the day-to-day operation of the organization—expressions such as "the customer is #1" and "we can be #1." As indicated in Figure 2.3, synecdochal expressions of the typical baseball structured organization might be: "staffing as key priority," "nonsequential tasks," and "limited member interaction," which are expressions that undergird more particular expressions at the denotative and connotative level. As such, these expressions represent not only an "organizing principle that prevails throughout the diversity of detail" (Burke, 1962, p. 259), but also an opportunity to access the motives found in other elements of the discourse as a whole (pp. 324, 507–509). Synecdochal expressions, in this sense, might be viewed as essential features of an organizing structure.

Ultimately, to the extent such expressions might be understood to underpin the basic design priorities of the organization, synecdochical expression could be approached as those most central to an organization's effective operation. As indicated in Figure 2.3, it is conceivable that both successful and unsuccessful baseball-structured organizations may strategically embrace the same synecdochal expressions. What may vary in the two organizations are the expressions that functionally spring from these signs. Successful baseball-structured organizations might be conceived of as those that share expressions at the connotative and denotative levels that are consonant with the synecdochal expressions.

Moreover, to the extent that a semiotic context is a message that determined how another expression is to be interpreted (Goffman, 1974), the notion of *macrocontext* would seem to be particularly important. Unlike a microcontext, which refers to that segment of the signifying chain that occurs when both signs are immediately present and evident, a macrocontext involves those parts of the signifying chain at work determining meaning for a sign when the referent is absent or nonevident. In this sense, a macrocontext functions to mediate an understanding of expressions that don't have an immediate mode for interpretation. A sender, for instance, creates meaning not with the expression "that a person is short," but leaves the creation of meaning to the receiver who, upon examination of the macrocontext (reality), realizes "the person" is 2 feet taller than anyone else in the room. Hence, the receiver derives meaning by realizing that the expression is irrevocably at odds with the circumstances evident in the macrocontext.

The significance of the macrocontext stems from its capacity to alter the necessarily desired interpretation, particularly as it may stem from an oppositional interpretation. *Irony* may result as a pattern of inter-

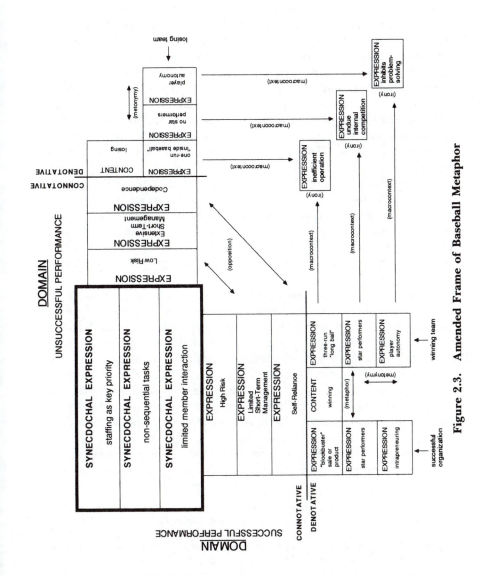

Figure 2.3. Amended Frame of Baseball Metaphor

33

pretation in the macrocontext to the extent that the original expression, mediated by an unintended expression housed in the mind of the receiver, may lead the auditor to derive an expression that is contrary to the intended.[5] Irony exists when two expressions possess one or more semantic features that are contrary when viewed in the macrocontext. An expression that derives its meaning through irony reveals alternate interpretations of what may have been the ideal or intended expression.

Figure 2.3 brings these two concepts together. Mediating the semantic extremes of winning and losing in Figure 2.3 is the macrocontext, or what the organizational member may construe as reality. For example, an organizational member might associate a denotative expression such as "three-run long ball" not with its intended metaphoric equivalent, "blockbuster sale or product," but instead with its ironic expression "inefficient operation." That is, in having observed the operation of the organization, the receiver of the message may draw on their personal impressions (macrocontext) and derive an interpretation notably at odds with the one intended. Similarly, an organizational member might associate a denotative expression such as "player autonomy" not with its metaphoric equivalent in the successful organization, "intrapeneuring," but because of recent difficulties encountered in interacting with others (macrocontextual cues), associate it instead with a propensity to "inhibit problem solving."

Incorporating these amendments into a semiotic frame increases the intricacy and potential accuracy of semiotic analyses. The many elements and processes that are involved in creating and refining organizational reality are, logically, more accessible with a more intricate tool. Accommodating a fuller range of expressions affords the investigator a better opportunity to understand how meaning is created and shared within an organizational setting. For instance, if investigators are able to diagnose the operative synecdochal expressions, they may find themselves peeping through a most revealing keyhole at primary elements of an organization's culture. Synecdochal expressions may, in fact, be linchpins to determining organizational wellness. As hinted at in the preceding paragraphs, a disconnect between the synecdochal expressions and the more

---

[5] Manning had incorporated irony into his analysis of organizational communication. Yet, his use of the trope seems to align more with the definition offered by poet Allen Tate, who observed that irony "was the arrangement of experience, either premeditated by art or accidentally appearing in the affairs of men which permits to the spectator an insight superior to that of the actor" (see Burke, 1962, pp. 513–515). Manning (1979) uses irony to describe his (spectator) impressions of the unusual similarities between the expressions of narcotic dealers and law enforcement officials (actors) in his study of the British constabulary (p. 667). Irony, as it is used here, functions as a trope that affects the interpretations of the organizational members (actors).

prevalent day-to-day expressions at the strictly connotative or denotative levels could be a primary indicator of a dysfunctional culture.

Beyond this, the amendments provide a basis for using semiotics in interpretive research venues other than culture studies. Incorporating synecdochal expressions, for example, permits the investigator to respond to individual symbols that characterize the entire organization. Identifying such expressions offers a researcher opportunity to explore the potential lineage of what may be the more commonly shared signs at the connotative and denotative levels. At one level, then, synecdochal expressions might be approached as a constraining force on the emergence of other expressions. Distinguishing the factions responsible for the creation and/or the dissemination of such expressions, or determining how these expressions function in confining the more commonly used connotative and denotative expressions, might give an investigator an enlightened view of the political milieu of the organization.

To the extent that synecdochal expressions might aid in identifying specific factions within an organization, they might also facilitate the identification of specific motives and, in turn, offer a first step towards identifying rhetorical intent. Operating from the core assumption that "organizations take the task of persuasion and the goal of employee identification very seriously," (Cheney, 1983a, p. 156), the agenda in rhetorical studies has been defined by its analysis of the role symbols play in the "inducement process" (see Cheney, 1983b), and an interest in how this inducement affects decision making (Tompkins & Cheney, 1983) and member commitment (Cheney & Tompkins, 1987). Synecdochal expressions, if understood as among the most "significant" expressions used in the organization, would appear a worthy concept for addressing many dimensions of the research questions driving this research agenda.

As investigators in the information-processing perspective begin to understand that information serves a more "symbolic" than "pragmatic" function in organizations (Putnam & Cheney, 1985, p. 145), messages that travel through the organization will come to be understood to be by-products of several forces. Technology, organizational tasks, and organizational roles, for instance, have been forwarded as defining and constraining forces offering organizational meaning. When synecdochal expressions are viewed as those that function connotatively to characterize the entire organization, they might be understood to be among such "metarules" that shape and constrain the interpretation of the vast majority of the messages that circulate throughout the organization.

Irony, generally, and macrocontext, specifically, permit the investigator to account more specifically for the affect setting plays in altering the relationship between the expression and the interpreter. The presence of ironic expressions, for instance, signals that there are forces working to create alternative interpretations of organizational reality. Chronicling the presence of such expressions and discerning how these expressions evolved offers the investigator insight into the creation of organizational meaning in two ways.

First, a prevalence of ironic expressions indicates that there are symbols capable of constituting a reality that runs counter to another preferred by certain organizational constituencies. To the extent that field research can effectively isolate ironic expressions, researchers will have identified message patterns that are refutive. If accomplished, such analyses might underscore not only why specific expressions failed to effectively bind members to the organization, but also permitting a closer scrutiny of the suasive factor and/or dysfunction of expressions that emerge as polysemous. Any work that exposes messages or expressions that are rife with antithetical interpretations would be advancing, even if serendipitously, the emancipation of organizational members who are "trapped" by such organizationally generated contradictions—traps that are clearly a part of the political perspective (Putnam & Cheney, 1985, p. 153).

Second, the tenor of the ironic expressions should tell the investigator much about the macrocontext, or those cues that function to shape the organizational member's interpretation of organizational events. Establishing a profile of the macrocontextual forces at work within an organization would be an inherent advantage for any interpretive investigator. A research method such as semiotics that not only allows for, but promotes the identification of intuitive ("deep structure") forces that shape meaning, is an interpretive methodology that would seem consonant with interests that are common to both information-processing and political perspectives. Indeed, if a dominant credo of the political perspective continues to be that political power stems from "the ability to guide the interpretation of organizational information and events" (Putnam & Cheney, 1985, p. 151), the seclusion of macrocontextual cues may provide the most privileged view yet of "who" controls message interpretation and "how" such control is achieved.

CONCLUSION

While questions undoubtedly remain regarding the use of semiotics as an interpretive research procedure, this chapter has addressed some of the issues with respect to how semiotics has served, and more significantly, might better serve the organizational researchers. In this regard, the proceeding pages have made it clear that the history of semiotic use in organizational research is, at best, scant. It has been the preferred procedure in but a handful of analyses; aiding primarily those investigators who have assumed organizational discourse functions to primarily to shape an organizational culture. By expanding the semiotic frame to incorporate a wider range of tropes and semiotic concepts, the procedure might be rendered one capable of attending to the needs of investigators operating in each of the predominant perspectives that currently drive organizational research. Semiotics thus exists as a viable and amendable procedure for focusing on how symbols or the forces that control symbol use not only explain and collaborate, but also induce and justify activity in organizational settings.

An important qualification remains. Amending current conceptualizations of semiotics in organizational analyses to be more readily adaptable to the variety of modes of discourse manifest in the organizational setting calls for a leap of faith on the part of the investigator. This chapter, if not the previous work of organizational investigators, has hinted at the sinuosity of semiotic research. Faith is necessary at that juncture when the investigator answers "yes" to the question, "does your innovation aid current understanding more than it adds to the quagmire of arcane methodological refinements?"

The preponderance of such a question, however, should not deter the organizational investigator from envisioning still other important revisions to semiotic application. Rather, the noteworthy difference in how Barley (1983b), Manning (1986, 1988), Fiol (1989), Bouissac (1976), and Tway (1976b) have chosen to wield semiotic procedures should hint at the variety of alternative emphases endemic to interpretive research. The amendments suggested here are, in this sense, limited, if not elementary, variations from a pool of potential alternations.

Interpretive procedures such as semiotics offer a unique access to the various systems of meanings and the forces that drive these systems within organizations. These procedures, however, are not to be simply set aside and cured over time. Accessing the intricate nuances in patterns of organizational communication dictates unremitting imaginative reassessment and reapplication of all research methodologies.

REFERENCES

Barley, S. (1983a). Semiotics and the study of occupational and organizational cultures. *Urban Life, 12*, 3–31.

Barley, S. (1983b). Semiotics and the study of occupational and organizational cultures. *Administrative Science Quarterly, 28*, 393–414.

Barthes, R. (1967). *Elements of semiology*. Boston: Beacon Press.

Bouissac, P. (1976). *Circus and culture*. Bloomington: University of Indiana Press.

Burke, K. (1962). *A grammar of motives*. Berkeley: University of California Press.

Cheney, G. (1983a). The rhetoric of identification and the study of organizational commu-
    nication. *Quarterly Journal of Speech, 69,* 143–158.
Cheney, G. (1983b). On the various and changing meanings of organizational member-
    ship: A field study of organizational identification. *Communication Monographs, 50,*
    342–362.
Cheney, G., & Tompkins, P. (1987). Coming to terms with organizational identification
    and commitment. *Central States Speech Journal, 38,* 1–15.
Clark, B. (1972). The organizational saga in higher education. *Administrative Science Quar-
    terly, 17,* 178–184.
Conrad, C. (1983). Organizational power: Faces and symbolic forms. In L. Putnam & M.
    Paconowsky (Eds.), *Communication and organizations: An interpretive approach.* Beverly
    Hills, CA: Sage.
Deal, T., & Kennedy, A. (1982). *Corporate culture: The rites and rituals of corporate life.*
    Reading, MA: Addison-Wesley.
Deetz, S. (1982). Critical interpretive research in organizational communication. *The West-
    ern Journal of Speech Communication, 46,* 131–149.
Eco, U. (1976). *A theory of semiotics.* Bloomington, IN: University of Indiana Press.
Eisenberg, E. (1984). Ambiguity as strategy in organizational communication. *Communica-
    tion Monographs, 51,* 277–242.
Fiol, M. C. (1989). A semiotic analysis of corporate language: Organization boundaries and
    joint venturing. *Administrative Science Quarterly, 34,* 277–303.
Gellner, E. (1985). *Relativism and the social sciences.* Cambridge, UK: Cambridge University
    Press.
Goffman, E. (1974). *Frame analysis.* Cambridge, MA: Harvard University Press.
Keidel, R. (1984). Baseball, football, and basketball: Models for business. *Organizational
    Dynamics,* pp. 5–18.
Keidel, R. (1985). *Game plans: Sports strategies for business.* New York: Berkeley Books.
Keidel, R. (1987). Team sports models as generic organizational framework. *Human
    Relations, 40,* 591–612.
Manning, P. (1979). Metaphors of the field: Varieties of organizational discourse. *Adminis-
    trative Science Quarterly, 24,* 66–671.
Manning, P. (1986). Signwork. *Human Relations, 39,* 283–308.
Manning, P. (1987). *Semiotics and fieldwork.* Beverly Hills, CA: Sage.
Manning, P. (1988). *Symbolic communication: Signifying calls and the police response.* Cam-
    bridge, MA: MIT Press.
Meyer, J., & Rowan B. (1977). Institutional organizations: Formal structure as myth and
    ceremony. *American Journal of Sociology, 83,* 340–363.
Morgan, G. (1980). Paradigms, metaphors and puzzle solving organization theory. *Admin-
    istrative Science Quarterly, 25,* 605–622.
Morgan, G. (1983). More on metaphor: Why we cannot control tropes in administrative
    science. *Administrative Science Quarterly, 28,* 601–607.
Morgan, G. (1986). *Images of organization.* Beverly Hills, CA: Sage.
Mumby, D. (1987). The political function of narrative in organizations. *Communication
    Monographs, 54,* 113–127.
Pacanowsky, M., & O'Donnell-Trujillo, N. (1982). Communication and organizational
    culture. *The Western Journal of Speech Communication, 46,* 115–130.
Peters, T., & Waterman, R. (1982). *In search of excellence.* New York: Harper & Row.
Putnam, L., & Cheney G. (1985). Organizational communication: Historical development
    and future directions. In T. Benson (Ed.), *Speech communication in the 20th century*
    (pp. 130–156). Carbondale, IL: Southern Illinois University.
Ramsey, D. (1987). *The corporate warriors.* Boston: Houghton-Mifflin.

Schofer, P., & Rice, D. (1977). Metaphor, metonymy, and synecdoche revis(it)ed. *Semiotica, 21*, 121–149.

Scott, R. (1967). On viewing rhetoric as epistemic. *Central States Speech Journal, 18*, 9–16.

Scott, R. (1976). On viewing rhetoric as epistemic. *Central States Speech Journal, 27*, 259–266.

Smircich, L. (1983). Concepts of culture and organizational analysis. *Administrative Science Quarterly, 28*, 339–358.

Smith, R., & Eisenberg, E. (1987). Conflict at Disneyland: A root-metaphor analysis. *Communication Monographs, 54*, 367–380.

Steiner, P. (1989). Semiotics. In E. Barnouw (Ed.), *The international encyclopedia of communication* (Vol. 3, pp. 46–50). Oxford University Press.

Tompkins, P., & Cheney, G. (1983). Account analysis of organizations: Decision making and identification. In L. Putnam & M. Pacanowsky (Eds.), *Communication and organizations: An interpretative approach* (pp. 123–146). Beverly Hills, CA: Sage.

Tway, P. (1976a). Verbal and non-verbal communication of factory workers. *Semiotic, 16*, 29–44.

Tway, P. (1976b). Cognitive processes and linguistic forms of factory workers. *Semiotica, 17*, 12–30.

3

The Symbolic Convergence Theory of Communication and Organizational Culture

Ernest G. Bormann

Each identifiable small group in the context of an organization has a culture. By culture I mean the total ways of living, organizing, and communicating built up in a group of human beings and transmitted to newcomers by verbal and nonverbal communication. The culture consists of the shared norms, reminiscences, stories, rites, and rituals that provide the members with a unique symbolic common ground. Some members from several or more small groups in the organization may share cultural features and these people will form larger communities of like-minded individuals. Finally, all or most members of an organization may share elements of a common culture that ties them together even though the cultures of their primary small groups and communities within the larger organizations have important differences. If most members of an organization share elements of a common culture, they have the basis for communicating and pulling together as a unified organization.

Currently there is an interest in the Western world in communication as it relates to organizational culture (Ott, 1989) and the relationship of that culture to the quality of production, morale, and productivity (Pacanowsky & O'Donnell-Trujiullo, 1982; Putnam & Pacanowsky, 1983). The interest in culture relates directly to the symbolic convergence theory. Symbolic convergence concerns the description and explanation of a communicative method by which groups create the symbolic features of their culture.

This chapter presents an overview of the symbolic convergence theory and indicates how studies using the theory have contributed to an understanding of organizational communication and to helping teachers, consultants, and participants understand and improve their analysis and practice of communication.

The symbolic convergence theory (Bormann, 1985) explains the appearance of a group consciousness with its implied shared emotions, motives, and meanings. The explanation is in terms of socially shared narratives and other imaginative discourse rather than of individual daydreaming.

OVERVIEW OF THE SYMBOLIC CONVERGENCE COMMUNICATION THEORY

The basic communicative process of the symbolic convergence theory is the sharing of group fantasies that brings about symbolic convergence for the participants. Investigators in small group communication laboratories (Bales, 1970; Bormann, 1975, 1990; Bormann, Pratt, & Putnam, 1978; Chesebro, Cragan, & McCullough, 1973; Dunphy, 1966; Gibbard, Hartman, & Mann, 1974) discovered the process of sharing fantasies when they investigated dramatizing messages and their effect on the group.

A dramatizing message is one that contains one or more of the following: a pun or other word play, a double entendre, a figure of speech, an analogy, an anecdote, an allegory, a fable, a narrative, or a story.

As they studied these dramatizing messages, investigators found that while observing members of either an informal social group or a task-oriented group meeting, they could isolate moments when the discussion dropped off and members were at a stalemate. The members often seemed tense and unsure of what to say next. Nonverbally they might slump down in their chairs, seem bored or distracted. At this point someone might dramatize by telling a joke, narrating a personal experience, or in another fashion portraying persona in action at some other place and time than the here-and-now meeting of the group. Some of these dramatizing messages made little difference to the lackadaisical atmosphere; the group members did not pay much attention to them. Some dramatizing, however, caused a symbolic explosion in the form of a chain reaction. As the fantasy chain begins a listener sits up and responds to the story. Something about it has caught the person's interest and attention. Another person responds with a laugh and adds onto the story. Still another joins in and soon the entire group comes alive. They all begin talking and they grow emotional. They may laugh or express fear or sadness. Then a member abruptly breaks off the episode by changing the subject, often by pulling the group back to work. The people who share in the imaginative enactment of the drama do so with appropriate responses. If the tone of the unfolding communication is humorous they laugh, if it is sad they appear dejected and melancholy. The technical term for such communicative episodes in which group members are pulled into sympathetic participation is a *fantasy chain*.

Fantasy chains take place not only during informal conversations as members of the organization take breaks, pass the time of day, or make small talk but also during business meetings and conferences. When people participate in a fantasy chain they come to symbolic convergence, they emotionally share symbolic common ground. They share a *group fantasy*. The content of the dramatizing message that sparks the fantasy chain is a *fantasy theme*. The fantasy theme is an observable record of the nature and content of the shared imagination. The theme is a social artifact that is public and that provides evidence of a small aspect of the common culture.

Not all dramatizing messages result in group apathy or in fantasy chains. Sometimes members express active disapproval when they hear the comment. They groan when they should laugh or laugh when they should be serious. This active rejection of dramatizing messages also provides data for the analysis of culture by showing the symbols, meanings, and emotions that members do not hold in common. Scholars and consultants can use differences among group members in terms of sharing, ignoring, or rejecting imaginative portrayals as evidence of symbolic divisions along rhetorical and cultural lines in the organizations under study.

The symbolic convergence theory distinguishes between the ongoing unfolding of experience and the messages that discuss events in other than the here-and-now. If several members in a company office begin to have a loud argument the situation might be dramatic. People watching the scene might become emotionally involved but, because the action is unfolding in their presence, it would not be a group fantasy for them. Suppose that some people who observed the argument present a structured dramatic account of the same event the next day while having coffee in the lunch room with several acquaintances. Their day-after dramatizations could lead to shared fantasies because the content is not about the here-and-now of their experience.

By reporting the events of the day before in dramatic terms, the observer is providing a plausible account of what happened and portraying the event so that it expresses emotions and motives. The dramatization might portray one of the disputants in a laudable light as defending right action while portraying the other as villainous and unethical. No matter how the speaker portrays the event the result is always an interpretation that puts a *spin* on what happened. Another observer might give an account of the event that interpreted it in different terms and reverse the characterizations of the two disputants making the hero of the first story the villain in the second person's account and vice versa. The sharing of group fantasies brings the participants into symbolic convergence in a way that explains what otherwise might be a confusing experience. In doing so the fantasy chain makes sense out of events and creates a common ground of meaning. Such shared meanings are an important component of culture and a prerequisite for members of the organization to achieve empathic communion, and also a meeting of the minds.

One result of symbolic convergence is that the participants have charged their emotional and memory banks with common meanings and emotions that can be set off by a shared symbolic cue. The communication phenomenon of the inside joke is an example of such a cue. Only those who have shared the fantasy theme that the inside joke refers to will respond in an appropriate fashion. The symbolic cue need not be an inside joke. The allusion to a previously shared fantasy may arouse tears or evoke anger, hatred, love, or affection as well as laughter and humor. Inside cues consist of code words, phrases, slogans, or nonverbal signs or gestures. Scholars and consultants who find that members share inside cues to trigger common cultural memories can use the discourse as evidence of previous fantasy chains and of symbolic convergence.

The communication dynamic of the inside cue makes possible the development of *types*. When members of an organizational unit share several similar themes, including particulars of scene, character, and situation, they have the basis for generalizing to a broader fantasy type.

Organizational members may generalize inductively from a series of specific fantasy themes to a more general drama. As a culture matures and grows more elaborate members tend to use some abstract and general fantasy types in their communication. Rather than dramatizing a fantasy theme they present a skeleton outline of stock scenario general enough to encompass several themes. An employee may say, "Upper management keeps asking for our opinions and when we give it to them, they ignore it and go ahead and do what they want anyway." The fantasy type works if the listeners have previously shared several fantasy themes about specific occasions when members of the "we" group have responded to the requests of upper managers, supplied information, and then heard nothing more about it. When group members use stock scenarios they are able to make quick summarizations of several similar cases. Such reminders recall for the members their common shared fantasy themes as well as using the precedent setting cases to explain new experiences and anticipate future events. The fantasy type explains the new request for information by suggesting *this is just like the other times when we have been asked.* The fantasy type also provides an implied anticipation of the future in terms of *we can anticipate that upper management will ignore our opinions and do what they want to do again.*

Scholars and consultants seeking evidence of symbolic convergence can find fantasy types in the public rhetoric that are signs of previously shared fantasy themes. The inductions require the specific dramas to be shared to form the basis of the more abstract dramas.

DIFFERING LEVELS OF ANALYSIS

Fantasy theme analysis is a contemporary movement to develop a broad-based program of critical studies in which some investigators use the same scholarly viewpoint and the same technical vocabulary so comparisons can be made across studies and generalizations about communication can be drawn on the basis of a number of investigations. Sufficient work has now been done using the symbolic convergence theory as a controlling perspective so a synthesis of findings is possible. The conclusions in this chapter are largely drawn from the Minnesota Studies of small group communication plus a series of doctoral dissertations and scholarly articles investigating organizational communication that used the symbolic convergence theory as an interpretative frame.

Studies using the symbolic convergence theory reveal that the organization is seldom a homogeneous culture in which most or all members share the same symbolic common ground. The typical organization exhibits a complex symbolic geography composed of a number of small and large conglomerates of consciousness living in greater or lesser harmony with one another. The symbolic geography provides the basis for an explanation of communication practices, successes, and failures as well as ways to anticipate future communication.

At the first level of analysis are clusters of a few employees who come together and communicate until they create a small group culture. These small groups may be formed by members who come together because they are part of the same organizational unit, such as an office force or a software development team. But, people also form small groups who come together informally in clusters that cut across organizational lines, such as the five people who usually have lunch together on the back loading dock or who like to go to a nearby bar after work.

The Minnesota Studies of small group communication (Bormann, 1990) reveal that when a clump of people communicate on the job regularly and begin to share fantasies that identify them as a separate group and that create a sense of history and cohesiveness, they will have created a separate small group consciousness and culture.

While some small groups will seldom communicate with others within the organization there are often group cultures that share considerable symbolic common ground and their members find it easy to talk across the group boundaries. On the other hand, the small group cultures may be antagonistic with one another, thus creating many problems in terms of talking across the group boundaries or in terms of talking with audiences composed of members of several groups.

If a communication consultant is studying a small group of people, (from 3 to 12 or 13), the investigator can examine the group's communication for shared fantasies, inside-cues, and fantasy types. He or she can then construct an overall description of the group's culture based on the textual analysis.

Since 1968, Bormann and his associates have been making case studies of the organizations that form the core of a course in small group and organizational communication. The organization is called Group Dynamics Institute and is a consulting, teaching, and research organization. The organization lasts for approximately three months and all of the meetings, written communication, and other communications are kept and become the basis for the case studies. Since 1970, the symbolic convergence theory and the study of the organizational culture has been a central rationale for much of the research.

An early finding of the case studies (Bormann, 1975) was related to intergroup competition within the organization. When groups within the organization came to competition their internal communication was characterized by dramatizing the insiders as heroes and the members of the opposing groups as villains. Typically, the shared fantasies emphasized the positive aspect of the insiders and denied any group weakness. They developed negative fantasy themes about the other group. The emotional tone of the fantasies encouraged hostility and anger towards the other groups. The dramas often included a theme of "They do not play fair like we do." Communication among groups tended to decrease under conditions of competition.

When one of the competing groups gained some outside recognition as having won or done better than a competitive group, the winning group sometimes fell prey to a "fat and complacent" stage. Their culture portrayed them as the best and the other units as less effective. The loser often began to chain into fantasies that denied or distorted the reality of their losing. They did not really lose. Someone outside the group stole the resources from them. If the group reevaluated its fantasies and accepted the loss the members sometimes splintered into hostile cliques, conflicts surfaced; blame for the loss was assigned. The group became more tense. The spiral sometimes continued until a tradition of losing (a loser's culture) became a way of group life. The converse also happened. The group then reexamined the situation and the members utilized the loss as a way to improve their social and task dimensions. They became more cohesive and effective.

The attempts to impose the structure of Group Dynamics, Inc. on the members of the organization as blueprinted by a formal table of organizations almost always failed. At first the investigators came to the conclusion that the formal structure was dysfunctional and not an important feature of the organizing activity. As time went on and more investigators made cultural analyses using the symbolic convergence theory it became apparent that the formal structure with the titles such as *supervisor, manager, director,* and so forth, remained symbolically important. The labels continued to be used in the dramatizing messages and in only one instance was there a rebellion that overthrew the formal structure and then created a different organization. The formal structure became a central symbolic force in the group's culture. Even when the members portrayed the formal structure as ineffective and no longer descriptive of what was happening, the structure remained a compelling feature of their discourse.

Members of the organization became preoccupied with power in every case. Rice (1963, 1965) examining unstructured large groups from the perspective of the Tavistock Workshops maintained that people found the unstructured group a terrifying experience because it was potentially unreasonable and violent.

The case studies of simulated organizations discovered similar forces at work among members of the larger groups. Repeatedly, they tested the limits of their power. The members' ambivalence to power and authority was a major feature of their early organizing effort. They wanted the security of norms and limits and clear jurisdictional boundaries and occasionally seemed willing to take orders from a strong authority figure. At the same time, whenever anyone or any group in the organization began to take power the other members would rise up and challenge the individual or group doing so.

Bormann, Pratt, and Putnam (1978) did a detailed case study of one of the simulated organizations that focused on "Power, Authority, and Sex." The GDI in this instance was one in which the shared fantasies played a significant role in the symbolic interpretation and resolution of the conflicts related to authority and power.

The organization was unusual in the dominance of female strength in the divisions of the organization as well as in the entire organization. The result was that women took over the leadership of the organization and controlled its direction. The predominant male response to female dominance was to withdraw from active participation in the organization. Other male responses included active striving for leadership followed by strong resentment and withdrawal, and active participation primarily in the socioemotional maintenance areas in either a joking or satirical vein.

The shared fantasies of the organizational members provided a key to the way the group members, male and female, tried to deal with issues of power, authority, and sex. The symbolic treatment of female leadership in terms of sexual symbols and dramas influenced and helped account for the male response.

A major finding was the recurrence of fantasy themes that linked leadership and male potency. The most common scenario depicted a male who, in his struggle for leadership, lost to a female competitor and in doing so, lost his sexual potency. One of the males said in an interview that a male leader undercut by the gender dynamic is castrated. Another man's diary reported that if the males did not go along with the women's plans they would be castrated. A woman noted that women should get used to being a "bitch" and a castrating woman. The males in one division used sexual teasing to try to counteract the power of an emerging female leader without success. Another woman emerged as a division leader as a result of a symbolic climate that supported her power with fantasies that were, for the most part, sexual. Among the fantasies that contributed to this climate were dramas about men who were drones, who fertilized the group process but might be killed as happens in the insect world with those male spiders who fertilize black widow spiders. These dramas were supplanted later in the group's life by a series of fantasies suggesting the unimportance of gender to task leadership. The fantasies of a group that no longer played games and that used some better way of judging a person than sexuality were generally shared by the group.

At a middle-range level of analysis, when most people within a communication subsystem, no matter what their official position or divisional membership, come to share several fantasies, inside cues, and fantasy types, they may come to share a rhetorical vision. A *rhetorical vision* is a unified putting together of the various scripts that gives the participants a broader view of things. Rhetorical visions are often integrated by a master analogy (McDonald, 1978) which structures the various elements together into a whole. When a rhetorical vision emerges, the participants in the vision come to form a *rhetorical community*.

The rhetorical visions may overlap to a greater or lesser degree some small group cultures in an organization. Such overlap creates commonalities that help communication among small group members who share a common rhetorical vision. Like small group cultures, however, rhetorical visions within the organizational context may be more or less antagonistic to one another and thus, create a host of communication conflicts and difficulties.

Dotlich's (1980) study illustrates the nature of organizational rhetorical visions. His research question related to organizational change resulting from more women moving into management positions. Dotlich used focus-group interviews in three organizations to study the shared fantasies, inside-cues, and types relating to female and male rhetorical portrayals of women in management. He interviewed samples of groups composed of male upper, middle, and lower managers and female upper, middle, and lower managers.

Dotlich found the men divided into two rhetorical communities. The first rhetorical vision he called the "traditional," and the second he named the "modern." The first vision portrayed the "good old days," while the second consisted largely of dramas set in the future. Dotlich was able to delineate the boundaries of both visions from the interview data. He found both visions in all three organizations. The visions were not correlated with formal position. Participants in both visions were to be found at all three levels of management.

The traditional male vision evoked frustration, anger, and outrage because of the actions of women who were pushy, aggressive, and rocking the boat. The modern male vision portrayed male frustration but attributed it to their personal responsibility and not to the presence of women in management. The modern male vision portrayed women in a favorable light with stories celebrating such qualities as male nurturing, personal interest, and fairness to women in their managerial careers.

None of the fantasies of the women interviewed matched the traditional male rhetorical vision. The women did share some overarching fantasies about how women managers should be treated and the opportunities they should have. They also dramatized the scene as one were they could pierce the veil of male buffoonery, ignorance, and refusal to accommodate to the changing role of women in society and in organizations. They portrayed women as having a clear view of how organizational decisions are made, how power is distributed, and how the network functions.

Although all the women in the interviews shared the vision of a basic awareness of what is the case, they developed alternative dramatizations of how best to proceed. Some women portrayed the ideal as one in which they would fight for women's rights. The fantasy type implied that they should challenge and change the male culture of the organization so it would become more congenial to female values and women in management. Other women chose to "fit in" and portrayed as laudatory a course that sought to adapt to the organizations as the protagonist found it. The second approach dramatized women as needing to learn the rules and the male culture and how to handle the problems of sexuality in the work place. If they learned the male culture and worked harder than their male counterparts there were opportunities in management and they would climb up the ladder to success.

Dotlich analyzed the four rhetorical communities to discover their communication implications. He concluded that the women who shared the fitting in strategy would find considerable symbolic common ground with those men who shared the modern male rhetorical vision. The women who shared the fight-back dramas and the men in the traditional male rhetorical vision had little in common. Their visions were symbolically so different that communication across their boundaries would be very difficult.

Dotlich's independent examination of the communication climates of the organizations bore out the inferences from the symbolic convergence theory. The organization that had many members sharing the modern male and the adaptive women rhetorical visions had the best communication climate of the three organizations studied. The organization that had more members sharing the traditional male and the fighting female visions had the poorest communication climate among the organizations.

In a series of studies of organizational cultures de Vries and Miller (1984) used the ideas of Wilfred Bion's basic assumptions groups (a psychiatric position that undergirds the Tavestock workshops) and found that the sharing of group fantasies resulted in three basic rhetorical visions.

The dependency assumption of Bion encouraged the sharing of group fantasies that resulted in a rhetorical vision whose central fantasy type featured an idealized charismatic leader. The hopes, ambitions, and goals of the vision all centered on the charismatic leader who often led the group to rapid success. In the organizations where the leader had passed from the scene there was a "bible" or some written legacy that group members had fantasized about until they had raised it to the level of holy writ. Dependency groups also had a vision characterized by a short time span. They focused on the current party line and the immediate call for action. The shared fantasy portrayed the charismatic leader as action-oriented, pragmatic, striving to achieve the desired results. The dependency groups did not do much deliberation in making decisions. What the leader ordered was what the followers did. The result was a trusting, unquestioning climate among the followers. Once the leaders were gone the shared fantasies kept the personae alive as important symbols. The vision then encouraged the bureaucratization of the organization in order to achieve success in the model of the original leader.

The pairing assumption of Bion encouraged the sharing of group fantasies that resulted in a rhetorical vision that was future oriented. Indeed, the participants spent so much time contemplating the future that they often neglected the pressing problems on which members of the other two visions would focus. The future emphasis in the rhetorical vision resulted in the members being preoccupied with goals rather than the means to achieve them. The pairing assumption encouraged the sharing of fantasies that resulted in a flexible decision-making style among the members. The culture was participative and democratic, emphasizing the social values of good human relations. The firms that exhibited the pairing rhetorical visions tended to be future-oriented, research and development, high-technology units or companies. Creativity, flexibility, and imagination were stressed in such organizational cultures.

The fight-or-flight assumption of Bion encouraged the sharing of group fantasies that resulted in a rhetorical vision that depicted a bi-valued world filled with threatening enemies for which the proper response was either fight or flight. The vision included a world sharply divided into friends and enemies. The predominant emotional evocation of the dramas was fear that made the vision rigid and inflexible. Organizational members developed avoidance and attack goals that became givens, and members did not discuss or change them. General goals were vague and the participants restricted their problem solving to immediate crises and to survival. The shared fantasies encouraged a decision-making style in which only the means to achieve the assumed goals were up for discussion. The fight-or-flight vision was preoccupied with the present and had a short time frame. The emphasis in the culture was on a specific battle with a clear villainous persona or a set of personae.

The rhetorical vision portrayed a narrow and rigid view of the world, one that did not change or develop. Dealing with the enemy mobilized energy and strong conviction among members as to the correctness of their actions and their interpretation of events. These shared fantasies often resulted in courageous action but they also resulted in noncoping wasted effort and a rigidity in decision making that often became escapist. Suspicion was rampant in the organization. Few were to be trusted. Those sharing the rhetorical vision associated with fight-or-flight were inclined to industrial espionage or other unethical behaviors.

Internal politics were rife with suspicion among departments, warring factions, and there was little teamwork. The vision had a tendency to result in organizational stagnation. When they failed, members blamed outsiders or internal villains, seldom themselves. The rhetorical vision featured battle metaphors in which victory went to the righteous. The vision often contained elements of paranoia and stressed member sacrifice and dedication to the goals of the organization.

At a macrolevel of analysis the employees of an organization may share more or less of the saga. A *saga* is a detailed narrative of the achievements and events in the life of a person, group, or community. The *organizational saga* (Baldridge, 1972; Clark, 1972) includes the shared group fantasies, the rhetorical visions, and the narratives of achievements, events, and the future dreams of the entire organization.

The saga provides the common symbolic ties that bind the participants to the organization and furnishes the symbolic aspects that relate to organizational culture and customs. To function, the saga, like a fantasy, must be shared.

The organizational saga answers such questions as: What kind of an organization are we? What kind of people are members of our organization? What do we do? What is our mission? Of what exploits of the past are we proud? Why are we admirable? What great things do we plan to do in the future? Answers to these questions provide an explanation of our better nature and our strength. They often are the aspects of their symbolic ground that organizational members emphasize when they develop messages for outside consumption. The organizational saga also will contain material aimed at insiders that emphasizes the heroic exploits and glorious future of the organization.

All or most of the employees of an organization may share the organizational saga. The saga, in such instances, overlaps to a greater or lesser degree the small group cultures and rhetorical visions within the organization. Some commitment to the organizational saga is important to the effectiveness and satisfaction that members experience in their communicative environment.

When there are several large rhetorical communities in the organization committed to different organizational sagas the result is often conflict. Conflict over policy, mission, decisions relating to future commitments, budget allocations, and the hiring and firing of new people are often battles fought in the war over the proper saga for our organization. In such circumstances organizational members will be attending many meetings to develop mission statements, plans for the future, and to clarify the basic purposes and functions of units and divisions.

Koval-Jarboe's (1986) longitudinal study over several years reveals how attempts by upper management to change an organization's saga affects the members' communication. Koval-Jarboe did an intensive study using the method of participant observations to track the sharing of fantasies associated with a major organizational change. She used

direct observation of meetings both formal and informal, written documents, memorandums, informal written messages, and interviews in her
study.

The chief executive officer of a division of a Midwestern University
left with his management team to be replaced by a new group. The new
management found an organization, according to Koval-Jarboe's analysis, in which most members shared a strong saga. The saga was organized by the analogy of the family. The organization's purpose was to
provide information and help to agriculture. The saga portrayed the
members as an extended farm family; informal, caring, and willing to
help one another. They saw themselves as people willing to jump in and
help do the work when someone was overloaded. They had strong
networks of informal communication. Members would often go from
workplace to workplace with a cup of coffee to pass the time of day when
things were quiet. The director of the organization was dramatized as
a father figure and there were strong paternalistic norms operating
through the organization with much participative decision making.
There was, however, a minority rhetorical vision whose members shared
in much of the saga but saw the participative features of decision making
to be something of a sham and that decisions of importance were really
made by the upper management.

The new management team had a group culture which identified the
members as professional managers. When they took over upper management positions and analyzed the current state of the organization,
they decided that it needed an overhaul to make it more businesslike and
competitive. They saw considerable laxness in the way members did
their duties and made decisions. They started promulgating their new
saga organized around the analogy of the educational unit to a business.

With the new management in place, the organization began to go
through several years of symbolic turmoil as employees sought to make
sense out of what was happening. Some clung to the family analogy and
tried to continue the old saga. Many of these began to share fantasies of
the victimage type. The new management team began changes in terms
of affirmative action and women's role in the organization. Some people
began to dramatize these and other changes as an improvement over the
old ways. These employees began to share in the new saga. The professors in the organization began to resist the new vision and make clear
a view they probably always held that portrayed them as different from
the others and more like professors in other university departments.
They did not share in the business analogy.

At the conclusion of Koval-Jarboe's study the organizational saga had
changed. The family saga was largely extinct although some members
still recalled it with nostalgia as they talked about the good old days. Most

of the employees now shared the new business vision with the professional vision claiming a minority.

Interestingly enough, although the new vision became the symbolic reality that provided the employees with their sense of identity, motivations, emotional evocations, and values, many participants in the new vision divorced the persona of the new director from the vision and portrayed him as the arch villain in their dramas. The director left for a new position at about the same time that Koval-Jarboe completed the study.

Koval-Jarboe's study provides a thickly textured account of the communication geography and its changes during the transition. Members of the organization could have been aided in their transition from one saga to another by an understanding of the symbolic convergence theory and the data collected by Koval-Jarboe.

Cragan and Shields (1992) report a consulting study concerned with the change in corporate symbolic realities resulting from mergers and buy outs. They argue that in such instances the identity of the company died and a new identity had to be developed. In the instance of Beta Company (masked identity), Cragan and Shields were contracted as paid communication consultants for a New York advertising agency in a competitive bidding situation. The agency hired the communication consultants because of a presentation stressing the symbolic convergence theory as a way to provide the necessary analysis and information. Beta Company was a manufacturer of nationally marketed agricultural feeds.

Cragan and Shields conducted internal and external research to find a viable corporate name and identity, to position the corporation in the marketplace, to segment the market for the products, and to determine pretested dramatizations to be used in internal and external communication.

They identified four corporate sagas that had been used internally over the years. Their research indicated that each of the four had outlived their usefulness and no longer reflected actual conditions within the corporation and in the external environment. There had been a series of negative chaining fantasies weakening the older sagas. Their study did reveal a series of fantasy themes and types that suggested the possible emergence of a new and unifying saga.

Beta company accepted most of the recommendations and tried to put them into effect. Cragan and Shields note the difficulty of assessing the results of their study. Sales of Beta Company increased by 18% despite a downturn in the economy. Still, parts of the intervention met with limited success. The consultants concluded that the symbolic convergence theory explained the chaos resulting from the takeover of the Beta Company. They also noted they could identify corporate sagas with relative ease. The more difficult problem was to try to create a useful unifying saga in an environment of symbolic chaos.

In the United States, organizations embroiled in internal battles among differing rhetorical communities will often decide to reorganize their structure. Reorganizing the formal structure of the organization seldom works if the problem is related to differing social realities based upon differing rhetorical visions. What is required is an understanding of the communication problems and a plan for organizational members to work cooperatively on a solution for their common symbolic difficulties.

Using the symbolic convergence theory as an explanatory account enables the organizational communication scholar to search for the boundaries of rhetorical communities. Discovering the boundaries of the typical business firm or religious or educational institution will reveal a complicated symbolic terrain. Such analysis is a strong antidote to interpretations that select out of the complexity a small cluster of ideas and suggest that this cluster represents the essence of an organization's communication and culture.

THE ORGANIZATION AS A COMMUNICATION SYSTEM

Consultants may well look at the organization as a communication system on the assumption that they are studying a complex process that has interrelated subparts and that important features emerge from the complex give-and-take of elements of the system.

One possible way to divide the total is to examine who has control of a subsystem of messages. For example, upper management will control some of the formal communications. Only those scripts that upper management approves are formally dramatized in such messages as quarterly reports, mission statements, and official policy statements. Large organizations often have professional communicators, such as public relations or media specialists, who develop press releases and speak for the organization at press conferences.

Upper management also may use these communication specialists for internal persuasive campaigns aimed at increasing motivation or productivity or compliance with safety regulations. The campaign may include a variety of messages and many dramatizations in slogans, posters, company newsletters, individual letters, or memos signed by various officials.

Some formal communication may be controlled by middle management and some by workers and technicians. The latter may include such things as letters to the company newspaper, recommendations in a suggestion box, or formal complaints through grievance procedures or legal channels.

Informal communication tends to be an open marketplace for dramatizations that is beyond the control of any special interest group, formal organizational unit, or management level. Within this informal system the carefully orchestrated campaign developed and planned by management may include dramatizations that become shared fantasies. On the other hand, people may reject, ridicule, or ignore the dramatizations. New and much different fantasies may chain through these informal systems and create a rhetorical vision for a community of people that cuts across organizational structures, management levels, and primary group memberships.

Eyo's (1985) investigation of a major multinational corporation reveals the communication effects of efforts by upper management to introduce organizational change. In addition, Eyo's study replicates Dotlich's investigation of rhetorical visions and provides further supporting evidence for their nature and importance in communication. Eyo used focus-group interviews of a sample of employees in involvement teams, their supervisors, and the facilitators of the groups to examine the sharing of fantasies related to the forming of the involvement teams that was a major organizational change.

Eyo found two important rhetorical visions in the populations he studied. Again, as in other studies (Dotlich, 1980; Kroll, 1981), the rhetorical visions cut across formal hierarchical levels and boundaries. The first vision he called "Participative Productivity" and the second "Victimization."

The first vision portrayed the instituting of the involvement teams as changing the organizational climate for the better. The change began a time of difficulties but with support from all levels of management and the willing efforts of the rank and file things had been improving ever since. Workers were given an opportunity to provide input into decisions relating to working conditions, quality improvement, and productivity increases. They had a chance to meet their supervisors in a setting that cut down on status barriers so real communication could take place and they often found that the supervisors were more human and more approachable than they had originally thought. Evidence was accumulating of increased morale, more organizational commitment, increased productivity, and higher quality work since the change.

The victimage rhetorical vision, on the other hand, portrayed the change as forced upon participants by the efforts of upper management. Upper management had foisted the change on them and then did not support the effort. Victimized by upper management the workers had been left with additional duties to add to their burden with no additional

reward. Supervisors were also victimized by having their tasks complicated so they no longer could devote full attention to their real job which
was to supervise their people to assure high levels of good quality work.
The newly added group facilitators were also victimized as they were
expected to work miracles without proper support from management or
the workers. Generally the participants in the victimage rhetorical vision
were cynical about what had happened and portrayed their communicative climate as bad before the change and getting worse because of it.

Upper management, trying to initiate communication to facilitate the
change, would find members of the first rhetorical vision open to persuasion because of the credibility of the personae of management. Upper management would face a much more difficult task communicating
with members of the victimage vision because they represented the arch
villains who had caused participants their problems. Much of the rancor
that is to be found in many organizations stems from the victimage
fantasy type that crops up repeatedly and in which the participants see
themselves as harassed and persecuted by upper management and often
by the Chief Executive Officer.

Another way to divide the subsystems as a consultant is in terms of the
network of communication of which a group of employees is a part. A
given employee may never hear some fantasies because he or she is not
part of a communication network through which the drama is flowing.

There are several forces that restrict the flow of messages to limited
subgroups or communities within the organization and thus make it
unlikely that all members will have access to all the dramatizations that
could form the basis for common symbolic ground.

Since information is often power in the organizational context, there
are many pressures for secrecy. Departments and division may not want
other units of the organization to know what they are up to because they
compete with them for resources, status, prestige, and power. Upper
management may feel that certain key information should not be made
generally available to everyone. Employees on the production line or in
the secretarial pool may not want supervisors or upper level managers
overhearing their communication about what they really feel and think
of the way things are going. People committed to various informal and
formal groups may not want to tell relative strangers about gossip,
rumors, or interpersonal relationships within these offices and divisions.

APPLICATIONS FOR ORGANIZATIONAL CONSULTANTS

The main task for someone employing the symbolic convergence theory
to study organizational communication is to find evidence that symbolic

convergence has taken place; that numbers of people have shared a group consciousness.

Communication consultants conducting an audit of an organization (Cragan & Shields, 1981) can use such techniques as individual and focus-group interviews to discover the dramatizing messages that members tell and retell to one another. Field observations of chaining fantasies in informal and formal meetings are also useful ways to gather data.

Consultants can find additional material by reading official written messages such as mission statements, or outlines of organizational and unit goals and plans. Unofficial written messages such as satirical poems, songs, and jokes are important if they spread rapidly and are shared. Jokes, cartoons, and other humorous messages on bulletin boards, in company newsletters and magazines, or as graffiti on rest room walls can be important.

Having gathered a representative or random sample of messages, the consultant should next investigate the messages to find similar dramatizing material that appears in the group's communication in different contexts. Such repetition is evidence of symbolic convergence and the resultant messages are useful for further analysis.

Cryptic allusions to symbolic common group provides other evidence of the sharing of fantasies. Employees who have shared a fantasy can recollect both the denotative and connotative meanings that resulted by using an agreed-upon cryptic symbolic cue. The communication analyst should trace back the inside cue to find the original fantasy theme for further analysis.

When communicators begin to use fantasy types or allusions to types in their messages it is further evidence that fantasy themes have been shared. People cannot generalize to the more abstract type without having first shared at least several themes of a similar nature.

Bormann, Nichols, Howell, and Shapiro (1982) have outlined a technique for making script analyses of fantasy themes and types within an organization. Once communication consultants have an accurate map of the symbolic landscape they can examine the common heroes and villains, the shared fantasy types, values, motives, and emotions to gain an understanding of the communication climate and culture.

Consultants can use the communication analysis to intervene (Bormann, 1982) with groups and units whose members share common symbolic elements and use such techniques as discussion and debate, confrontation and working through to get consensus, or compromise on issues that cause disagreement and conflict within the organization.

Where the rhetorical fantasies approach mirror images of one another, the lack of common ground often makes the use of data, evidence, and argument ineffective in managing intergroup conflict. In such circumstances, consciousness-raising communication designed to convert members of one rhetorical vision to the other is a possibility. Consciousness raising, or conversion communication, is time-consuming and raises a host of ethical problems (Bormann, 1986).

REFERENCES

Baldridge, J. V. (1972). Organization change: Institutional sagas, external challenges, and internal politics. In J. V. Baldridge & T. Deal (Eds.), *Managing changes in educational organizations* (pp. 123–144). Berkeley, CA: McCutcheon.

Bales, R. F. (1970). *Personality and interpersonal behavior*. New York: Holt, Rinehart & Winston.

Bormann, E. G. (1975). *Discussion and group methods: Theory and practice* (2nd ed.). New York: Harper & Row.

Bormann, E. G. (1982). Symbolic convergence theory of communication: Applications and implications for teachers and consultants. *Journal of Applied Communication Research, 10*, 50–61.

Bormann, E. G. (1985). Symbolic convergence theory: A communication formulation based on homo narrans. *The Journal of Communication, 35*, 128–138.

Bormann, E. G. (1986). Small group communication and consciousness creating, consciousness raising, and consciousness sustaining. In E. Slembek (Ed.), *Miteinander Sprechen und Handeln* (pp. 35–45). Frankfurt: Scriptor Verlag.

Bormann, E. G. (1990). *Small group communication: Theory and practice* (3rd ed.). New York: Harper & Row.

Bormann, E. G., Nichols, R. G., Howell, W. S., & Shapiro, G. L. (1982). *Interpersonal communication in the modern organization* (2nd ed.). Englewood Cliffs, NJ: Prentice-Hall.

Bormann, E. G., Pratt, J., & Putnam, L. (1978). Power, authority, and sex: Male response to female leadership. *Communication Monographs, 45*, 119–155.

Chesebro, J. W., Cragan, J. F., & McCullough, P. W. (1973). The small group technique of the radical revolutionary: A synthetic study of consciousness raising. *Communication Monographs, 40*, 136–146.

Clark, B. (1972). The organizational saga in higher education. *Administrative Science Quarterly, 17*, 178–184.

Cragan, J. F., & Shields, D. C. (1981). *Applied communication research: A dramatistic approach*. Prospect Heights, IL: Waveland Press.

Cragan, J. F., & Shields, D. C. (1992). The use of symbolic convergence theory in corporate strategic planning. *Journal of Applied Communication Research, 20*, 199–218.

de Vries, M. F. R. K., & Miller, D. (1984). Group fantasies and organizational functioning. *Human Relations, 37*, 111–134.

Dotlich, D. L. (1980). *Worlds apart: Perceptions of opposite sex managers in three modern organizations*. Unpublished doctoral dissertation, Department of Speech-Communication, University of Minnesota.

Dunphy, D. C. (1966). Social change in self-analytic groups. In P. J. Stone, D. C. Dunphy, M. S. Smith, & D. M. Ogilivie (Eds.), *The general inquirer: A computer approach to content analysis* (pp. 287–340). Cambridge, MA: MIT Press.

Eyo, B. (1985). *Quality circles, involvement teams, and participative management in modern business culture: A study of the rhetorical visions of line-unit managers, employees, and facilitators*. Unpublished doctoral dissertation, Department of Speech-Communication, University of Minnesota.

Gibbard, G. S., Hartman, J. J., & Mann, R. D. (Eds.). (1974). *Analysis of groups.* San Francisco: Jossey-Bass.

Koval-Jarboe, P. (1986). *An analysis of organizational culture during change.* Unpublished doctoral dissertation, Department of Speech-Communication, University of Minnesota.

Kroll, B. S. (1981). *Rhetoric and organizing: The Twin Cities' women's movement 1969–1976.* Unpublished doctoral dissertation, Department of Speech-Communication, University of Minnesota.

McDonald, J. (1978). *Rhetorical movements based on metaphor with a case study of Christian Science and its rhetorical vision.* Unpublished doctoral dissertation, Department of Speech-Communication, University of Minnesota.

Ott, K. (1989). *An historic explanatory study of the evolution and development of organizational culture in speech communication.* Unpublished doctoral dissertation, Department of Speech-Communication, University of Minnesota.

Pacanowsky, M., & O'Donnell-Trujillo, N. (1982). Communication and organizational cultures. *Western Journal of Speech Communication, 46,* 115–130.

Putnam, L., & Pacanowsky, M. (Eds.). (1983). *Communication and organizations: An interpretive approach.* Beverly Hills, CA: Sage.

Rice, A. E. (1963). *The enterprise and its environment.* London: Tavistock.

Rice, A. E. (1965). *Learning for leadership: Interpersonal and intergroup relations.* London: Tavistock.

4

An Alternative Approach to Using Interpretative Theory to Examine Corporate Messages and Organizational Culture*

Cornelia A. Freeman
George A. Barnett

Within organizational communication, organizational culture is most commonly studied from a symbolic perspective (Bormann, 1983; Pacanowsky & O'Donnell-Trujillo, 1982; Pondy, Morgan, Frost, & Dandridge, 1983; Putnam, 1982; Putnam & Pacanowsky, 1983). This theoretical position defines the organization as a system of shared meanings and symbols. It treats the concepts of organization and communication as essentially interchangeable, and research focuses on how to "read" or decipher the organization as a culture (Smircich, 1983). Interpretive theory is commonly used as the basis for studying "the sense-making practices of organizational members, as manifested in their use of organizational symbolism" (Mumby, 1987, p. 113). The symbolic approach centers on the meanings organizational members attach to events based on their interpretations. Key concepts include meaning, belief, and faith (Bolman & Deal, 1984). The goals of research are to generate insights, explain events, and seek understanding (Putnam & Pacanowsky, 1983).

In its simplest form, organizational culture has been defined as "the way we do things around here" (Deal & Kennedy, 1982). An organization's culture includes the shared norms, reminiscences, stories, rites, and rituals that provide members with unique symbolic common ground (Bormann, 1983). Clearly, when culture is defined in this way, the symbolic perspective lends itself well to interpretation of the meanings

* A paper presented at the Organizational Communication Division of International Communication Association, Chicago, Illinois, May 23–27, 1991.

The authors would like to thank Barry Roach and James Danowski for their assistance in this research.

of events such as rites and rituals, and to the significance of the beliefs and values shared by organizational members.

The primary research methods used in studying organizational culture from a symbolic perspective are naturalistic and include qualitative methods, ethnography, and hermeneutics (Putnam, 1982). Research is subjective, interpretive, and critical. Corporate rhetoric and its link to the organization's culture is most frequently examined from a rhetorical-critical perspective.

The concept of culture, however, remains rather vague and has been defined in a variety of ways. Wuthnow (1987) writes, "Culture remains, by many indications, vaguely conceptualized, vaguely approached methodologically, and vaguely associated with value judgments and other sorts of observer bias" (pp. 5–6). Wuthnow argues that culture continues to have widely different connotations ranging from consisting of beliefs and attitudes to representing an objectified ontological system. As a result, problems arise with regard to the degree to which culture can or should be approached scientifically versus interpretively. Wuthnow further argues that the radical subjectivity with which the traditional study of culture has been associated clearly leads to problems of evidence, method, and interpretation that many researchers would like to avoid or minimize where possible.

One alternative view of organizational culture defines culture as "an emergent property of the [organizational] members' communication activities which, in turn, acts to restrict future communication" (Barnett, 1988, p. 101). Such a view suggests culture is learned, evolves with new experiences, and can be changed if one understands the dynamics of the learning process (Schein, 1985).

Organizational members learn the culture from the messages they hear and read. Thus, it follows that an analysis of an organization's messages will reveal much about its culture. Cheney and Frenette (1990) write, "If representative and rich samples of corporate public discourse are examined, we should be able to draw some interpretive conclusions . . . about the values of contemporary corporate America" (p. 9). If this is valid, then an analysis of a specific organization's written messages should provide information about its values, which relates directly to its corporate culture.

Institutional theory suggests that the messages produced by the institution form the culture of the institution. "Effective leaders are able to define . . . the organization's institutional values—its distinctive mission" (Scott, 1987, p. 494), and they do so in large part through the messages they generate. Scott (1987) further states that,

institutionalization is viewed as the social process by which individuals come to accept a shared definition of social reality—a conception whose validity is seen as independent of the actor's own views or actions but is taken for granted as defining the 'way things are' and/or the 'way things are to be done.' (p. 496)

This social reality, in essence, represents the culture of the institution, and it is shared through the communication of organizational messages.

An organization's culture is communicated through a variety of channels (i.e., informal interpersonal networks, formal and informal written communication), for example, memos, bulletin boards, employee newsletters, annual reports and policy manuals, and external mass media communication on television, radio, and in print (Barnett, 1988). The corporate rhetoric of an organization necessarily communicates its culture (i.e., its language patterns, values, attitudes, beliefs and thoughts). While many messages in an organization are communicated verbally, it is the written messages that are more lasting and permanent and which do not vary across individuals. A written message does not change in form regardless of who reads it and when it is read.

It is also important to consider the source of an organization's written messages. Schein (1985) suggests that it is the leaders in an organization who determine and define the culture. It is these same leaders— corporate executives, department directors, managers—who compose and/or guide the creation of most of the internal written communication. It is for these reasons that it is useful and appropriate to study these written messages as part of the process of examining organizational culture. "We need to broaden our view of organizational rhetoric/persuasion to include the actual range of 'internal' and 'external' messages produced by/in/for organizations" (Cheney & Frenette, 1990, p. 3; emphasis omitted).

This chapter offers a method for analyzing written corporate messages and describing organizational culture. While culture has traditionally been approached interpretively, this chapter discusses a less subjective, more precise method for examining the actual permanent recorded messages produced by an organization and for describing its culture. A content analysis was conducted of various written corporate messages produced by an organization. The content analysis identified key words and language patterns. A description of the company's culture was then generated from the quantitative analysis of the company's written messages.

METHOD

The Organization

The organization whose corporate messages were analyzed is a medical equipment manufacturing company located in a small northeastern city.

Founded in 1915, the privately held, family-operated company employs 1,300 people. It designs, manufactures, and sells high-technology instruments and equipment for use in health care and industry. The company markets its instruments and equipment worldwide and has manufacturing and distribution centers in Canada, Ireland, and Germany.

The Content Analysis Software

Content analysis of the organization's messages is a first step toward a more objective examination of an organization's culture. "Content analysis techniques can be used to establish the existence and frequency of relatively straightforward cultural categories and to demonstrate empirical correlations among the distribution of these categories" (Wuthnow, 1987, p. 340). Two different computer-based content analysis programs were used to analyze the organization's mediated messages, CATPAC (Woelfel & Holmes, 1982) and NETIMAGE (Danowski, Andrews, & Edison-Swift, 1985).

Barnett (1988) discusses the use of CATPAC to identify the critical symbols out of which an organization's culture is composed. It operates as explained below. The CATPAC program reads the text of the organizational media. Every sentence (or other grammatical unit) is separated from every other by a delimiter. This guarantees that the words are analyzed as parts of sentences rather than only as single words. The program then reads the words and deletes any of a list of articles, prepositions, transitive verbs, conjunctions, and other words as specified by the analyst that have proven problematic in the past or distort the description of the organization's culture.

At this point the program counts the occurrences of the remaining words. The infrequently occurring words are deleted, such that only the one hundred (or slightly less) most frequently occurring words remain. From this pool, a words-by-units matrix of frequencies is created. This matrix is then postmultiplied by its transpose, resulting in a words-by-words matrix of co-occurrences. A hierarchical cluster analysis is performed on the cooccurrence matrix (Johnson, 1967). The results of CATPAC is a list of the frequencies of the one hundred most prevalent words and how these words cluster. In this way, the organization's culture can be more precisely interpreted.

Network analysis may also be used for computer-based content analysis to describe an organization's culture (Danowski et al., 1985). Mediated messages are first passed by a sliding window 3 to 10 words wide. If two words co-occur in this window, they are assigned a link. This procedure is repeated by moving the window one word at a time until the entire text is read. These data are then entered into the NEGOPY network analysis program (Richards, 1988) which identifies groups of words, words which link groups of words, and others which are structurally isolated. These groups of words may be used in the same way as in the cluster from CATPAC.[1]

Procedures

Approximately 40 pages of text produced by the organization were selected. The documents analyzed included internal employee newsletters, recruitment materials, product advertisements, and human resources materials. All messages were communicated to employees or potential employees during 1988 and 1989. These messages were typed into a personal computer[2] using a standard word processing package and then uploaded into a mainframe computer for analysis.

CATPAC eliminated conjunctions, prepositions, and similar terms from the analysis to reduce the amount of information to be addressed and to yield theoretically useful generalizations. Table 4.1 lists the words that were eliminated from the analysis.

CATPAC provided the frequencies of occurrences of the 91 most widely used words and the categories of words that describe the organization's culture. The unit of analysis used was the sentence, because the sentence is the recording unit most frequently used when one is interested in words or phrases that occur together (Weber, 1985).

RESULTS

CATPAC

A total of 3,137 words were analyzed, resulting in the identification of 91 unique words which occurred more than 16 times. These words were listed in terms of their frequency of occurrence. Word clusters were also presented. Table 4.2 lists the words of the corporate messages in descending order of occurrence.

From this information, the language patterns used by the organization begin to emerge. The key words (those occurring most frequently) used in the written messages are presented along with how frequently they occurred within the total messages analyzed. For example, in the

---

[1] It is recognized that these categorizations are not mutually exclusive; however, this is the tone that is set in the organizational communication and culture literature.

[2] Two more efficient methods would have been to obtain the text in electronic form directly from the company or to use an optical scanner and character recognition software to produce machine readable code.

Table 4.1. Words Omitted from CATPAC Analysis

AND	ABOUT	ALSO	AN	AND
ARE	AS	AT	BECAUSE	BUT
BY	ELSE	FOR	FROM	HAS
HERE	HOWEVER	IN	ITS	IT'S
OF	ONE	OR	SINCE	THAN
THAT	THAT'S	THE	THESE	TO
UNTIL	WAS	WERE	WHY	WILL
WITH				

present analysis, the most frequently occurring word, "our," occurred 285 times (27.26%). Such frequent use of the term "our" suggests a group or family orientation in the organization's written messages. The founders' names were the next most frequently occurring words at 158 times and 149 times (15.11% and 14.25%, respectively), suggesting frequent reference to the founders in the organization's written messages. This is in keeping with Schein's (1983) position that the founder of an organization creates a culture within the organization.

Table 4.3 lists the word clusters that emerged from the present analysis. These word clusters are believed to represent the cultural categories communicated in the organization's written messages which allow for a more objective, precise description of its culture. Clusters were identified as those groups of words that cooccurred at least as many times as the least frequent of the 91 most frequent words (i.e., at least 16 times).

For example, the two words that cooccur most frequently in the organization's written messages are "cofounder and part of the company name" and "fiber," which form the first cluster. The next cluster is composed of six words: "medical," "have," "all," "cofounder and current president's name," "your," and "manufacturing." The third identifiable cluster consists of the words "how" and "employees." This information suggests the company's written messages focus heavily on describing itself and referring to its past (references to founders' and president's name, type of business). The company also tends to see itself as a family (references to "your," "all," and "employees"). It is interesting to note that currently one of the organization's objectives involves focusing its messages toward the future; indeed, the organization feels its current messages tend to refer heavily to the past and past accomplishments.

The next most frequently cooccurring words are "sales" and "applications," which suggests the company is focusing on business goals involving sales and application for the instruments and equipment it manufactures.

The largest cluster of words—"optic," "use," "division," "product," "you," "products," "company," "first," "their," "problems," "specific

Table 4.2. Descending Word Frequency List

Word	Frequency	Percent
OUR	285	27.26
(NAME OF FOUNDER 1)	158	15.11
(NAME OF FOUNDER 2)	149	14.25
PRODUCTS	99	9.00
QUALITY	97	9.00
FIBER	68	6.50
HAVE	64	6.00
PRODUCT	62	5.00
YOU	58	5.00
MEDICAL	57	5.00
CAN	56	5.00
SALES	55	5.00
NEW	54	5.00
ALL	46	4.40
YOUR	44	4.00
TIME	44	4.00
MANUFACTURING	43	4.00
DIVISION	42	4.00
MORE	41	3.00
COMPANY	39	3.00
FIRST	39	3.00
THEIR	37	3.00
LIGHT	34	3.00
EQUIPMENT	31	2.96
BEEN	31	2.96
DESIGN	31	2.96
PROCESS	30	2.00
LINE	29	2.00
OPTICS	29	2.00
ONE	28	2.00
WHEN	28	2.00
INSTRUMENTS	27	2.00
INDUSTRY	27	2.00
PRODUCTION	27	2.00
LAMP	27	2.00
OTHER	26	2.49
OPTIC	26	2.49
CUSTOMERS	26	2.49
SERVICE	26	2.49
DATA	25	2.39
CUSTOMER	25	2.39
WELL	24	2.00
NEEDS	24	2.00
MARKET	24	2.00
MARKETING	24	2.00
MOST	23	2.00
INTO	23	2.00
(POSSESSIVE NAME OF FOUNDER 2)	23	2.00

Table 4.2. Descending Word Frequency List
(Continued)

Word	Frequency	Percent
THEY	22	2.00
MEET	22	2.00
INDUSTRIAL	22	2.00
MANY	22	2.00
HOW	22	2.00
EMPLOYEES	21	2.00
TECHNOLOGY	21	2.00
THROUGH	21	2.00
DEVELOPMENT	21	2.00
MAKE	21	2.00
NOT	20	1.00
OUT	20	1.00
JUST	20	1.00
WHAT	19	1.00
COLLECTION	19	1.00
USE	19	1.00
COMPONENTS	19	1.00
RIGHT	19	1.00
PROBLEMS	19	1.00
[SPECIFIC DIVISION]	18	1.72
BUSINESS	18	1.72
VIDEO	18	1.72
BAR	18	1.72
ENGINEERING	18	1.72
TEAM	18	1.72
INTERNATIONAL	18	1.72
TRAINING	18	1.72
WORK	18	1.72
HIGH	17	1.63
APPLICATIONS	17	1.63
SPECIAL	17	1.63
SOME	17	1.63
HELP	17	1.63
BOTH	17	1.63
DISTRIBUTORS	17	1.63
DIAGNOSTIC	16	1.00
WORLD	16	1.00
THEM	16	1.00
GOOD	16	1.00
PROVIDE	16	1.00
CAPABILITIES	16	1.00
EVERY	16	1.00

division"—also focuses on the business the company is in, namely, developing optic products for use and being a leader "first" in the field. Reference to "problems" is reflective of the company's current difficulties in meeting these challenges.

Table 4.3.   Word Clusters

(from most frequent to least frequent co-occurrence clusters)

1.   [COFOUNDER AND PART OF COMPANY NAME] – FIBER
2.   MEDICAL – HAVE – ALL – [COFOUNDER AND CURRENT PRESIDENT] –
     YOUR – MANUFACTURING
3.   HOW – EMPLOYEES
4.   SALES – APPLICATIONS
5.   OPTIC – USE – DIVISION – PRODUCT – YOU – PRODUCTS – COMPANY
     – FIRST – THEIR – PROBLEMS – [SPECIFIC DIVISION]
6.   WELL – NEEDS – MARKET – MARKETING – NEW – SPECIAL

(When the frequency of co-occurrence is lowered from 16 to 13 times, the following
  words also become part of Cluster 6: LAMP – CUSTOMER – TUNE –
  CUSTOMERS)
When the frequency of co-occurrence is lowered to 12 times, the word WORK also
  becomes part of Cluster 4, and the following clusters also appear:

7.   OTHER – ENGINEERING
8.   PEOPLE – TRAINING
9.   DIAGNOSTIC – WORLD

The final cluster that includes words that cooccur at least 16 times—
"well," "needs," "market," "marketing," "new," "special"—suggests the
company is currently focusing on its marketing efforts and may be
looking for new ways to advertise.

NETIMAGE

Five distinct groups of words were identified using network analysis. In
this study, a group was defined as a set of at least three words that have
more than 50% of their linkage with one another, are connected by some
path lying entirely within the group to each of the other words in the
group, and that remain so connected when up to 10% of the group is
removed.

Table 4.4 lists the five groups of words that emerged from the network analysis, and the isolated words that attached to each of the groups
but were not actually part of the groups. Groups 1, 2, 4, and 5 were all
connected to isolated words, as well as to the name of one of the
founders and part of the company name; Group 3 had no outside
connections.

Group 1 includes six words and reflects the company's past medical
history (i.e., reference to "first," "hand," and "held" represent the company's reputation as a leader in the design and development of its
medical instruments).

The nine words in Group 2 refer to the core optical business of the
company (i.e., "electronic," "light," "fiber," "optics").

Table 4.4. Network Analysis Word Groups and Isolated Attached Words

Group 1: FIRST – HAND – HELD – TIME – JUST – RIGHT
Group 1 Attached Words: OPHTHALMOSCOPE – FULL – PRODUCT – NOT – ONLY – COULD

Group 2: ELECTRONIC – LIGHT – SUCH – FIBER – OPTICS – OPTIC – COMPONENTS – DISTANCE – SHORT
Group 2 Attached Words: SOURCE – OPTICAL – TRANSMISSION – BUNDLES – ILLUMINATION – ELECTRONICS – TRANSMIT – LAMP – TECHNOLOGY – SOPHISTICATED

Group 3: BOARD – ASSEMBLY – FINAL
Group 3 Attached Words: None

Group 4: NEW YORK – PRODUCT – LINE – FULL – CENTRAL – COMPUTER – DESIGN – AIDED
Group 4 Attached Words: BASIC – MUST – SYSTEM – MANUFACTURE – MARKETS – MANUFACTURING – PROCESS – ENGINEER – SERVICE – EVERY – BEST – STATE – GOOD – NEWS – DEVELOPMENT – RESEARCH – WHILE – REDUCING

Group 5: MARKETING – SALES – MANAGER
Group 5 Attached Words: PEOPLE – SUPPORT – DISTRIBUTORS – SCOPE – SERVICES – ADMINISTRATION – COORDINATION – INTERNATIONAL

Group 3 includes three words that refer to assembly operations. This group has no connections with other words in the organization's written messages nor is it connected to the founder or company name, which suggests this word group has a narrow, internal focus.

Group 4 consists of nine words that describe the company and its location. This information is frequently found in the organization's recruitment literature. The three words in Group 5 reflect an external marketing and sales focus.

The isolated words attached to Groups 1, 2, 4, and 5 represent links to the word groups but with insufficient strength to be part of the groups. These attached words are helpful in interpreting the meaning of the word groups. For example, Group 5 includes three words— "marketing," "sales," "manager"—and eight isolated words are attached to this group—"people," "support," "distributors," "scope," "services," "administration," "coordination," "international"—which provide additional meaning to the word group.

Additional words that were identified as being heavily involved in the culture of the organization but not part of any group are listed in Table 4.5. In network analysis, nodes of this type are generally labeled liaisons.[3] These words have less than 50% of their linkage with members

---

[3] Liaisons are words that have less than 50% of their linkage with members of groups. Most links will be with other liaisons. They connect groups indirectly.

Table 4.5.   Liaison Words Identified Not Belonging to a Group

[SPECIFIC DIVISION]	BAR	REQUIREMENTS
MANUFACTURING(4)*	MORE	CAPABILITIES
INSTRUMENTS	MEET	LAMP(2)*
COMPANY	APPLICATIONS	CUSTOMER(S)
MEDICAL	NEEDS	ENGINEERING
PRODUCTS	INDUSTRY	CONTROL
PROCESS(4)*	INDUSTRIAL	INTERNATIONAL(5)*
[COFOUNDER AND	DATA	SERVICE (4)*
COMPANY NAME]	COLLECTION	CODE
EQUIPMENT	SPECIAL	DIVISION
TODAY	[COFOUNDER	WHICH
DIAGNOSTIC	NAMES]	CAN
IMPROVEMENT	RECOGNIZED	SAID
RECENTLY		

*Words that are also isolated attached words to groups are identified by the group number in parentheses.

of groups and, therefore, do not meet the criteria for group membership. Some of these words are attached to the five groups while most are not. It is possible that a larger sample of written messages may result in more and larger groups of words being identified as well as a smaller number of unattached words.

Describing the Organization's Culture

A comparison of the content analysis and the semantic network analysis results reveals those words and word groups that are identified as the critical concepts in the organization. While the word frequencies are valuable in providing an initial description of the messages generated by the organization, an examination of how these words cluster together offers greater insight into the organization's culture. By identifying what terms cooccur or are linked together, a more precise description of the organization's language patterns emerges, and by influence, its values, attitudes, beliefs, and thoughts. Those words that appear most frequently and those that appear together in both analyses can be used as the basis to begin to describe the organization's culture. For example, both analyses identify a word cluster or group that represents the organization's medical history and frequent references to its past. Both analyses also identify word groups that refer to the company's core business. Finally, both analyses suggest the company is focusing on its sales and marketing efforts.

While the above similarities provide important indicators of the critical concepts in the organization, there are differences between the content analysis and network analysis results. Clearly, the word groups identified by both procedures are not identical, which suggests the word groups are not absolute or constant and are subject to various clustering relationships. However, it is important to recognize that it is not critical that the word groups be identical, but rather that the groups or clusters identified represent similar meanings.

DISCUSSION

A complete review of all the word patterns that emerge from a content analysis of an organization's written messages may provide a more precise view of the beliefs, attitudes, values, and thought patterns of the organization. By objectively and systematically identifying the key words and word patterns used by the organization in its written messages, it is possible to gain a more precise description of an organization's culture than by relying solely on interpretive methods. Such an approach strives to make the concept of culture a more objective focus of inquiry by treating the elements of culture almost as if they were tangible objects— word patterns that can be identified in corporate messages.

In this example, key words and word groups identified reflect the organization's frequent reference to its past history and accomplishments, its focus on the core business, current sales, and marketing efforts. This initial analysis of the organization's messages provides information about what the company values, and these values relate to its corporate culture. This particular organization appears to value its heritage, its core business of designing and developing new optical instruments and equipment, and marketing and selling these items. Additionally, this company appears to see itself as a family even though it has worldwide interests.

While this approach also contains elements of interpretive analysis in that the meanings of the word clusters and groups must be interpreted, this approach does more objectively identify those word groups that should be examined. As such, quantitative content analysis of written messages minimizes the reliance on rhetorical-critical analysis. Such an approach attempts to objectify the study of culture by quantitatively examining messages produced by an organization and potentially reducing the value judgments and other types of observer bias inherent in culture research.

Quantitative analysis of written messages may be used as a first step in organizational culture research. One could use the content analysis of organizational messages as part of the cultural analysis described by Barnett (1988). In that case, indepth interviews of a representative sample of organizational members may also be analyzed with the two computer programs described in this chapter. Then the critical cultural symbols from the written messages and the interviews as identified by this method can form the basis for a second, more precise stage of cultural measurement. The symbols can be selected for a series of paired-comparisons which will precisely describe the relationships among the symbols. This represents the meaning system or culture of the organization from which messages can be developed to alter the culture according to organizational goals.

Future research includes expanding the content analysis procedures to the mass media messages about the organization by gathering stories about the company from online databases (*New York Times*, *Business Week*, *Dow Jones*) as well as the local daily and weekly newspapers in the community where the company is located. Such an analysis will provide information on how the organization is perceived by the external public. Employees also receive media information, either directly, or through their interpersonal networks. Messages received interpersonally may be altered by the people in the networks. Both types of information may impact on the way in which the organization is perceived by its members, thus altering its culture. A content analysis of what the external media is saying about the organization may also assist the organization in developing its public relations efforts as well as its internal culture.

The major shortcomings in research of this type lie in the difficulty of obtaining sufficient written materials for analysis and, subsequently, in sampling of materials for use in such studies. A substantially larger sample than 40 pages of written text should be analyzed to obtain a clearer picture of the organization's culture. Ideally, the sample should include written messages from a variety of sources across the organization to minimize any sampling effect created by the inclusion of one type of communication (e.g., recruitment or orientation materials). Also, this study examined only one organization. It will be important in future studies to demonstrate the utility of this approach on more than one organization.

SUMMARY

This chapter suggests applying quantitative content analysis and network analysis procedures to analyzing written corporate messages as a more objective, precise first step in describing organizational culture than through solely interpretive methods. Analyzing written corporate messages in a less subjective, more precise manner may strengthen the link between the messages produced by an organization and the understanding of its corporate culture. An example of the proposed method is provided. Results of the content analysis and network analysis are presented, and a description of the corporate culture is offered based on the word patterns identified in the corporate messages. Implications of objectifying the culture through the quantitative analysis of mediated messages are discussed.

REFERENCES

Barnett, G. A. (1988). Communication and organizational culture. In G. M. Goldhaber & G. A. Barnett (Eds.), *Handbook of organizational communication* (pp. 101–130). Norwood, NJ: Ablex.

Bolman, L., & Deal, T. (1984). *Modern approaches to understanding and managing organizations*. San Francisco, CA: Jossey-Bass.

Bormann, E. G. (1983). Symbolic convergence: Organizational communication and culture. In L. Putnam & M. Pacanowsky (Eds.), *Communication and organizations: An interpretative approach*. Beverly Hills, CA: Sage.

Cheney, G., & Frenette, G. (1990, June). *Persuasion and organization: Values, logics, and accounts in corporate public discourse*. Paper presented at the Organizational Communication Division of the International Communication Association, Dublin, Ireland.

Danowski, J. A., Andrews, J. R., & Edison-Swift, P. (1985, February). *A network analysis method for representing social concepts: An illustration with words co-occurring across electronic mail*. Paper presented to the Sunbelt Social Networks Conference, Palm Beach, FL.

Deal, T. E., & Kennedy, A. A. (1982). *Corporate cultures: The rites and rituals of corporate life*. Reading, MA: Addison-Wesley.

Johnson, S. C. (1967). Hierarchical clustering schemas. *Psychometrika, 32,* 241–254.

Mumby, D. (1987). The political function of narrative in organizations. *Communication Monographs, 54,* 113–127.

Pacanowsky, M., & O'Donnell-Trujillo, N. (1982). Communication and organizational cultures. *Western Journal of Speech Communication, 46,* 115–130.

Pondy, L., Morgan, G., Frost, P., & Dandridge, T. (1983). *Organizational symbolism*. Greenwich, CT: JAI Press.

Putnam, L. (1982). Paradigms for organizational communication research. *Western Journal of Speech Communication, 46,* 192–206.

Putnam, L., & Pacanowsky, M. (1983). *Communication and organizations: An interpretive approach*. Beverly Hills, CA: Sage.

Richards, W. D. (1988). Negopy. *Connections, 11,* 80–83.

Schein, E. H. (1985). *Organizational culture and leadership*. San Francisco: Jossey-Bass.

Schein, E. H. (1983). The role of the founder in creating organizational culture. *Organizational Dynamics, 12,* 13–28.

Scott, W. R. (1987). The adolescence of institutional theory. *Administrative Science Quarterly, 32,* 493–511.

Smircich, L. (1983). Concepts of culture and organizational analysis. *Administrative Science Quarterly, 28,* 339–358.

Weber, R. P. (1985). *Basic content analysis*. Beverly Hills, CA: Sage.

Woelfel, J., & Holmes, R. (1982, May). *CATPAC demonstration*. Paper presented at the International Communication Association, Boston, MA.

Wuthnow, R. (1987). *Meaning and moral order: Explorations in cultural analysis*. Berkeley: University of California Press.

5

The Structuring of Organizational Climates*

Marshall Scott Poole

INTRODUCTION

Organizational climate is an important, but engimatic concept. It is important because it refers to members' molar perceptions of the internal environment of the organization. Such perceptions are widely acknowledged as an important link between member behavior and organizational context. Climate is also something of an enigma, because these "molar perceptions" have proven to be conceptually elusive. Researchers have resorted to the atmospheric or climatic metaphor to capture some sense of the pervasive, generalized character of the environment, but the implications of this metaphor are not clear, even after years of research.

Climate is slippery, in part, because it is a lay construct appropriated for scientific purposes. The media have long used stock phrases like "political climate," "a charged atmosphere," and "a changed climate for business." Gossips and novelists alike refer to the mood of a party or "the smell of trouble in the air." In his testimony at the Watergate hearings, Jeb Magruder reported: "Because of a certain atmosphere that had developed in my working at the White House I was not as concerned about (Watergate's) illegality as I should have been." Scientific definitions are more precise, but they are grounded in lay usages. Indeed, the many divergent definitions of climate may stem from different "cuts" taken from the rich, complex, unexplicated lay construct.

No precise or widely accepted definition of climate exists. Here, we will initially define climate as a relatively enduring quality of the environment that is experienced and perceived by individuals, influences individual interpretations and actions, and can be described in terms of a particular set of characteristics which describe system practices, pro-

* The author would like to thank Ann Goodell, Julie Brown, Lisa O'Dell, Sandra Petronio, Jim Helmer, and Ken Martin for their useful discussions and comments.

cedures, and tendencies (Taguiri, 1968; Schneider, 1975; Woodman & King, 1978). This definition highlights several points:

1. Climate is a molar abstraction that is meaningful to organizational members. This abstraction is reflected in members' perceptions of climate.
2. Climates are associated with organizational or unit practices. Because an organization has many different sets of practices or procedures, there may be many climates in the organization (Schneider, 1975; Schneider & Reichers, 1983).
3. Climate is construed as a system-level and not an individual property (Glick, 1985). Although the study of individual psychological climate has made important contributions (James & Jones, 1974; Jones & James, 1979; Joyce & Slocum, 1984), this chapter focuses on system-level climates—organizational, unit, and group climates. Individual climates are considered only insofar as they relate to system-level climates.
4. Climate is a component of the organization's culture. Climate and culture are often assumed to be synonymous, but to equate the two terms is to adopt much too narrow a definition of culture, and to make climate overly broad. Climate serves as one, among many, reservoirs of common knowledge and expectations for an organizational culture. It is akin to what Bateson (1958) has referred to as the culture's *ethos*.

This chapter attempts to sharpen this definition by developing a theoretical analysis of climate structuring. This process-based analysis has several advantages. It eliminates conceptual ambiguities through synthesis, rather than through introducing additional distinctions to further fragment climate research; it spells out the relationships between organizational and subunit climates; it sets out the beginnings of a theory of how individual perceptions result from collective climates; it shows how climates can have varying levels of agreement depending on the structural context; it clarifies the link between climates and "objective" features of organizations, particularly organizational structure; and it draws a picture of climate consistent with the common-sense stock of knowledge lay actors have about climate.

This chapter is divided into two parts. The first section discusses the status of the climate construct in current theory, points out several unanswered questions, and suggests how these might be addressed. The second section develops a model of climate structuring and discusses how it might be tested or evaluated. The model is based on the theory of structuration, which focuses on the interplay of action and structure in a continuous structuring process (Barthes, 1971; Bourdieu, 1977; Giddens, 1976, 1979; Ranson, Hinings, & Greenwood, 1980). This chapter builds on several ideas and distinctions presented in earlier papers by Poole and McPhee (1983; Poole, 1985).

STATUS OF CLIMATE

Many definitions of climate are marked by a seeming paradox. It is exhibited in Taguiri's (1968) classic definition:

> Climate is the relatively enduring quality of the total environment that (a) is experienced by the occupants, (b) influences their behavior, and (c) can be described in terms of the values of a particular set of characteristics (or attributes) of the environment. (p. 25)

Similarly, Woodman and King (1978) note, "Phenomenologically, climate is external to the individual, yet cognitively the climate is internal to the extent that it is affected by individual perceptions" (p. 218). In these and other definitions, climate is construed as both external to the individual *and* to individual cognition. This tension can also be observed in lay usage. Climate is an atmosphere and, therefore, external to the individual; yet it is invisible and intangible and therefore a product of the individual's perceptions. How climate can have this dual nature is puzzling.

The two-valued logic of quantitative social science seems to have pushed earlier researchers toward construing climate as *either* psychological and subjective or public and objective (Payne & Pugh, 1976). This dualism is reflected in the distinction between psychological climate and organizational climate (James & Jones, 1974). Psychological climate refers to the individual's perceptions of organizational climate and can be measured through psychological questionnaires. Organizational climate is considered to be a systemic property, but it has often been measured by aggregating individual perceptions. Glick (1985) indicates several problems with this method of measurement. He argues that organizational climate must be measured specifically at the system level and recommends several methods for improving the validity of organizational climate assessment, including the use of larger samples of organizations, orientation of questions to the organization or unit rather than to psychological concerns, and "treating respondents as key informants . . . describing organizational characteristics, not as individual actors revealing unique experiences" (p. 608). Glick's approach directs research efforts toward assessing the system's rather than aggregate perceptions. Individual reports are still useful, but as indicators of system properties rather than in their own right. Agreement among member perceptions is still an important indicator, but contrary to some arguments (Jones &

James, 1979; Joyce & Slocum, 1984), agreement alone is not sufficient to define organizational climates. Unit boundaries, organizational practices, and informant biases, among other things, must be taken into account (Glick, 1985).

Several empirical studies suggest that Glick is correct in his claim that organizational climate is distinct from individual perceptions of the organization. Generally, variance in climate scores is greater between organizations than within organizations, suggesting climate is an organizational property (Drexler, 1977; Zohar, 1980). In an explicit comparison, Paolillo (1982) investigated the relative strength of personal characteristics (sex, age, educational level), situational variables (organization, size, number of hierarchical levels, and specialization), and joint personal-situational variables (position tenure, hierarchical position, and time spent in supervisory activities) on research climate, as measured with Pelz and Andrew's instrument. He found that the four situational variables accounted for more than 60% of the variance in climate scores, lending support to the proposition that climate is a system property, and not a property of individual members.

Clarification of unit of analysis is an important move, but several important questions remain to be answered:

1. While we may acknowledge that climate is a system-level construct, it remains unclear what type of system-level construct climate is. There are several different ways to conceive of system constructs, and each has its own implications concerning how climate relates to individual-level constructs and other system variables.
2. How do climates at various system levels (group, unit, organizational) relate to each other? This issue has seldom been addressed.
3. What is the nature of the linkage between individual agreement and collective climates? This degree of collective agreement about climates is important, because it influences how individuals behave with respect to the collective. The relationships of agreement to climate is even more complex than Glick portrays it, and should be explored further.
4. What is the relationship between climate and other system-level variables, especially organizational design? The evidence regarding such relationships is mixed (Payne & Pugh, 1976). Theories of climate should attempt to provide an account of this variation.

CLIMATE AS AN INTERSUBJECTIVE CONSTRUCT

Neither the objective nor the subjective interpretations of organizational climate are adequate. Glick's (1985) criticisms of individual-based climate measures have been mentioned. Regarding climate as a purely objective organizational property is equally untenable. Climate cannot be adequately measured with the objective, observer-based variables advocated by ecological psychologists, such as measures of organizational structure, turnover, goals, or management styles (e.g., Forehand & Gilmer, 1964). As James and Jones (1974) pointed out, the objective approach makes climate "synonymous with organizational situation and seems to offer little more than a semantically appealing but 'catch-all' term" (p. 1099). Climate is an important term in organizational theory for the very reason that distinguishes it from variables such as organizational structure. It pertains to general qualities of the organization *for its members*, and not in a purely objective sense. Climate is a social construct.

Social philosophers have posited a third ontological category, specifically with reference to social constructs. Rather than objective or subjective, socially mediated constructs are regarded as *intersubjective* (Taylor, 1971). This chapter proposes to recast climate as an intersubjective construct and to develop a systematic analysis of intersubjective climates.

The *Oxford English Dictionary* defines intersubjective as "existing between conscious minds." Thus, an intersubjective construct is collective, constituting a supraindividual linkage of members' perspectives. This move introduces a new level of theoretical construct, intermediate between objective and subjective variables. This level is particularly useful in the study of common cultural or social properties, particularly those assumed to be meaningful to members (Morris, 1938).

Many different definitions or theories of intersubjectivity have been advanced by philosophers, literary critics, and social theorists (Grossberg, 1979). These can be divided roughly into two camps. Some writers regard intersubjectivity as a more or less stable *state* of shared knowledge or feeling. Others maintain that intersubjectivity is precarious and variable over time, and that it can only be understood in terms of the *processes* which create and reproduce shared perspectives. After evaluating several alternative approaches to the study of intersubjective constructs, Poole and McPhee (1983) concluded that it was necessary to focus on the *processes* creating intersubjectivity in the study of climate. To regard social constructs as static is to risk reifying them. A processual approach gives an account of how individual perspectives are linked into a supraindividual climate that has the same force as objective variables, yet it is not itself objectifiable. An implication of this view is that an adequate definition of climate must include not only a statement of climate's static attributes, as in the definition offered at the beginning of this chapter, but also a model or theory of the process that creates and maintains the climate.

Several converging lines of work (Ashforth, 1985; Dandridge, Mitroff, & Joyce, 1980; Poole, 1985; Poole & McPhee, 1983; Schneider &

Reichers, 1983; Zeitz, 1983) analyze climates as an intersubjective or socially defined phenomenon.

Zeitz (1983) has proposed what might be termed an "amplification" model. In this view climate is an emergent collective trait which

> can also operate on the individual level, but becomes collective when possessed by multiple interacting members. For example, when individual behaviors and attitudes are reinforced and amplified through imitation, social rewards, or sanctioned and communicated through widespread interaction, they become pervasive, organization-wide characteristics. (p. 1089)

This account is similar to Smelser's (1962) theory of generalized belief formation in social movements. Common experience with organizational practices reverberates through a collective, via widespread interaction, and becomes an organizational property by virtue of being commonly held by members of the collectivity. However, Zeitz's account is not clear on how this reverberation occurs or on how it could create organizational characteristics.

Schneider and others (Ashforth, 1985; Deiterly & Schneider, 1974; Schneider, 1975; Schneider & Reichers, 1983) have developed an insightful account of the etiology of climates based on symbolic interactionist theory. They argue that members develop and sustain their organizational identities through interaction and that a key aspect of members' identity is an orientation toward the organized activities of the work group. As members are socialized, they adopt the attitudes and beliefs of coworkers, adjust their expectations to the work situation, and work out the meanings of the situation. This understanding, which enables members to situate themselves in the organization, is the organizational climate.

> The same processes that act to socialize newcomers into the setting also give rise to climates. Specifically, social interactions in the workplace help newcomers to understand the meaning of various aspects of the work context. And it is through social interactions that individuals in the workplace come to have similar perceptions of that context. (Schneider & Reichers, 1983, p. 31)

Workers who have common communication networks develop shared climates. Organizational structure, the organization's selection and training processes, organizational culture, the physical setting, and the organization's management of symbols have been proposed as influences on climate development (Ashforth, 1985; Schneider & Reichers, 1983).

This is an important advance, but it leaves a number of unanswered questions. First, Schneider and Reichers (1983) do not consider how structure enters into the symbolic interaction that create shared climates. Recognizing the role of interaction in climate is useful, but their analysis fails to show how actors are constrained by structure. By their model each group can develop its own climate. But how do we account for consistency of meaning across groups, the shared themes ubiquitous in any organization? Why do the various groups, each of which enacts its own climate, converge so often and share at least some aspects of organizationwide climate? According to Schneider and Reichers's analysis, convergence would be due to selection of similar people and exposure to the same structural characteristics. This is true, as far as it goes, but it portrays actors as passive perceivers of structure who react to it in their interactions. In essence, Schneider and Reichers posit a two-stage process in which actors are influenced by selection and assimilation processes and organizational structure and, after this, they symbolically interact to create climates. It would be beter to consider how structure enters into symbolic interaction (i.e., how it acquires meaning and is enacted in groups and how it directly enters into and constrains interaction). This issue has been emphasized in recent symbolic interactionist research (Maines, 1977; Strauss, 1978).

Second, the conceptual status of climate remains unclear in this work. In Schneider and Reichers's (1983) analysis there are statements that meaning is not in the individual perceiver, but "in interaction" (p. 30), but also statements implying an individual focus—meaning is learned. Individuals "attach meaning" (pp. 29–31). In Ashforth (1985) climate is a "joint property of the individual and organization" (p. 838) and meaning is in the episode, not in the setting or the actors. On the other hand, climate is a "molar perception meaningful to individuals" (p. 837). This tacking between an individual and interactional locus for climate may be due to an attempt to ground symbolic interaction in individuals. Schneider and Reichers (1983) refer to Mead's essays on meaning and self. However, other writings of Mead and later symbolic interactionists (Maines, 1977; Strauss, 1978) emphasize the inseparability of the individual and society. Moving to a systemic viewpoint rather than one grounded in individuals would give a clearer picture of climate as an interactional emergent.

The symbolic interactionist view of climate is a major advance. However, there is still a need to situate climate in the organizational system. At its present state of development, the symbolic interactionist view gives no detailed sense of processes that create intersubjectivity. These processes must be tied to broader organizational processes. To this point analysis has focused on the immediate creation of climate, but has treated climate as separable from the system. To spell out the processes that create and maintain intersubjectivity in the organizational system, it is necessary to address the remaining three questions, concerning how various subsystem climates relate to each other and to an overall system climate, how individual beliefs fit into systemic climates, and how the larger organizational system interacts with climate.

RELATIONSHIPS AMONG SYSTEM AND SUBSYSTEM CLIMATES

Distinct climates have been identified for entire organizations, for subunits within organizations (Powell & Butterfield, 1978), and for groups that do not conform to formal subunit boundaries (Johnston, 1976). Can all of these types of climate exist simultaneously in an organization? Or does the existence of subsystem climates preclude the existence of an overall system climate? Current theory is largely silent on this point, though Powell and Butterfield (1978) argue there can be no system climate if there are subsystem climates.

However, it seems reasonable to uncouple system and subsystem climates completely. It certainly seems possible for an entire organization to share some beliefs, yet have subunit differences on others. If, following Schneider (1975), we accept that an organization may have different climates for different practices, such as communication, safety, or customer service, it seems possible to have the same climate in the whole organization for one practice, such as communication, and different climates for others, such as safety. Various writers have offered explanations for why subunit climates exist (Powell & Butterfield, 1978; Schneider & Reichers, 1983), but these explanations pertain to individual unit climates and do not address relationships among climates. If climates are system-level properties, it is important to have a common generation point in the system, an explanation of how whole-system climates develop and how they differentiate. This explanation should incorporate factors that cause systems to differentiate.

INTERSUBJECT AGREEMENT AND CLIMATE

Studies of psychological climate have shown wide variation in the degree of intersubjective agreement on climate. Some studies have found a low degree of agreement (Bass, Valenzi, Farrow, & Solomon, 1975; Jones & James, 1979; Payne & Mansfield, 1973; Schneider, 1975); others have found high degrees of agreement (Drexler, 1977; Howe, 1977; Joyce & Slocum, 1984; Paolillo, 1982; Pritchard & Karasick, 1973; Zohar, 1980).

Glick (1985) has criticized the individual-based measures of intersubject agreement used in most of these studies. He argues instead that a different index of mean-rater reliability based on intraclass correlation is more appropriate for assessing organizational characteristics, on the assumption that these are best measured by aggregated-rater judgment. Glick seems to be correct in his argument, but this does not mean that measures of individual intersubject reliability do not have a place in the study of climate as well. Individual reliability coefficients tell us how homogeneous subject perceptions are, and that the degree of perceptual homogenity is an important system property, especially when we are attempting to study processes that create and sustain climates. The degree of consensus or dissensus in members' individual perceptions of climates may tell us important things about how climate is produced and reproduced and how climate figures in members' behavior.

Some researchers have advocated that climate should only be attributed to those units or organizations in which there is consensus on climate (Jacofsky & Slocum, 1986; Joyce & Slocum, 1984; Powell & Butterfield, 1978). However, dissension among organizational members does not always imply the absence of a coherent climate. Members may all share common beliefs, but react differently to these beliefs. And such reactions may well result in different responses on a climate questionnaire. For example, consider an organization with an achievement-oriented climate. As Kanter's (1977) study showed, members on their way up may well describe this organization as supportive, reward-oriented, and fairly low in terms of activity structuring; on the other hand members who are not being promoted (yet who also sees the emphasis on achievement) are likely to describe the organization as nonsupportive, nonrewarding, and highly structured. In this case, a shared, commonly experienced climate would give rise to highly divergent responses on a questionnaire.

Instead of considering degree of agreement as a dichotomous criterion for the existence of climate, researchers can consider it as a possible clue to how the organization operates. Theories of climate should explain how differing degrees of agreement come about.

RELATION OF ORGANIZATIONAL STRUCTURE AND CLIMATE

As a system-level variable, organizational climate should relate to other system constructs. Schneider and his colleagues have emphasized the links between climate and system practices, work, and procedures. The relationship between climate and macrolevel system properties is not so clear. Some studies have found relationships between organizational design variables such as centralization and formalization and climate, and others have found no relationship (Payne & Pugh, 1976). Indeed, one of the striking features of research on design and climate is the mixture of findings.

Differences can to some extent be traced to methodological differences and problems in some studies. However, 20 years of research should not be written off. Perhaps under some conditions design influences climate and in others design and climate are uncoupled. A theory of climate should take the inconsistency of the design–climate relationship as a given, which is in need of explanation.

A MODEL OF THE STRUCTURATION OF CLIMATES

Schneider and Reichers, Ashforth, Zeitz, and others advance a convincing view of climate at the microlevel. However, if climate is a systemic property, it is necessary to consider the macrolevel as well. This requires us to clarify the relationships among climates at different system levels; to specify how climate relates to macrolevel variables, especially organizational structure; and to work out how microlevel individual beliefs link with system-level climates (i.e., how climates affect intersubject agreement and vice versa).

This section develops a theory of climate that holds onto the insights of recent microlevel analysis, but also considers how climates, and the microprocesses that generate and maintain them, figure in the larger organizational system. Rather than simply shifting our attention from the micro to the macro, the theory explicitly addresses the linkage between the two levels (Knorr-Cetina & Cicourel, 1981). It is absolutely necessary to ground any theory in interaction, because interaction is the locus of the production and reproduction of climates. There is abundant evidence that the character of climate depends on members' experiences with organizational practices, which are mediated by interaction processes (Campbell, Dunette, Lawler, & Weick, 1970; Indik, 1965; Schneider, 1975; Schneider, Parkington, & Buxton, 1980; Zohar, 1980). Through the cumulation of repeated individual encounters, interaction is also the site on which climate has an impact on macrolevel variables. There is no metaphysical impact of climate on organizational structure or structure on climate at the macrolevel. All influences are mediated by interaction, and if we rise too far above the level of organizational practices, we risk losing our grasp of the climate construct. One key is to consider how organizational structures enter into practices, and how

they intersect with climate in practices. The strength of the organizational structure-climate relationship can then be traced to the nature of the
interaction system, the type of practice, and the context.

The model advanced here undertakes a formal reconceptualization
of climate as an intersubjective construct. Previous work has done this
implicitly, but has no taken a position on whether intersubjectivity is a
state or a process. However, as the earlier review by Poole and McPhee
(1983) concluded, it is necessary to construe intersubjective constructs as
processes, or we risk reification of climate. In current literature, the
references to climate as a "shared" construct and the emphasis on consensus as a means of defining climates, may lead us to buy into the static
view of intersubjectivity.

What is needed is a model of climate that explains the processes
involved in attaining and maintaining intersubjectivity. This may seem
like simply clothing old ideas in new terminology. However, it represents
a key conceptual advance because it focuses attention not only on the
content of climate, but also on the processes that create and change
climates. This promises several advantages: (a) It can help us understand
the effects of climates on members. Some processes are set up so that
climate can influence members' attitudes and behaviors, while in other
cases the influence of climate is counteracted or dissipated by other
features of the process. (b) It can help us understand the links between
climate with macrovariables such as organizational structure and culture. Some processes tightly link climate and other macrolevel variables,
while in other cases, they are only loosely coupled or not coupled at all.
(c) It can help us understand how negative aspects of climate might be
changed or how positive aspects might be preserved by altering the
processes which structure them.

The model will be presented in three sections. The first describes
some basic concepts of the theory of structuration, as developed by
Giddens (1976, 1979, 1981), Ranson, Hinings, and Greenwood (1980),
and Poole, McPhee, and Seibold (McPhee, 1985; Poole, Seibold, &
McPhee, 1985a, 1985b). The second section lays out a schematic description of the structure of climate and its relation to practices and other
structures. The third section discusses the processes involved in the
structuration of climates and the forces that influence structuring processes.

THE THEORY OF STRUCTURATION

A number of social theorists and literary critics have studied structuration (Barthes, 1971; Bordieu, 1977; Coward & Ellis, 1977; Giddens,
1976, 1979). Applied to social organizations, structuration refers to the

production and reproduction of social systems via actors' application of generative rules and resources (Giddens, 1979). This definition rests on a distinction between system and structure. *Systems* are observable, "regularized relations of interdependence between individuals and groups" (Giddens, 1979, p. 66). Examples of systems include families, complex organizations, and nation states. *Structures* are rules and resources used in the production and reproduction of systems. Examples of rules are language structures and the norms that govern authority relationships in organizations. Resources include formal authority, money, and knowledge, things that can be used to support action or to exert power.

A central assumption of the theory of structuration that structures have a dual nature: They are both the *medium* and the *outcome* of action. They are the medium of action, because people must draw on rules and resources to act or interact. They are the outcome of action, because rules and resources exist only by virtue of being used in social practices; whenever the structural feature is employed, the activity reproduces it (and associated structures as well) by invoking and confirming it as a valid basis for action. System and structure are a duality, codetermining each other in a continuous process of structuration (Poole, 1983).

Here we will analyze climate as a structure underlying observable organizational systems. As a set of generalized beliefs and expectations about system practices, procedures, and tendencies, climate can be construed as a structure of rules and knowledge resources. Members use climate in the structuration of the organizational system. As generalized knowledge structures, climates serve as common frames of reference for member activity. They enable members to apprehend order in the work environment (Schneider, 1975), to adapt to novel situations and problems, to understand others, and to organize and plan activities (Folger, Poole, & Stutman, 1993). In general, climates facilitate coordination and consistent execution of organizational practices. Climate thus serves a key role in the production of organizational systems. At the same time, by invoking climate, as well as by socializing new members to it, members are also *reproducing* and perpetuating the climate.

Because structural features are produced by organizational practices, they will persist only if some aspect of the activity system reproduces them. As Poole, Seibold, and McPhee (1985) note:

> Structurational theory shifts the focus from systems or structures to structuration and emphasizes their dynamic interrelationship in interaction: "To study the structuration of social systems is to study the conditions governing their continuity, change, or dissolution" (Giddens, 1981:27). Neither stability nor change is taken as a "basic state" by structurational theory. Both must be explained in terms of definite mechanisms or processes that create and reproduce them. On this view, neither the descrip-

tion of systems and their relationships nor the enumeration and analysis of structures is the central object. System properties can only be explained by looking at their production and reproduction; simply describing them yields little understanding of stability or change (Hernes, 1976). Nor can rules and resources merely be listed or arrayed in structural or taxonomic diagrams. Because they are meaningful only in relation to other rules and resources in an ongoing practice, it is not only necessary, but more informative to study structuration than to attempt to isolate static structures. The description of systemic and structural components and relations is a useful component of any analysis, but it is subsidiary to exploration of the conditions and mechanisms governing structuration. (p. 248)

Structurational theory addresses a central problem in social theory, the relation of action to social institutions. The structures members use in interaction are generally grounded in established social institutions, such as language, the economic system, or the family. Occasionally, actors create totally new structural features, but this is rare. More often, actors appropriate existing institutional features for their own uses. For example, the president of a company facing motivational and deadline problems might install a management by objectives program and tailor it to the organization through prolonged experimentation. In so doing, the organization would be adapting the structuring rules associated with Management by Objectives to its own situation. The result may depart considerably from textbook descriptions of Management by Objectives.

The linkage of institutions and action is accomplished in *modalities* of structuration. Modalities are *the appropriation of institutional structures in concrete, situated practices*. Three general types of modalities can be distinguished: structures may serve as *interpretive schemes* in communicative interaction, as *norms*, supplying a moral order for interaction, or as *facilities* supporting power moves in interaction. Giddens (1979) distinguishes three general types of social institutions that the modalities draw on and constitute—orders of signification (language, symbolic structures), legitimation (religion, ethics, law), and domination (privileges, resource allocation). Giddens (1976) provides the following diagram which illustrates the place of modalities mediating between interaction and institutions:

INTERACTION	Communication	Power	Morality
(MODALITY)	Interpretive Scheme	Facility	Norm
STRUCTURE	Signification	Domination	Legitimation

As the diagram shows, modalities are structures appropriated for action. A given structure may be used in all three modalities, although some structures are more appropriate for certain modalities. To extend our example, management by objectives, as described by textbooks, articles, and consultants, is now an important part of the institution of modern management. In adopting M.B.O., the organization mentioned above is appropriating the structure of rules and knowledge involved in M.B.O. This structure can serve as an interpretive scheme to help members define and "understand" the problems facing the organization, as a set of norms that provides recommendations for behavior, and as a facility that enables the redistribution of authority and the restructuring of the organization.

At the same time interaction draws on these institutional structures in the modalities, it is also reconstituting the institutions. M.B.O., as we know it, exists because there are many organizations that have adopted it and act as exemplars and instances. Depending on how the structurational process is organized, the instantiation of institutions in interaction either preserves their stability or promotes change. Individual interactions aggregate and accumulate to yield institutional consequences. The modalities are the sites at which the production and reproduction of interaction systems and structural formations occur.

Climates are structured by the appropriation of institutions in two respects. First, the themes in climates reflect general social themes. Litwin and Stringer (1968), for example, have defined motivational climates which are similar to the achievement and power motivations McClelland (1961) found for entire societies. Second, climates arise in response to other structural features adopted by organizations. The climate of the organization adopting M.B.O. is likely to change radically if the program succeeds. The details of how climate is shaped by appropriation will be worked out below.

Several levels of structure may be involved in structuration. Climates, themselves, can serve as organizational institutions, subject to appropriation by members. As such, they are immediate between the broader institutions of society at large and organizational activities. As we will see later, climate has a unique place in the organization: *Climate sets the tone for the appropriation of other structures.*

To understand structuration we must delineate the forces that influence the appropriation of structures and the production and reproduction of systems. Structurational processes are shaped by two major classes of factors: (a) forces that influence action, at both micro- and macrolevels; and (b) structural dynamics, in which different structural features shape, constrain, and change one another.

Three features of interest to climate research influence action. The nature of the *interaction system* is the first and most important factor. Since structuration occurs through interaction, the formal and informal networks that pattern and control the flow of interaction have great impact on structuring processes. For example, members in central network positions can usually exert more influence over structuring than less central members. In addition to the pattern of interaction, the quality of interaction—the nature of relationships and style of interaction—is important. A system in which coercion and authority are often used will structure climate in a very different way than will one in which the common currency is democracy and egalitarian relations. A second constraint on action are members' *individual traits* and *capacities*. Differences in intelligence, skill, experience, and insight into the organization translate into differential control over structuration. A third influence is *historical precedent*, including sociocultural rules and resources, as well as structures reproduced earlier by members. Because preexisting structures are salient to the actor and assumed by others, they tend to be drawn on and reproduced in present conduct, and in this way they circumscribe and condition that conduct. Previous structures constrain later ones and perpetuate themselves, thus limiting members' ability to alter or adapt them. Once established, a climate tends to have presumption in the organization.

It would be misleading to analyze action only on the microlevel. All three of the forces just mentioned are shaped by both macro- and microlevel influences. An interaction system evolves through multiple microtransactions, but it is also influenced by macrolevel forces such as the organization's design and the nature of work. A highly centralized organization, for example, will tend to have a more formal, less dense network. Individual traits and capacities are shaped by macrolevel influences, as well as by the individual's experience. For example, there is evidence that empowering members enhance their skills and motivations (Kanter, 1977; Tannenbaum, 1966).

In any complex system action will also be influenced by its unintended consequences. Because of the complexity of social systems, many consequences of action are unintended and even unknown, thus, escaping control of members. The consequences of action can "loop back" in a variety of ways, often reinforcing or otherwise conditioning later action, as Masuch (1985) has shown.

Multiple structural formations are involved in any organization, and their interrelationships are a second important influence on structuration. For example, there is mutual influence between climate and structures underlying organizational design—norms about how decisions are made; interpretive schemes given by formal structural diagrams; formal authority. Several types of structural influence relations are possible: structures may determine how other structures operate; they may serve as a metaphor for another structure, facilitating interpretation of the structure; or they may contradict and work against another structure. As mentioned earlier, there may be "layers" of structures, in which some structures are "deeper" than others (i.e., less accessible to researchers). Generally, more accessible structures are less fundamental and are in an intermediate position between the interaction system and deeper structures (social institutions). Climates, which are produced and in relatively narrow systems, have been mentioned as one structure that mediates between broader social structures and organizational behavior.

Relations between structures are not "effects at a distance." They are mediated by interaction. One structure can only influence another through structurational processes, which are accomplished in interaction. Structural influence occurs through the cumulation of many interactions that bring structures into contact.

In the remaining two sections we will develop a model of climate based on these distinctions. The next section lays out a schematic description that shows the "layers" of structure directly involved with climates. This schematic also provides a basis for exploring how broader, more "distant" institutions are involved in climate structuring. In the third and final section, we will discuss some dynamics of climate structuration, putting the schematic description "into motion." This final section will attempt to develop specific propositions regarding climate structuration.

A SCHEMATIC DESCRIPTION OF CLIMATE STRUCTURE

Climates are part of a nested set of structures, shown in Figure 5.1. This set can be divided into several "layers" which differ in degree of generality (i.e., in the presence of practices and contexts they apply to), and in their "depth" (i.e., in how evident or accessible they are to an analyst). Generally, deeper and more abstract layers have greater influence on the system, but any layer may influence any other, depending on the nature of the structuring process. Figure 5.1 depicts the structural hierarchy in general terms, and Figure 5.2 gives a specific example, using a work climate reported in Johnston's (1976) study of a consulting firm. What we refer to as climate forms the middle layer of this hierarchy. The deepest layer, basal constructs, mediates the linkage of climate to the larger institutional structure of the organization, while the top layer, practical structures, mediates the linkage of climate to practices. Climate is one of the constructs that stands between the institutional environment and day-to-day organizational practices.

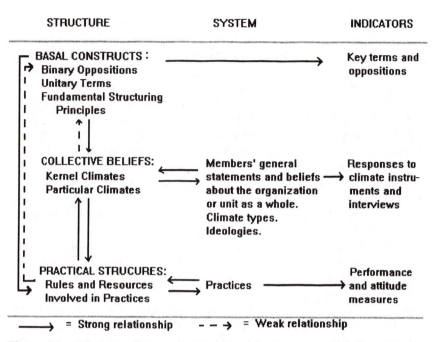

Figure 5.1. Diagram of Structural Relations in the Structuration of Climate

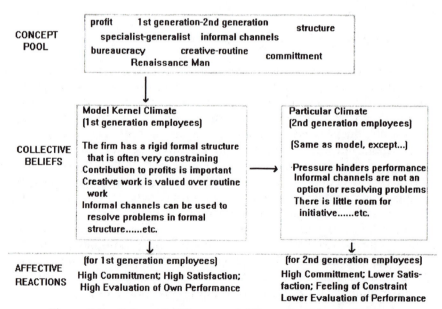

Figure 5.2. Schematic Diagram of Climate in Johnston's Firm

Basal Constructs

The most fundamental level of the hierarchy are the organization's basal constructs, the key terms, distinctions, and structuring principles which define the organization. Included in this "pool" of concepts are unitary terms, such as "profit," "committment," and "structure" and binary oppositions along which organizational members range themselves and others (Turner, 1977). The unitary terms refer to basic features of the organization, the institutions, properties, and preoccupations members must deal with in their work. Binary oppositions are fundamental to the social categorization process that enables members to position themselves and others in the organization (Doise, 1978; Tajfel & Turner, 1979). The basal constructs define the space of possible meaning for the organization; there are implicit backgrounds for all organizational activities.

In addition to concepts and distinctions, the basal level includes fundamental structuring principles which organize structuration throughout the system (Clegg, 1975; Giddens, 1981). Clegg (1975), for example, found evidence that the principles of appropriation and reproduction of capital underlie the organization of work interaction on several construction sites. These principles shaped intermediate, more accessible structures which preserved the dominance of managers over workers. For example, the structuring principles created a bias toward economic rationality that favored arguments cast in terms of managerial and production issues over those based on worker's personal needs or concerns. The impact of fundamental principles resonates throughout the system, as they shape more immediate structures and practices.

Collective Beliefs

The middle tier of the hierarchy is comprised of collective beliefs, which are less general and abstract than basal constructs, and also more accessible to researchers and actors. An important structure at this level is the *kernel climate*, the basic structure of beliefs, values, and expectations collectively held by most or all members of an organization or unit. Basal constructs provide key terms and distinctions for kernel climates. Kernel climates, in turn, constitute much of members' immediately available knowledge and beliefs about basal constructs. Kernel climates are common stocks of generalized knowledge that give a system its overall character and indicate to members in what manner they can use rules and resources that constitute the system. The propositions or elements of the kernel climate are organized in definite relations; a symbolic calculus or map of relations among climate elements could be derived (Axelrod, 1976; Bougon, Weick, & Binkhorst, 1977). Under certain

conditions there may be more than one kernel climate in an organization.

There may also be variations on kernel climates. The differentiation
of general climates into subgroup climates occurs in the development of
particularized climates, which result from qualifications, elaborations of
kernel climates by subgroups. Structural ambiguities in the premises of
kernel climates permit different subgroups to reinterpret and elaborate
them in a manner consonant with their own particular situations and
goals. Previous findings of differences in climate due to subunit, position, pay level, tenure, and level of authority (Powell & Butterfield,
1978) may be due either to separate kernel climates or to particularized
versions of the same kernel climate.

Various permutations of kernel and particular climates are possible.
First, there is the case where there is a single kernel climate shared by all
members, with no particular climates. Second, one group might define
the kernel and other subgroups might modify it to derive particular
climates. In this case one group serves as a model or ideal for the whole
organization. Other groups either adapt the model climate to their own
circumstances or they rebel against the model and create an "inverted"
version of the model. In both cases the model sets the parameters for
particular climates. Third, in the case where there is not a single kernel,
but instead a number of kernel climates, each of which may have particularized versions. In each of these three cases the nature of the structuring process is different. We will explore how and why below.

Climates are carried by numerous vehicles in the organizational system. They are reflected in members' general statements about what the
organization or its practices are like, in stories and rumors, in advice, in
company creeds, in jokes, and in "sensitive areas," to name a few.
Climate structures are generally unified around one or more central
themes (Folger, Poole, & Stutman, 1993). So, for example, an autocratic
climate would organize a number of specific themes or beliefs subject to
an order of domination. The degree of coherency in these structures
and the degree to which this coherency transmits itself to member
behavior determines how definite the type is. A major issue in the study
of climate is how coherency is maintained. This determines whether
particular climates exist and the relation between particular and kernel
climates. It also determines how pervasive the effects of climates are.

Practical Structures

The third tier of the hierarchy is composed of structures directly related
to the conduct of organizational practices, such as communication and
performance appraisal. Since the various practices are generally restricted to certain contexts and cover a relatively small range of the

totality of organizational behavior, these structures are not as general and are usually more accessible than the other two tiers. Structures governing communication practices, for example, include rules for routing messages and for addressing superiors, and resources, such as network centrality.

The relation between climate and practical structures is this: Climates influence how members appropriate practical structures in modalities of structuration. Climates influence members' expectations about the organization and lend a general tenor to work and interaction. They also serve as interpretive schemes to help members make sense of the organization. As such, they influence the types of structural features members select out of the repertoire of possible structures. For example, in a power-oriented climate, members will use political resources, such as coalitions, more often than in creativity-oriented climates, where they might instead rely on knowledge and reputation. More important than their influence over selection, climates influence *how* members use structures. In a power-oriented climate, members are likely to turn rules and resources to political ends, whereas in a creative climate rules and resources are likely to be used to advance ideas. So, climate influences the manner in which practical structures are appropriated and used. This will be discussed in the next section.

Interactions organized around practices give rise to member's behavioral and affective reactions to the organization, reactions such as feelings of committment, a positive evaluation of performance, or lack of attachment to coworkers. Through their effects on practices, climates affect members' reactions. For example, Stern (1970) found that student attitudes and performance varied with variations in college climates. A classic study by Lewin, Lippitt, and White (1939) demonstrated behavioral differences among authoritarian, democratic, and laissez-faire leadership climates. A number of studies have shown strong relationships between climate and job satisfaction (Hellreigel & Slocum, 1974, p. 263; Pritchard & Karasick, 1973; Woodman & King, 1978; Zeitz, 1983). The relationship between climate and performance is more complicated. Hellreigel and Slocum (1974) reported nine studies showing a significant relationship between organizational climate and job performance. However, these depended on several moderating factors, including compatibility of climate with member needs (Pelz & Andrews, 1976; Stern, 1970), whether the climate indicates appropriate behaviors in a clear and unambiguous manner (Fredericksen, Jenson & Beaton, 1972), and how specifically the climate measure related to behavior (Schneider et al., 1980). As several have commented, some climate instruments actually measure phase reactions, rather than climate *per se* (Payne, Fineman, & Wall, 1976). Such measures are at best indirect indices of climates, because they are affected by many other factors.

An Example

Reanalysis of Johnston's (1976) study provides an example of this hierarchy, illustrated in Figure 5.2. The firm Johnston studied was about five years old and had grown from an original staff of twelve—which had coordinated most activities informally—to 180 employees. Along with this growth came increased bureaucratization: the firm's hierarchy was elaborated, there was increasing task specialization, and there were attempts to formalize roles, information systems, and evaluations. As a result, Johnston found two "generations" of employees; one composed of employees from the early years, who were plugged into the old informal system and had helped evolve the bureaucratic structure; and one composed of newer employees, who were not tied into the informal system and had to accept the organization's structure.

To assess climate, Johnston conducted a content analysis of unstructured interviews with 40 employees. He identified 25 basic themes describing work climate, and found different response patterns on these themes for first- and second-generation employees. Johnston concluded that his firm had two separate climates which were a function of situational and personal factors.

The distinctions developed in the previous section permit an informal reanalysis of Johnston's findings that shed additional light on the organization. Instead of two separate climates, the firm can be seen to have a single, model kernel climate which is controlled by the long-term employees. The newer cadre of employees has developed its own particular adaption of the kernel climate.

From Johnston's account, the relevant portion of the basal constructs might be composed of several unitary terms—including profits, commitment, and structure—and three key oppositions: specialist/generalist, creative work/ routine work, and older employees/newer employees. These concepts appear in the kernel climate in beliefs such as "The firm has a rigid formal structure" and value statements such as "creativity is the firm's cornerstone," and "contributing to company profits is crucial." These beliefs are consistent with the action of the fundamental structuring principles of capitalist economy, as defined by Clegg (although there is no way to determine this without further data).

The kernel climate is set by first generation employees. They can use their ties to the informal network to bypass logjams in the formal structure. The formal structure also makes sense to them and is likely to be designed in line with their needs and preferences. Also, by virtue of their position, first generation employees had the opportunity to do creative work. These members felt pressure, but the pressure was interpreted as constructive and helpful. Second generation employees were brought into an established climate and had to adapt to the prevailing atmosphere. But different experiences in the organization led them to qualify and adapt the kernel climate to their own particular situation. Second generation employees, who were not tied into the informal system and could not get past routine channels, felt great pressure to produce and believed it hurt their performance. They also perceived bad superior-subordinate relationships, because they did not have well-developed informal friendships. They were aware of the informal system, though their awareness was vaguer than that of first generation employees (Johnston, 1976, p. 100). The kernel and particular climates led to different affective and behavioral reactions, as Figure 5.2 illustrates.

The kernel and particular climates are social constructs shared by members of the subgroups. Johnston's methodology is unusual in that it allows identification of specific themes held by various groups. If we had come into his organization with a traditional climate questionnaire, we might well have found either low agreement and conclude there was no coherent climate, or two separate climates, unrelated to each other. As this reanalysis suggests, there are cases in which there could be low agreement levels, despite the presence of shared constructs.

Considered as a static picture, the scheme merely serves as a reinterpretation of Johnston, and a post hoc interpretation at that. The key advance comes when we consider the structuring of climate through interrelation of the levels. This set of structures is not static, but exists only because there is a process producing intersubjectivity. We will discuss the nature of this process in the next section. At this point, however, it is helpful to mention two points concerning possible climate-structuring processes in this example.

First, the first generation employees have some control over climate, because they have participated in its evolution and therefore have a degree of understanding. They are comfortable with the climate and can act effectively within it. Because of their success, the second generation employees look to the first generation employees as models. They act in ways similar to first generation workers and these actions reproduce the climate. Unless a countermovement develops that specifically rejects the first group and attempts to undermine the existing climate, it is likely the reproduction of the model will continue. Second, Johnston's discussion suggests that the design of the organization, as differentially experienced by the two generations, actively contributed to the evolution of the particular climate of the second generation employees. The problems with the bureaucratic design are not particularly salient to first generation employees, who lived through its evolution. Therefore, bureaucracy does not figure in a negative way in the kernel climate. Because they had to deal with a design that was not of their making and which they could not circumvent, second generation employees were continuously reminded of it. Their failures and frustrations led them to qualify the expectations in the model kernel climate in a discouraging manner.

These two points contribute a partial explanation of how the climate in Johnston's firm was structured. A more detailed explanation would require us to go well beyond the data he provides, and the reanalysis here probably "stretches" Johnston's results somewhat in any case. But as these points illustrate, climates are best understood and explained in terms of the social processes that generate and maintain them. In the next section we will discuss these processes in more general terms.

THE STRUCTURING PROCESS

The scheme just outlined must now be set in motion: to fully grasp the genesis and influence of climate it is necessary to study how they figure in the structuration of organizational systems. We will consider two levels of analysis. First, we discuss the processes immediately involved in climate structuration—the relationships among practices, interaction, and climate. Interaction systems influence members' interpretations of their experiences and practices in organizations and therefore set climate. Second, we consider the influence of macrolevel organizational design variables on climate. Organizational design plays an important role in determining the nature of practices and constrains the interaction system, thereby shaping climates. In particular, we will focus on organizational units explicitly designed to produce and influence climates—climatic apparati. The relationships discussed in this section are diagrammed in Figure 5.3. The climate—practical structure/practice relationships—discussed in the previous section are also illustrated in Figure 5.3 and form the starting point for this discussion.

Interaction, Practices, Climates

Climate is important both in the production and reproduction of practice systems. Climate enters into all three modalities of structuration in the production of action systems. It serves as a common interpretive scheme, enabling members to engage in, adapt, and coordinate their activities. Climates provide general norms and expectations to guide member's behavior. They also influence resources available for action; expectations and beliefs and power lend credibility to some member's power moves and undermine others' (Apfelbaum, 1979; Pfeffer, 1978).

As a collective generalization applicable across settings and occasions, climate also enters into the *reproduction* of organizational systems. Their very generality lends stability to climates, and this stability tends to reinforce the practices climate is linked to. For example, the safety climates identified by Zohar (1980) create expectations about safety that guide member's behaviors in the same "grooves" that generated the climate in the first place. Even high innovation climates, as much as they may change other parts of the organization, have one stable characteristic—they tend to reproduce innovative interaction patterns. So, other things equal, climates generally serve as a conservative force in organizational interaction systems.

Climate is both a medium of action and its outcome. Climate is produced by organizational practices, and it only persists if some aspect of the activity system reproduces it. In part, the reproduction of climate is a natural consequence of its place in a body of ongoing practices that are repeated many times. To the extent that this body of practices has a unified character, the climate will be unified and pervasive.

An organization has many practices and hence, in principle, it could have many climates. Some theorists, like Schneider (1975), have argued that separate climates should be identified for each distinct genre of practices. However, this conclusion seems premature. Seemingly diverse practices may still be conducted under a common philosophy. And sometimes a single concern can wash out the influence of particular practices on climates, as happens when a firm perceives itself to be in crisis. If conditions are such that organizational practices converge or are patterned after each other, there is likely to be a single coherent kernel climate, which has a strong impact on the organization. If, on the other hand, practices are fragmented, diverse kernel climates or particularized climates are likely to result, and they may have more circumscribed impact. In our discussion of macrolevel structural influences, several factors that determine the nature and convergence of practices will be discussed.

Because they are outcomes of social practices, climates can be changed by appropriate actions. In the study of climate, it is important not to forget the importance of the actor, who carries out the practices which constitute the system. Actors' control over these practices depends on their own abilities and limitations. These are determined, to a large extent, by the system itself and by structures in the larger society. But actors are not simply puppets: They have degrees of freedom that enable them to introduce innovation into practices, innovations which may become permanent if the structuring process perpetuates them, or if actors alter the structuring process. Actors may choose to act in ways inconsistent with prevailing climates, and this can ultimately alter them.

Traditionally, social scientific theory has focused on individual traits or differences as key constraints on individuals' scope of action. Inherited traits, such as intelligence, and individual characteristics linked to social class, such as level of education, are important determinants of capacities. But these only have an impact insofar as they are activated in interaction networks, the locus of the production and reproduction of climates. The interaction system is the constraint of the first order on structuration, and, hence, on the structuring of climates and their impact on the organization.

Schneider and Reichers (1983) and Ashforth (1985) have noted the importance of interaction in the creation of climates. Three central properties of interaction systems can be identified.

First, the *pattern* of the organization's communication network determines how unified and pervasive climates can be. If the organization's network is highly interconnected and carries a high volume of messages, a unified kernel climate will result. The higher the volume, the stronger and more pervasive the climate. Particular climates will result in less-connected sectors of this network. In networks which are broken into cliques or fragmented, multiple kernel climates will result, and there will also be many particular climates. These results occur, in part, because a densely connected network tends to result in unified practices (Feld, 1981), just as a fragmented one signals divergence. Since interconnected networks often create unified attitudes (Monge & Eisenberg, 1987), we would expect the influence of climate on individual appropriation of rules and resources to be stronger and more pervasive in high density networks than in fragmented networks. However, a pilot study by Contractor (1986) suggests that the effect of network patterns on climates may be more complex than these hypotheses suggest.

Who *controls* the flow of communication is also important. In most networks some actors or units have greater control over the system than others. Actors or units which control-key linkages or central routing points can regulate the amount and content of communication and thereby influence the content and strength of climate. With strong control we would expect either a single kernel climate or a kernel that serves as a model for particular climates. Indeed, control over networks is what gives a group the power to project itself as a model (Apfelbaum, 1979). Franklin (1975a, 1975b; Dennison, 1982) showed that climates in managerial groups determined the climates in work groups directly below them. In line with Likert's linking pin theory, Franklin explained this as a product of downward interaction between higher level groups and lower participants.

A third important property of interaction systems is the mode of *coorientation* they promote. Coorientation was introduced by Newcomb (1953) to refer to the simultaneous orientation of two persons toward each other and toward external objects, concepts, or issues. Scheff (1967) has generalized coorientation to represent prevailing states of agreement or consensus in social systems. Coorientation can be defined in terms of two concepts important for our purposes: agreement and accuracy. To the extent that two people's beliefs are similar, they are in *agreement*; independent of this, to the extent that one correctly knows the other's beliefs, he or she has *accuracy*, about the other. The coorientation in a system can be described in terms of the degree of agreement and accuracy members have. Scheff described four cases: consensus (high agreement, high accuracy), dissension (low agreement, high accuracy—people disagree and they know it), pluralistic ignorance (high agreement, low accuracy—people agree, but they don't realize it), and anomie (low agreement, low accuracy).

Coorientation plays an important role in the structuration of climates. It influences the form climates take, the pervasiveness of their effects throughout the organization, their relationship to organizational structure, and the strength of their impact on member behavior. Table 5.1 summarizes the effects of coorientation on climate structuring.

The form of climates will be quite different, depending on mode of coorientation, as Table 5.1 indicates. Consider, for example, an achieve-

Table 5.1.   Relation of Co-orientation States to Climate Effects

COORIENTA-TION STATE	FORM OF CLIMATE	PERVASIVENESS Strength of Climate Effects on Organization	COUPLING of Climate with Macro-Structures and Processes	RELATION-SHIP of Climate to Member Behavior
CONSENSUS: High Agreement, High Accuracy	Single Kernel; Model Kernel with Particular Climates	High	Uncoupling Possible	May Be High
DISSENSUS: Low Agreement, High Accuracy	Multiple Kernels; Model Kernel with Particular Climates	Medium to Low	Uncoupling Possible	Low
PLURALISTIC IGNORANCE: High Agreement, Low Accuracy	Single Kernel; Model Kernel with Particular Climates	High	Uncoupling Not Possible	May Be High
ANOMIE: Low Agreement, Low Accuracy	Multiple Kernels; Many Particular Climates	Low	Uncoupling Not Possible	Low

ment-oriented climate. Under consensus, a unit's supervisor might, for instance, openly encourage retraining and post pictures of those who won promotions in order to inspire others. There would be a great deal of rhetoric supporting high achievement and its attendant rewards. Unit members would probably exhibit high morale, agree that achievement was important, and encourage each other in the pursuit of higher productivity. There would be a single kernel climate or a model kernel with particular climates. In the case of pluralistic ignorance with an achievement-oriented climate, we might find the sort of situation described by Kanter (1977). Members believe the organization and their coworkers value achievement and they work for it, but in their hearts many do not value it. This pluralistic ignorance fosters cynicism in workers; they learn to act busy and competent, while actually worrying more about political maneuvering than about productivity. Again, there would be a single kernel or model kernel, but members' attitudes toward the climate and how the climate influences the system differ from the case of consensus. Under dissensus we might find open disagreement about the value of achievement; achievement would still be a concern of the unit, but factions with discrepant climates would arise and there would be an implicit struggle over whether achievement should guide the unit's actions. In the case of dissensus, then, there would be multiple kernel climates or model kernels with "inverted" particular climates. With anomie, a coherent climate could not be maintained. Achievement might still be stressed by higher levels of the organization, but the message (if attended to at all) would be likely to create highly individualized motivations. Each member would concentrate on his or her gains, because collective beliefs would not exist. In the case of anomie there would be multiple kernels with many particular climates, if there was any consensus on climates at all.

Coorientation also affects the *pervasiveness* of climate's influence, that is, how strong and widespread their effects are throughout the organization. The degree of intersubject agreement on climate is a particularly important determinant of their pervasiveness. Climates with high consensus and pluralistic ignorance would have pervasive effects, because they are widely shared (although, as noted in the previous paragraph, these effects might be quite different for the two cases). Climates with dissensus would have medium to low pervasiveness. Low levels of agreement would work against strong and widespread influence of any single climate, but high levels of accuracy would permit members of different subgroups to orient to each other, thereby giving the climates some influence. In cases of dissensus, climate would have little pervasive influence; subgroup climates may have some influence within their kens, but it may be washed out by other factors.

As the third column in Table 5.1 shows, coorientation also influences the *degree of coupling* between the climate and other macrolevel organizational features, on the one hand, and practices, on the other. If climate and other organizational features are coupled, then each can influence the other: the structures associated with organizational features shape climate and climate shapes features in a reciprocal influence process. It is possible, on the other hand, for climates and other structures to be uncoupled. In this case, climate would develop as an ideology, independent of other structures and work. In general, low degrees of accuracy make it difficult for climates to uncouple from other organizational structures. Climates can only attain functional autonomy from ongoing practices if the members of subgroups are aware of each others' beliefs and work together to sustain climate as a symbolic creation. To sustain a climate uncoupled from day-to-day practices, members must consciously or unconsciously make climate promulgation a practice in its own right, a common organizational activity. This might be done, for example, by a group of managers who attempt to introduce an open participative climate into their transaction with other members in a repressive, autocratic organization. They will only succeed in this if other members have accurate perceptions of their climate and take these into account in interaction. If others inaccurately perceive the managerial unit to have the same untrusting, closed climate as the rest of the organization, they will act in an untrusting way. The managerial unit will have to react in line with this and the open climate will be hard to sustain. Accuracy is essential if climate is to survive independent of other structures and practices. Hence, for climates with consensus and dissensus, climate and other organizational features *may* be uncoupled. This does not guarantee that they will be uncoupled; it merely opens the possibility. In cases of pluralistic ignorance and anomie, it will be difficult to uncouple climates from other organizational features or practices. Members cannot sustain climates independent of practices if they do not perceive others' climatic perceptions accurately. Differences in coupling can explain, in part, the inconsistent relationship found between climate and organizational design in previous research. In some organizations climate and structure may be uncoupled, resulting in low-structure climate correlations. In others, they may be coupled, resulting in higher correlations.

As the fourth column in Table 5.1 shows, coorientation mode also determines the *strength* of the relationship between climate and individual behavior. Other factors may prevent climate from influencing members' behavior, but coorientation places an upper bound on possible linkages. In the case of consensus and pluralistic ignorance on climate, the link between climate and behavior can be quite strong. If members have agreement on climate, they act on the same grounds and appropriate practical rules and resources in similar ways. Consistent behaviors resonate as described by Zeitz (1983), reinforcing the practice system and thereby reinforcing climate effects. In the case of dissensus, the climate-behavior link will likely be weaker because different subunit climates may work against each other. There will not be the resonance found when there is high agreement. In cases of anomie, the relationship between climate and behavior would be weak.

The climate-interaction relationship cuts both ways. Behavior also influences climate, and this, too, depends on coorientation. Coorientation mode influences members' understanding and penetration of their situation, and hence, their appropriation of organizational rules and resources. At one extreme, members may accept the organization and its climate unreflectively. At the other, they may understand the attempts of various groups to create climates and the role of various structural properties in climate processes. In the latter case, members would be able to exert greater control over climate and, more generally, over their appropriation of organizational structures. They could even take a role in shaping climate themselves or, at least, disregard or reinterpret prevailing beliefs and values. One oft-cited example of this are workers who sneer at company efforts to motivate "open communication," because they know that giving information may be harmful to their careers. Obviously, degree of penetration and control will differ across members, depending on their formal position, duties, and personal needs (among other things). However, coorientation mode set limits on the penetration members can achieve, and this determines the degree to which they can actively control climate.

Coorientation depends on the nature of the interaction system, particularly what is said, who interacts with whom, and how clear, consistent, and univocal the messages are. However, once a mode of coorientation is firmly established, it becomes a structuring force in its own right. Coorientation modes tend to reinforce themselves by setting up interaction patterns that regenerate them. The full understanding of consensus tends to promote interaction among members, leading to further understanding. In systems with dissensus or pluralistic ignorance, subgroups with different beliefs tend to avoid interaction, often without realizing they do, which reinforces lack of agreement and understanding.

Together, the three characteristics of interaction systems—network patterns, control over networks, and coorientation mode—constitute a basic framework for action in climate structuring. Two important factors which are not discussed in this section are the specific interaction patterns and symbolic moves that constitute climates. Although these deserve detailed examination, this essay has focused on more general, summary properties of interaction systems. This section gives a partial

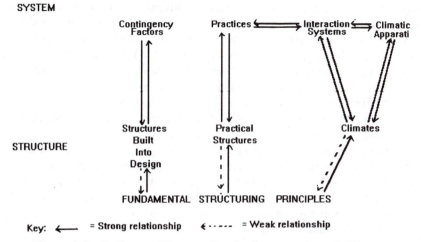

Key: ←——— = Strong relationship   ←····· = Weak relationship

Figure 5.3.   Influence Diagram for the Structuration of Climates

answer to Questions 1 and 2, concerning how intersubjective climates are created and maintained, and how various system and subsystem climates relate to each other. It also addresses Question 3 by distinguishing four modes of coorientation which represent different types of "agreement" about climate members may have. Finally, propositions developed here also provide several pieces of the puzzle laid by Question 4, concerning how climates relate to other macrolevel variables. As Figure 5.3 shows, to fully answer this last question, it is necessary to consider macrolevel linkages as well.

Macrostructural Influences on Climate

As a system-level construct, climate is connected with macrolevel factors, such as organizational design, environment, and organizational culture. Here we will focus on the two most important and immediate macrolevel factors, climatic apparati and organizational design.

In addition to deriving from interaction organized around practices, climates may be directly structured by climatic apparati. An important feature of organizations is the existence of institutional apparati for creating and maintaining climates, as well as symbols, attitudes, ideologies (cf. Althusser, 1977). These apparati include socialization and training programs, work groups, sponsors, newsletters, internal "publicity agencies," and figureheads. In some cases—training programs, sponsorship systems, newsletters—the apparatus is consciously designed to control climate; other apparati—work groups, key managers, figureheads—emerge as crucial "institutions" and control climate on their own terms.

Apparati govern the communication and interaction systems which produce climates and, hence, not only introduce climate themes directly, but also mediate some effects of other macrolevel properties on climate. If apparati produce a pervasive message and emphasize unity, they create a single kernel or model kernel climate; if they set up differentiations, multiple kernels or particular climates will result.

The effectiveness of climatic apparati depends on the nature of the organization's interaction system. Most climatic apparati are located at points that control a network. Often these points "create" apparati since their incumbents either are asked to promulgate general beliefs or do so for political reasons. The credibility of the apparatus in the interaction system is an important determinant of how influential it will be. And in organizations with "weak" forms of coorientation—anomie, pluralistic ignorance, and to a lesser extent dissensus—climatic apparati may play a particularly important role.

Climatic apparati can generate climates independent of the influence of the existing practice system, especially if the apparatus has high control over the network and high credibility. In this case, the climate is uncoupled from the macrolevel factors and practices. It could serve as a "middle-range ideology," masking the true nature and consequences of organizational practices.

The influence of *organizational design* on climate has received a great deal of attention (Payne & Pugh, 1976). Here we will consider two aspects of organizational structure, the commonly studied dimensions of organizational design and less studied, but more fundamental "structuring principles."

Several properties of organizational design, including centralization, formalization, and size have been shown to be related to climate perceptions. But there is evidence that practices mediate the influence of macrolevel design variables on climate. Correlations between climate dimensions and variables describing organizational practices (e.g., role routines, supervisory style) are typically higher than those between climate dimensions and macrolevel structural variables, such as size, centralization, and formalization (Payne & Pugh, 1976), a finding consistent with the hypothesis that practices mediate the effect of macrolevel variables on climate. Using path analysis, Child and Ellis (1973) found that role routines and level of perceived authority—two variables implicated directly in organizational practices—mediated the influence of centralization on perceived innovative climate.

Organizational design properties influence climate structuring in several ways. First, they are to some degree responsible for the nature of the interaction system. They affect the pattern of communication linkages and whether communication flow can be controlled by a few positions.

Second, organizational design also partially determines the unity of the organization's practices. The more practices converge, the more pervasive the influence of the climate and the more likely there is to be a single kernel or model kernel climate. Practices will be more likely to converge if they are similar, so organizations with a restricted range of practices will exhibit greater unification of climate. Several design characteristics determine the degree of unity practices. Practices are likely to be restricted in: (a) small organizations, (b) service as opposed to production organizations (managerial and executive practices are in many ways similar to human service practices, whereas they may differ from production practices), (c) organizations designed to maximize control over member activities (i.e., those with high centralization and formalization), and (d) organizations with a single overriding purpose, either a strong sense of mission or determination to survive a crisis.

Third, design properties influence whether climatic apparati exist and how influential they can be. For example, an organization with a well-developed information and control system has a excellent infrastructure for the operation of climatic apparati.

A central assumption of structurational theory is that the influence of organizational design on climate is mediated by members' appropriation of structural features carried by the design. Hence, design influences climate via its effect on practices and interaction, as Figure 5.3 shows. For example, if an organization has a large body of written rules, these are likely to influence climate. But this influence will be mediated by the meaning of rules to members and members' attitudes toward rules (are they useful, or a burden, or made to be broken?), as well as the types of coorientation in the interaction system. Depending on mediating interpretive and interaction processes, written rules will be used differently and have different effects on climate. Differences in interaction systems will lead to differences in how the same design features influence climate. This, in part, accounts for inconsistent findings in studies of the design-climate relationship.

Underlying the operation of design characteristics are fundamental structuring principles. There is substantial evidence that the configuration of design properties depends on the pattern of contingency variables, including the nature of the organization's environment and its work technology (e.g., Mintzberg, 1979). Although this relation is often portrayed as a simple determination of one set of system properties (design configuration) by another (contingencies), more often it is assumed to be mediated by some structuring process (Drazin & Van de Ven, 1985), such as strategic choice (Child, 1972) or structuring of work (Mintzberg, 1979). This process is shaped by fundamental structuring principles, basic assumptions, and modes of operation which underpin capitalist institutions. This sequence and its effect on climates are illustrated in Figure 5.3.

The most common fundamental deep structure underlying the modern capitalist structure—economic rationalization—has been described by Weber (1947) and more recently by Clegg (1975). Clegg shows in some detail how this principle determines the nature and organization of work and power on a construction site. The principle of economic rationalization shaped and constrained "intermediate" structures governing decision-making and managerial activities, creating a unified basis for action. In a similar vein, such a principle would be expected to shape climate as part of a unified action system.

It is beyond the scope of this chapter to discuss the operation of societal-level structuring priciples. But it is important to acknowledge and investigate their operation, because they serve as a unifying generative base for the structuration of climates, organizational design, and other seemingly diverse macrolevel features.

It is also worth noting that several more or less inconsistent structuring principles may operate together. Of interest is how they interact to counteract or reinforce one another.

This discussion of macrolevel influences on climate structuring directly addresses Question 4. It clarifies the connection of climate to the larger organization and emphasizes the importance of going beyond the boundaries of the organization to consider the role of broader social institutions in climate structuring. It also contributes another piece of the puzzle regarding the relationship of system and subsystem climates.

DISCUSSION

Progress in science is marked by progressive criticism and redefinition of concepts and models in an effort to increase the accuracy with which our theories represent the world. Studies of the specifically human world face particular problems, because they must define concepts reflexively and models may change when people become aware of them. This chapter attempts to contribute to the current move toward reconceptualizing organizational climate. In recasting climate as an intersubjective process-based construct, the chapter attempts to push recent studies by Schneider, Ashforth, Zeitz, Joyce, and Slocum toward their logical conclusion. Rather than viewing climate as a more or less static system of beliefs, the model construes climate as both medium and outcome of structurational processes. The "sharedness" or intersubjectivity of climates, which may vary in degree and quality, is a product of these structurational processes. Climate is viewed as an integral part of organizational practices, a structure which serves as a medium for the structuration of practice systems and which is an outcome of this process as well.

The structuration of climates involves the convergence of a number of elements at various levels in a common process of production and reproduction, mediated by interaction. In the strictest sense, then, the model must be evaluated as a whole. Neither the schematic diagram or the influence diagram or any relationship in them should properly stand alone. However, the preceding discussion implies a number of propositions or predictions that can be studied and evaluated individually. The pattern of results can shed light on the validity of the whole edifice. These propositions can be organized under the four questions raised at the beginning of the chapter.

The Nature of Systemic Climates

The model portrays climate as an intersubjective as opposed to an objective or subjective construct. The intersubjectivity of climates is not a stable state, but is generated and maintained by a continuous structurational process that produces and reproduces the climate along with the rest of the organization. In the study of this process the stability of climates is as much in need of explanation as is their change. Climate plays a key role in the structuring of organizations, because it guides how members appropriate all organizational structures. Depending on the nature of the structurational process, there can be various types of intersubjectivity in climates. We defined four different modes of coorientation that represent different degrees of intersubjectivity—consensus, dissensus, pluralistic ignorance, and anomie. It should be possible to find at least the first three variants of climates and the character and content of climate should differ for each of them. There should also be cases where climate is an ideology, uncoupled from important features of the organization and its ongoing work, that is, where members' beliefs about the organization differ from its "reality." In these cases, there should be a climatic apparatus which can generate high levels of agreement on climate beliefs in contradistinction to actual states of affairs.

System and Subsystem Climates

The model defines three different climate configurations—single kernel, model kernel with particular climates, and multiple kernel climates. These represent different types of relationships between system and subsystem climates. We have also defined "bundles" of conditions which determine which configuration results:

A single kernel climate is most likely when practices are unified, when there is a dense, highly connected network, when a few actors or units can control the network, under consensus and pluralistic ignorance coorientation states, and when there is a strong climatic apparatus.

A model kernel with particular climates is most likely when practices are fairly unified, when there is a dense network with moderate degrees of clique formation and division, when a few actors or units can control the network, under consensus and dissensus coorientation, accompanied by a strong climatic apparatus.

Multiple kernels with particular climates are most likely when practices are diverse, when the network is fragmented, with many cliques and sub-cliques, when control over the network is not concentrated, under dissensus or anomie coorientation states, and where there are either weak climate apparati or where there are several competing apparati.

The more these conditions occur together, the stronger the predictive power regarding climate. These conditions influence structurational processes and thereby have an impact on the form climates take; but the climate they create also has a role in the production and reproduction of conditions.

Agreement on Climate

While groups of members must share a climate in order for it to exist, there need not be agreement on all particulars, nor in members' affective or behavioral responses to climate. Indeed, many climate questionnaires may have tapped these surface disagreements, leading researchers to conclude there is little agreement on climate, when in fact there was. As the discussion of coorientation showed, "agreement" is more complicated than definitions of "shared" climates imply. Four different types of agreement can be distinguished, and it is likely there are intermediate forms as well. Coorientation mode has important effects on the organization. The higher the level of accuracy, the more pervasive the climate, and the higher the level of agreement, the more likely it is that the climate can achieve functional autonomy and exist uncoupled from other organizational structures and practices.

Relationship of Climate to Macrolevel Constructs

All relationships of climate with other macrostructures are mediated by the interaction processes which carry structuration. Organizational design influences climate by: (a) affecting interaction patterns, (b) determining the unity of practices, and (c) determining the existence of climate apparati. Climates influence organizational design and other macrolevel constructs by shaping members' appropriation of design and other macrolevel structures. Coorientation mode determines the degree to which macrostructure and climate must be coupled. Under some conditions—high accuracy and strong action of climatic apparati—climate, other macrostructures, and practices may be uncoupled. In addition, the relationships between organizational macrostructures and climate are shaped by broader social-level structuring principles.

Implications for Climate Research

Measurement of most of the factors discussed here would be fairly straightforward, and most of the hypotheses just delineated could be tested. However, this approach would not be sufficient to evaluate the model. The theory indicates the necessity of studying climates with longitudinal research designs rather than more typical cross-sectional designs. Any description of climate which focuses only on a structural map would be seriously incomplete, because it omits the generative processes which lend cohesion to the climate. The explanation of climates has to account for several overtime processes of structuring.

The model also implies the need to ground data collecting systems (whether the questionnaires, interviews, or direct observation) in the participants' perspectives. If climates have an impact because they shape the meaning of the organization for its members, and if the structuring of climates depend on meaningful systems of action, then researchers are omitting the crux of the construct if they view climate only from their own, rather remote perspective. Payne and Pugh (1976) argue with respect to studies using researcher-concocted questionnaires:

> Future research can ignore most of these studies and utilize a completely different approach. We need deep involvement from members of a complex system to gather meaningful data which accurately reflect these people's experiences. . . . The researcher needs to swap data interpretations with his subjects so that interpretations are more realistic. (p. 1168)

This conclusion may be a bit extreme; there is certainly much of value in previous research, but it must be supplemented with interpretive methods. Johnston's study suggests one pattern for future climate research. The case study by Folger, Poole, and Stutman (1993, pp. 166–173) illustrates a complementary approach for the identification of a climatic scheme and the processes that produce and reproduce it. The emerging combination of new theories and new methods promises a change in climate in the near future.

REFERENCES

Althusser, L. (1977). Ideology and state ideological apparatuses. In *Lenin and philosophy and other essays*. London: New Left Books.

Apfelbaum, E. (1979). Relations of domination and movements for liberation: An analysis of power between groups. In W. G. Austin & S. Worchel (Eds.), *The social psychology of intergroup relations*. Belmont, CA: Wadsworth.

Ashforth, B. (1985). Climate formation: Issues and extensions. *Academy of Management Review, 10*, 837–847.

Axelrod, R. (1976). *The structure of decision: The cognitive maps of political elites*. Princeton, NJ: Princeton University Press.

Barley, S. R. (1986). Technology as an occasion for structuring. *Administrative Science Quarterly, 31*, 78–108.

Barthes, R. (1971). *S/Z*. Paris: Seuil.

Bass, B. M., Valenzi, E. R., Farrow, D. L., & Solomon, R. J. (1975). Management styles associated with organizational, task, personal, and interpersonal contingencies. *Journal of Applied Psychology, 60*, 720–729.

Bateson, G. (1958). *Naven*. Stanford, CA: Stanford University Press.

Bougon, M., Weick, K., & Binkhorst, D. (1977). Cognition and organizations: An Analysis of the Utrecht jazz orchestra. *Administrative Science Quarterly, 22*, 606–639.

Bourdieu, P. (1977). *Outline of a theory of practice*. Cambridge, England: Cambridge University Press.

Campbell, J., Dunette, M., Lawler, E. E., & Weick, K. (1970). *Managerial behavior, performance, and effectiveness*. New York: McGraw-Hill.

Child, J. (1972). Organizational structure, environment, and performance: The role of strategic choice. *Sociology, 6*, 2–22.

Child, J., & Ellis, T. (1973). Predictors of variation in managerial roles. *Human Relations, 26*, 227–250.

Clegg, S. (1975). *Power, rule, and domination*. London: Routledge & Kegan Paul.

Contractor, N. S. (1986). *Formal and emergent structures as predictors of agreement on organizational climate*. Unpublished manuscript, University of Southern California, Annenberg School of Communications.

Coward, R., & Ellis, J. (1977). *Language and materialism: Developments in semiology and the theory of the subject*. Boston: Routledge & Kegan Paul.

Dandridge, T. C., Mitroff, I., & Joyce, W. F. (1980). Organizational symbolism: A topic to expand organizational analysis. *Academy of Management Review, 5*, 77–82.

Deiterly, T. C., & Schneider, B. (1974). The effect of organizational environment on perceived power and climate: A laboratory study. *Organizational Behavior and Human Performance, 11*, 316–337.

Dennison, D. A. (1982). Multidimensional scaling and structural equation modelling: A comparison of multivariate techniques for theory testing. *Multivariate Behavioral Research, 17*, 447–470.

Doise, W. (1978). *Groups and individuals: Explanations in social psychology*. Cambridge, England: Cambridge University Press.

Drazin, R., & Van de Ven, A. (1985). Alternative forms of fit in cotingency theory. *Administrative Science Quarterly, 30*, 514–539.

Drexler, J. A. (1977). Organizational climate: Its homogeneity within organizations. *Journal of Applied Psychology, 62*, 38–42.

Feld, S. (1981). The focused organization of social ties. *American Journal of Sociology, 81*, 1015–1035.

Folger, J. P., Poole, M., & Stutman, R. (1993). *Working through conflict*. New York: Harper-Collins.

Forehand, G. A., & Gilmer, B. V. H. (1964). Environmental variations in studies of organizational behavior. *Psychological Bulletin, 62*, 361–382.

Franklin, J. L. (1975a). Down the organization: Influence processes across levels of hierarchy. *Administrative Science Quarterly, 20*, 153–164.

Franklin, J. L. (1975b). Relations among four social-psychological aspects of organizations. *Administrative Science Quarterly, 20*, 422–433.

Frederiksen, N., Jensen, O., & Beaton, A. E. (1972). *Prediction of organizational behavior*. New York: Pergamon.

Garfinkel, H. (1967). *Studies in ethnomethodology*. Englewood Cliffs, NJ: Prentice-Hall.

Glick, W. H. (1985). Conceptualizing and measuring organizational psychological climate: Pitfalls in multilevel research. *Academy of Management Review, 10*, 601–616.

Giddens, A. (1976). *New rules of sociological method*. New York: Basic.

Giddens, A. (1979). *Central problem in social theory*. Berkeley, CA: University of California Press.

Giddens, A. (1981). *A contemporary critique of historical materialism*. Berkeley, CA: University of California Press.

Grossberg, L. (1979). *Intersubjectivity and the conceptualization of communication*. Unpublished manuscript, University of Illinois, Urbana-Champaign.

Guion, R. M. (1973). A note on organizational climate. *Organizational Behavior and Human Performance, 9*, 120–125.

Halpin, A., & Crofts, D. (1963). The organizational climate of schools. *Administrator's Notebook, 11*.

Hellreigel, D., & Slocum, J. W. (1974). Organizational climate: Measures, research, and contingencies. *Academy of Management Journal, 17*, 255–280.

Hernes, G. (1976). Structural change in social processes. *American Journal of Sociology, 82*, 513–547.

Howe, J. G. (1977). Group climate: An exploration of construct validity. *Organizational Behavior and Human Performance, 1*, 106–125.

Indik, B. P. (1965). Organizational size and member participation: Some empirical tests of alternative explanations. *Human Relations, 18*, 339–350.

Jackofsky, E., & Slocum, J. W. (1986). *A longitudinal study of climate*. Unpublished manuscript, Southern Methodist University.

James, L., & Jones, A. (1974). Organizational climate: A review of theory and research. *Psychological Bulletin, 81*, 1096–1112.

Johnston, H. R. (1976). A new conceptualization of source of organizational climate. *Administrative Science Quarterly, 21*, 95–103.

Jones, A. P., & James, L. R. (1979). Psychological climate. Dimensions and relationships of individual and aggregated work environment perceptions. *Organizational Behavior and Human Performance, 23*, 201–250.

Joyce, W. F., & Slocum, J. W. (1984). Collective climate: Agreement as a basis for defining aggregate climates in organizations. *Academy of Management Journal, 27*, 721–742.

Kanter, R. M. (1977). *Men and women of the corporation*. New York: Harper.

Knorr-Cetina, K., & Cicourel, A. (Eds.). (1981). *Advances in social theory: Toward an integration of micro- and macro sociologies*. Boston: Routledge & Kegan Paul.

Lawler, E. E., Hall, D. T., & Oldham, G. (1974). Organizational climate: Relationship to organizational structure, process, and performance. *Organizational Behavior and Human Performance, 11*, 139–155.

Lewin, K., Lippitt, R., & White, R. (1939). Patterns of aggressive behavior in experimentally-created social climates. *Journal of Social Psychology, 10*, 271–299.

Litwin, G., & Stringer, R. (1968). *Motivation and organizational climate*. Cambridge, MA: Harvard University Press.

Maines, D. (1977). Social organization and social structure in symbolic interactionist thought. *Annual Review of Sociology, 3*, 235–259.

Masuch, M. (1985). Vicious circles in organizations. *Administrative Science Quarterly, 30*, 14–33.

McClelland, D. C. (1961). *The achieving society*. Princeton, NJ: Van Nostrand.

McPhee, R. D. (1985). Formal structure and organizational communication. In R. D. McPhee & P. K. Tompkins (Eds.), *Organizational communication: Traditional themes and new directions*. Beverly Hills, CA: Sage.

Mintzberg, H. (1979). *The structuring of organizations*. Englewood Cliffs, NJ: Prentice-Hall.

Monge, P. R., & Eisenberg, E. (1987). Formal communication networks. In F. Jablin, L. Putnam, L. Porter, & K. Roberts (Eds.), *Handbook of organizational communication* (pp. 515–548). Beverly Hills, CA: Sage.

Morris, C. (1939). *Foundations of a theory of signs*. Chicago, IL: University of Chicago Press.

Newcomb, T. M. (1953). An approach to the study of communicative acts. *Psychological Review, 60*, 393–403.

Paolillo, J. G. R., & Paolillo, D. (1982). Subsystem climate as a function of personal and organizational factors. *Journal of Management Studies, 19*, 327–334.

Payne, R., Fineman, S., & Wall, T. D. (1976). Organizational climate and job satisfaction: A conceptual synthesis. *Organizational Behavior and Human Performance, 16*, 45–62.

Payne, R. L., & Mansfield, R. (1973). Relationships of perceptions of organizational climate to organizational structure, content, and hierarchical position. *Administrative Science Quarterly, 18*, 515–526.

Payne, R., & Pugh, D. (1976). Organizational structure and climate. In M. Dunnette (Ed.), *Handbook of industrial psychology*. Chicago: Rand-McNally.

Pelz, D., & Andrews, F. (1976). *Scientists in organizations*. Ann Arbor, MI: Institute for Social Research.

Pfeffer, J. (1981). *Power in organizations*. Marshfield, MA: Pitman.

Poole, M. S. (1983). Structural paradigms and the study of group communication. In M. Mandler (Ed.), *Communications in transition*. New York: Praeger.

Poole, M. S. (1985). Communication and organizational climate. In P. Tompkins & R. D. McPhee (Eds.), *Organizational communication: Traditional themes and new directions*. Beverly Hills, CA: Sage.

Poole, M. S., & McPhee, R. D. (1983). A structurational example of organizational climate. In L. Putnam & M. Pacanowsky (Eds.), *Communicational organization*. Beverly Hills, CA: Sage.

Poole, M. S., Seibold, D. R., & McPhee, R. D. (1985). Group decision-making as a structurational process. *Quarterly Journal of Speech, 71*, 74–102.

Poole, M. S., Siebold, D. R., & McPhee, R. D. (1985). A structurational approach to theory-building in group decision-making research. In R. Y. Hirokawa & M. S. Poole (Eds.), *Group decision-making and communication*. Beverly Hills, CA: Sage.

Powell, G. N., & Butterfield, D. A. (1978). The case for subsystem climates in organizations. *Academy of Management Review, 3*, 151–157.

Pritchard, R. D., & Karasick, B. (1973). The effects of organizational climate on managerial job performance and job satisfaction. *Organizational Behavior and Human Performance, 9*, 126–146.

Ranson, S., Hinings, B., & Greenwood, R. (1980). The structuring of organizational structures. *Administrative Science Quarterly, 25*, 1–17.

Reynolds, J., & Reynolds, L. (1973). Interactionism, complicity, and the astructural bias. *Catalyst, 7*, 76–85.

Scheff, T. J. (1967). Toward a sociological model of consensus. *American Sociological Review, 32*, 32–46.

Schneider, B. (1975). Organizational climates: An essay. *Personnel Psychology, 28*, 447–479.

Schneider, B., Parkington, J., & Buxton, V. (1980). Employee and customer perception of service in banks. *Administrative Science Quarterly, 25*, 252–267.

Schneider, B., & Reichers, A. (1983). On the etiology of climates. *Personnel Psychology, 36*, 19–39.

Smelser, N. J. (1962). *Theory of collective behavior.* New York: Free Press.

Strauss, A. (1978). *Negotiations: Varieties, contexts, processes and social order.* San Francisco, CA: Jossey-Bass.

Stern, G. C. (1970). *People in context: Measuring person-environment congruence in education and industry.* New York: Wiley.

Taguiri, R. (1968). The concept of organizational climate. In R. Taguiri & G. Litwin (Eds.), *Organizational climate: Explorations of a concept.* Cambridge, MA: Division of Research, Harvard Business School.

Tajfel, H., & Turner, J. (1979). An integrative theory of intergroup conflict. In W. G. Austin & S. Worchel (Eds.), *The social psychology of intergroup relations* (pp. 33–48). Monterey, CA: Brooks/Cole.

Tannenbaum, A. S. (1966). *Social psychology of work organizations.* Belmont, CA: Wadsworth.

Taylor, C. (1971). Interpretation and the sciences of man. *Review of Metaphysics, 25*, 1–52.

Taylor, J. C., & Bowers, D. G. (1980). *The survey of organizations.* Ann Arbor, MI: Institute for Social Research.

Turner, S. P. (1977). Complex organizations as savage tribes. *Journal of the Theory of Social Behavior, 4*, 99–125.

Weber, M. (1947). *The theory of social and economic organization* (T. Parsons, Ed.). New York: Free Press.

Woodman, R. W., & King, D. C. (1978). Organizational climate: Science or folklore? *Academy of Management Review, 3*, 816–826.

Zeitz, G. (1983). Structural and individual determinants of organizational morale and satisfaction. *Social Forces, 61*, 1088–1108.

Zohar, D. (1980). Safety climate in industrial organizations: Theoretical and applied implications. *Journal of Applied Psychology, 65*, 96–102.

6

Communication Competence in Organizations: Conceptualization and Comparison Across Multiple Level of Analysis

Fredric M. Jablin
Roger L. Cude
Ann House
Jaesub Lee
Nancy L. Roth

Although the communication competence construct is one that has traditionally been of interest to organizational communication researchers *and* practitioners, it has received relatively little theoretical development or empirical study as applied to the organizational context. The handful of investigations that have explored the construct in the organizational setting have typically adapted applications of communication competence developed for the study of interpersonal communication relationships. While there is some validity to such applications, there are also a variety of unique attributes of the organizational context which make such extrapolations problematic. In addition, extant studies have only considered the notion of communication competence at the individual and/or dyadic levels of analysis, and have not explored the attributes of competence at the group and organizational levels of analysis. As a consequence, this chapter develops theoretical, empirical, and pragmatic dimensions of the communication competence construct as it applies to various levels of analysis in the organizational setting (i.e., individual/dyadic, group, and organization levels of analysis). Based on our research critique, a general model for investigating communication competence in organizations at various levels of analysis is proposed and explicated with specific examples for the group and organizational levels of analysis.

ORGANIZATIONAL COMMUNICATION COMPETENCE: STATE OF THE ART

In order to develop a sense of the theoretical and empirical directions of extant research exploring communication competence, we conducted a literature review across the communication, management/administrative sciences, organizational behavior, psychology, and sociology disciplines for the period of 1975 to 1990. We considered studies as focusing on communication competence in organizations if they either explicitly stated they were examining *communication* competence, attempted to identify communication skills that contemporary research frequently associates with competence, or identified communication competencies as part of more general studies of competence in organizations (e.g., managerial competence). This literature review is not intended to be inclusive of all communication competence or competence-related studies reported from 1975 to 1990, but rather to be representative of research in the area.

Communication Competence in Organizations

Although researchers have been exploring various dimensions of communication competence in organizations for several decades, it is quite apparent that conceptual and theoretical development of the construct is a fairly recent phenomenon. In evaluating research exploring communication competence in organizations, we believe two major approaches epitomize the literature: (a) performance or skills-based conceptualizations, and (b) social cognition/symbolic interaction models.

Performance/Skills Approaches. Studies that have explored the performance aspects of competence assume that a competent communicator is one who "maximizes his or her goal achievement through communication" (Parks, 1977, p. 1). Accordingly, Monge, Bachman, Dillard, and Eisenberg (1982), early proponents of this perspective, argue that communication competence in organizations "ought to focus on observable communication behaviors and omit or minimize social and interpersonal factors" (p. 507). Along these lines, Monge et al. (1982) proposed and tested a competence construct containing two general dimensions: encoding and decoding ability. Implicit in their approach, as well as that of many others who have explored competence from a behavioral perspective (though utilizing self-report measurement methods), is the notion that competence is cross-situational. They also argue that since goals are typically "public and explicit because they are prescribed by the role of the individual within the organizational structure . . . the perennial problem of determining communication behavior which is 'appropriate for the context' [Larson, Backlund, Redmond, & Barbour, 1978] is reduced in the organizational setting" (Monge et al., 1982, p. 506).

In contrast to the Monge et al., two-factor, workplace communication competence model, a number of other researchers have adapted behaviorally oriented models of *interpersonal* communication competence to the organizational setting. For example, Wheeless and Berryman-Fink (1985) developed a model that is similar to that of Spitzberg's (1983) conceptualization of competence, which contains two factors: (a) altercentrism (empathy, listening, supportiveness, other-orientation), and (b) interaction management (appropriate turn-taking, episode punctuation patterns, etc.). On the other hand, Snavely and Walters (1983), extract a five-dimensional organizational communication competence model from their analysis of the interpersonal communication literature (empathy, listening, self-disclosure, social anxiety, versatility). In brief, although variations in findings are evident across these types of studies, most include at least three basic dimensions in their conceptualizations of interpersonal/organizational communication competence; empathy or other-orientation, interaction management, and behavioral flexibility (Sypher, 1984).

Another group of studies which fall within the general classification of the performance-based competence approach are those which have attempted to develop inventories of communication *skills* required by organizational members. Generally speaking, "skills" studies can be divided into two basic types: (a) research exploring in somewhat of an evaluative/prescriptive fashion the communication performance requirements of organizational roles, and (b) research attempting to identify in a descriptive manner the "actual" communication behaviors of persons in various roles.

Many of the studies summarized by DiSalvo (1980), in his collation of research identifying communication skills required in organizations, are representative of investigations attempting to prescribe organizational communication skill requirements. Data are typically collected via self-report questionnaires and: (a) request respondents to rank and rate the "importance" of lists of communication skills necessary for "success" in their jobs and organizations (e.g., DiSalvo & Larsen, 1987; DiSalvo, Larsen, & Seiler, 1976; Morse & Piland, 1981; Rader & Wunsch, 1980), or (b) ask respondents to identify communication skills in which they or another group of organizational members are deficient (areas that need improvement, where training is needed) (e.g., Bennett & Olney, 1986; Berryman-Fink, 1985; Hanna, 1978; Meister & Reinsch, 1978; Staley & Shockley-Zalabak, 1986), or (c) ask participants to assess the communication skills of others whom they consider to be "effective" (e.g., Clark et al., 1985; Downs & Conrad, 1982). For example, such studies ask respondents to describe supervisor or subordinate communication behaviors which are "important" and facilitate effectiveness. Based on the results of such surveys, lists of important communication skills required in various occupations and/or organizational roles are offered. Frequently included in these lists are skills such as listening, giving feedback, advising, persuading, instructing, interviewing, motivating, being clear and concise, and so on. While results of studies usually suggest commonalities across occupations and organizational roles with respect to communication skill requirements, distinctions in skills across occupations/roles are also often noted.

The other tradition of "skills" research has been oriented at discovering in descriptive fashion the "actual" (assessed by observation, self-report communication logs, etc.) communication behaviors of persons in organizations. In almost all cases, such studies have focused on the communication skills displayed by management personnel (e.g., Burns, 1954; Kotter, 1982; Luthans & Larsen, 1986; Luthans, Rosenkrantz, & Hennessey, 1985; Mintzberg, 1973; Stewart, 1976; Whitely, 1984, 1985). In addition, researchers frequently attempt to identify persons who are considered to be "effective"/"ineffective" in their jobs (usually based on judgments of management) and then distinguish the "actual" communication behaviors displayed by persons in each of these groups. The more micro-oriented research in this area summates the characteristics of specific interaction episodes, thus, providing "profiles" of the communication activity in which (typically) managers engage; data often include descriptions of the duration of communications, context of interaction, number of interactants, contact person, source of initiation (self, other), medium of communication, and content/purpose of interactions. On the other hand, most of the observation and interview studies in this area provide in-depth profiles of the communication activity of a select group of (typically) managers. Results of these studies often show that the communication activity of managers is not as systematic, formal, reflective, organized, or "clear cut" (for example, with respect to topics that are discussed) as conventional wisdom often suggests.

Social Cognition/Symbolic Interaction Perspectives. Social cognition/symbolic interaction approaches to communication competence in organizations assume that individuals create and sustain organizational realities, and consequently, the contextual nature of communication must be considered in exploring competence. Research from this perspective has developed in several directions.

The work of Sypher and colleagues (Sypher, 1984; Sypher & Sypher, 1983; Sypher & Zorn, 1986) has focused on answering the following question: "What kinds of skills are important in helping organizational members understand self and other role expectations and thus perform successfully in organizational situations?" (Sypher, 1984, p. 105). In attempting to answer this question they have investigated individual differences among organizational members with respect to a variety of social cognitive abilities including cognitive differentiation, self-monitoring, perspective taking, and persuasive ability. Generally, research results suggest that persons with more developed social-cognitive abilities tend "to be found at higher levels in the organizational hierarchy and tend to be promoted more often than persons with less developed abilities" (Sypher & Zorn, 1986, p. 420).

The research of Harris and Cronen (1979) and Wellmon (1988), based on rules theory (e.g., Cushman & Whiting, 1972; Shimanoff, 1980), also fits within the general category of social-cognitive approaches to the study of communication competence in organizations. According to this perspective, individuals make sense of and negotiate meaning with others through rules ("guidelines for what is appropriate in a given situation" [Wellmon, 1988, p. 519]). In particular, communication competence within organizations is considered a byproduct of an individual's understanding of the organization's "master contract" (shared beliefs or culture that define the organization), as well as the constitutive rules (which allow members to assign meaning to communicative acts) and regulative rules (standards for "appropriate" action to bring about outcomes) which guide interaction. In brief, from the rules perspective communication competence is a consequence of the extent to which individuals possess varying levels of "strategic" (knowledge of what things mean in the organization) and "tactical" competence (knowledge of how to communicate given meaning structures).

Communication and Overall Managerial Competence. Finally, it is important to the note that for most of this century, in one form of another, academicians as well as practitioners have attempted to distinguish the characteristics of competent from incompetent managers. Frequently studies that seek to identify such characteristics conclude that communication abilities play an important part in a manager's overall competency. As Boyatzis (1982, p. 235) observes, in perhaps the most thorough and theoretically sound study of managerial competence to date, "certain activities, such as communicating . . . are essential tasks involved in the performance of each of the five basic functions of management" (planning, organizing, controlling, motivating, and coordinating). In addition, it would appear that communication abilities play important functions in at least four of the six macrocompetency clusters Boyatzis (1982) identified in his research: goal and action management, leadership, human resources management and directing subordinates.

While there are exceptions (e.g., Boyatzis, 1982), most research exploring managerial competence is atheoretical, considers communication ability from a "skills perspective" and does not develop other dimensions of communication competence (e.g., cognitive aspects). Not surprisingly, there is a heavy emphasis in this literature on exploring ways of assessing managerial competencies (e.g., Brush & Schoenfeldt, 1980; Byham, 1971; Moses & Byham, 1977), and on programs for developing competencies via management training (e.g., Kolb, Lublin, Spoth, & Baker, 1986; Lorenzo, 1984; Powers, 1987).

Assessment of the Literature

As has been noted by others (e.g., Monge et al., 1982; Sypher, 1984), research that has explored communication competence in organizations has borrowed heavily from investigations of interpersonal communication competence in nonorganizational contexts. However, as Monge et al. (1982) suggest, "in attempting to apply past work on interpersonal competence to organizational research a problem arises: many of the above (interpersonal) skills lose their importance" (p. 507). While this criticism is certainly appropriate, we believe there is a related problem even more basic than this one in extant conceptualizations and studies of communication competence in organizations: Research has focused on only the individual and/or dyadic-interpersonal levels of analysis whereas organizations contain higher level collectives that should also be considered with respect to communication competence. In other words, we need to recognize that workgroups and organizations as entities can be described in terms of their communication competence, and that while the communication competencies of higher and lower order entities are somewhat distinct they are also related to one another. Thus, consistent with open systems theory (Katz & Kahn, 1966), in studying the communication competence of individuals, groups and organizations as entities, we need to recognize that: (a) higher order collectivities are more than just the sum of their parts (i.e., group and organizational competence is *not* merely the summation of individual competencies), and (b) some form of interdependence or embeddedness exists among levels (dyadic/interpersonal, group and organization) of communication competence in organizations. As numerous critiques of organizational research have argued (e.g., Dansereau & Markham, 1987; Farace & MacDonald, 1974; Jablin & Krone, 1987; Rousseau, 1985), the only way in which we can learn much about any particular level of analysis in organizations "is if we know how they are tied together, that is, how one level interacts with another level" (Weick, 1969, p. 45).

Our research review also suggests another very basic limitation in current research exploring communication competence in organizations: A tendency to emphasize the skills or capabilities (an entity's repertoire of communication skills) dimension of competence and ignore the *knowledge* component of communication competence. In essence, the great bulk of research in the area has focused on developing inventories of communication skill capabilities that are important in organizational settings, and has ignored the process by which entities develop the capability to know when to use various communication behaviors, the likely ways in which such behaviors will be interpreted by others, beliefs about communication behavior-outcome expectancies, and the like.

As a result of the heavy emphasis that researchers have placed on delineating communication capabilities/skill repertoires, the great bulk of our understanding of competence is limited to what might be considered "threshold" communication competencies. Threshold organizational communication competencies are generic capabilities which are essential to performing jobs, but which are not sufficient to cause superior levels of effectiveness in communication (we are indebted to Boyatzis [1982] for the notion of threshold competency; however, we have altered his conceptualization to adapt to the focus of this chapter). For example, the repertoire of language skills and even persuasive tactics that a salesperson might possess could be considered threshold competencies since: (a) articulateness and possession of tactical capabilities does not necessarily imply that one can use them strategically so as to achieve goals, and (b) possessing tactical capabilities does not imply that one will actually perform/enact these skills (assuming there is a successful strategy) in an effective manner. Knowing what to do and how to do it, and actually doing it, are quite distinct.

Relatively speaking, almost all organizational members possess minimally satisfactory threshold communication competence upon or shortly after organizational entry (or after passage into new roles within the organization). In other words, occupational education/socialization, organizational selection processes and initial socialization and training experiences screen out persons who do not meet minimal threshold competency levels (i.e., minimum capacities to encode and decode messages) related to their organizational roles. Threshold encoding capacity includes the capacity to send messages in a situationally appropriate fashion via various media and codes; however, message sending capacity does not require that an individual (or higher order entity) be capable of sending messages via all organizational channels and codes, just those required by job demands and other relevant organizational constraints. Threshold decoding capacity includes the ability to receive messages via relevant channels and codes and assign basic (a surface vs. deep structure) meaning to them, relative to the particular situation. Consequently, one factor that distinguishes threshold from "proficient" decoding ability is the capacity to assign multiple meanings to messages. Moreover, since almost all entities in organizational systems possess minimal threshold competence, it is likely that judgments about competence are based on the presence or absence of capacities above or below the threshold level of competence. To summarize, if all the entities in a given organizational system possess threshold capabilities, then assessments about competence will be based on the degree to which capabilities exceed or fall short of expectations at the threshold level.

In addition to the above limitations, extant research exploring communication competence seems plagued by several other problems. While we do not necessarily have *the* answers to all these dilemmas, it is quite clear that these concerns need to be considered in research exploring communication competence in organizations. Among the problems/dilemmas which require consideration are: (a) clarification of the roles of values and ethics in conceptualizing competence, (b) questionable assumptions about rationality associated with most conceptualizations of competence, (c) the tendency to view levels of competence in static versus dynamic terms, and (d) variations in definitions of key constructs (competence, performance, effectiveness). Each of these issues is briefly discussed below.

Values and Ethics. Generally speaking, when researchers study communication competence in organizations they do not place sufficient emphasis on the role of values and value structures in their conceptualizations of competence. Values (and how they may vary at different levels of analysis) are important to consider since value structures embedded within the organization are a primary determinant of what we have conceptualized as above threshold levels of communication competency. Thus, while one might learn about threshold-level competencies via "job descriptions and performance evaluations" (Monge et al., 1982, p. 506), the deep-structure values of the organization inform members of the capabilities they need to possess, beyond the threshold level, in order to be optimal communicators in the organization. Since it is quite evident that values often differ across organizations (as well as among levels within the same organization), what is considered competent communication (beyond the threshold level) in one organization (or at a lower order level of analysis within an organization) may not necessarily be the same as in another organization (or a different level of analysis). Thus, while there may be commonalities in definitions of competence across organizations and levels of analysis (characteristics associated with threshold competence), there will also be variations as a consequence of distinctions in organizational cultures and value systems (what Harris & Cronen [1979] term "master contracts").

Our reading of the literature also suggests that researchers frequently assume that assessments of the competence of individuals, groups and organizations are made against some fairly static, absolute set of optimal standards/values. As Pavitt and Haight (1985) observe, a basic assumption underlying many theories of competence is that competence is based on a conception of an "ideal communicator." For example, Habermas (1970) describes competence in terms of a mastery of linguistic rules and the production of a communication interaction which constitutes an "ideal" speech situation. He considers an ideal-speech situation to be one in which: (a) interactants communicate so that the truth claim of an utterance is shared by both the speaker and hearer, (b) the hearer is led to understand the speaker's intention, and (c) each speaker adapts to the hearer's world view. While the notion that competence is judged against standards/values is reasonable, the issue of whether or not ideal standards are utilized to assess competence is more problematic. Such a perspective does not recognize the dynamic nature of organizations and the possibility that ideals/standards of evaluation change over time as a byproduct of communication; hence, while standards/ideals for judging competence are being reproduced through interaction, they may also be newly produced (Ranson, Hinings, & Greenwood, 1980).

Finally, as the above quotation from Habermas (1970) suggests, conceptualizations of communication competence in organizations should also consider relationships between competence-related standards and ethical standards of communication. Habermas's conceptualization assumes some sort of objective truth as the end state of any competent communication interaction while Harris and Cronen (1979), Parks (1985), and others suggest that maximizing objectives epitomizes the goal of interaction. As these contrasting approaches suggest, conceptualizations of communication competence pivot around the age old question: Do the ends justify the means? Like it or not, as scholars we are obligated to consider the issue of whether or not a competent communicator is an ethical communicator. Consideration of this issue seems especially crucial given the apparent importance of impression management and political skills to success within organizations (e.g., Giacalone & Rosenfeld, 1991; Hayes, 1984; Leary & Kowalski, 1990; Wexley, 1986). As Wexley (1986) observes, "A predominant preoccupation of those of us who seek not only to be but to be viewed as competent is in learning the delicately strategic art of impression management (p. 247). If this is the case, then we must address the question: Is possessing the capability of controlling the manner in which information to others is received about oneself (or workgroup or organization), whether or not the information to be communicated is accurate ("the truth"), a hallmark of communication competency?

Relatedly, we need to examine more carefully how other work/task competencies may effect perceptions of communication competency. Since communication competence is just one dimension of an individual's (or group's or organization's) overall competency in performing a task, a "halo effect" may occur such that being highly competent in noncommunication task areas may foster inaccurate beliefs about competence in communication as well.

Assumptions of Rationality. In general, most conceptualizations of communication competence in organizations assume that communicators think and act in very rational ways (i.e., communicators will carefully analyze situations, consider relevant contextual rules and interaction norms, and then select from their behavior repertoires communication acts that will maximize their goals). Unfortunately, while this may be true in some situations it is quite apparent that it does not apply in other contexts. As Pearson and Daniels (1988) note, "In many day-to-day episodes of communication, people may well 'know' what kinds of behaviors will be both appropriate and effective, yet act in ways that deviate considerably from the behavior that their knowledge would seem to prescribe" (p. 99). In essence, in our conceptualizations of competence we need to recognize that people don't always use their communication capabilities in logical ways and that relationship history factors, motives, emotions, etc. can affect competence levels.

In addition, our conceptualizations of competence should consider the extent to which communication behavior in organizations is *mindless* versus *mindful* in origin (e.g., Langer, 1978). Since a growing body of research suggests that knowledge of behavior in organizations is cognitively structured in the form of "scripts" (e.g., Gioia, 1986), which are brought forth unconsciously and automatically by situational cues, the assumption that people are actively using knowledge to adapt communication behavior comes into question. Moreover, as Gioia (1986) observes, the use of scripts as guides to behavior may be efficient, but not necessarily lead to effective outcomes. In other words, because situational characteristics in new situations are similar (but not exactly the same) to those which we have experienced before, we may not mindfully/consciously analyze the new context, and as a consequence activate a script which is not appropriate in the new situation. Thus, while the possession of a cognitive repertoire of organizational communication scripts may facilitate competence, it may also limit competence.

It also seems reasonable to speculate that another factor distinguishing a communicator at the threshold level of competence from one whom is above that level, is that the more proficient communicator not only possesses a repertoire of scripted communication knowledge, but is also capable of knowing when to shift from mindless (scripted-guided) to mindful behavior (active consideration of multiple interpretations/meanings of the situation). Hence, it is likely that individuals whose communication is frequently mindless in origin, despite the fact that unique features of interaction situations are apparent, have fallen into what March (1988) terms the "competency trap" (a condition where previous learning undermines the generation of new learning).

Dynamic Nature of Competence. Even a cursory reading of the literature indicates that researchers frequently consider communication competence in very static versus dynamic terms (i.e., they do not adequately consider that communicators are constantly developing new competencies and reformulating existing competencies). In other words, the dynamic process of learning about competence requires more attention, and, in particular, how one's strategic knowledge of appropriate communication develops over time. Further, it also seems apparent that in our studies of competence we need to be more careful about: (a) falling into the trap of viewing competence in discrete versus continuous terms (i.e., classifying communicators as *either* competence *or* incompetent), and (b) recognizing that in any particular interaction situation communication competence can be displayed in many different ways (principle of equifinality). In fact, a sign of above threshold communication competency may be knowledge of not just one best communication strategy for any particular interaction context, but knowledge of and the capacity to enact several alternative strategies that might be equally appropriate for the situation. As Anderson (1984) observes, citing the notion of equifinality, "the more of each (competence) component and the more components one masters, the more competent one becomes (p. 358).

Distinguishing Among Concepts. As quite apparent in our review of the organizational communication competence literature, there is little consensus among scholars in their constitutive and operational definitions of competence and other key terms (e.g., skills, performance, and effectiveness). In particular, researchers frequently equate competence with effectiveness or competence with performance/enactment of appropriate communication behaviors. Although we can take solace that this problem exists among researchers exploring communication competence in other settings (e.g., McCroskey, 1982, 1984; Van Hoeven,

1985), if we are to ever advance our understanding of communication competence in organizations some consensually agreed upon definitions need to be established.

Based on our analysis of definitions existing in the literature, we cautiously enter the fray by offering a set of definitions which distinguish among the constructs of communication competence, performance, and effectiveness. We believe these definitions may help reduce some of the confusion associated with these concepts and represent conceptualizations that are applicable across multiple levels of analysis (as we show in later sections of this chapter).

Communication Competence. This may be defined as the set of abilities, henceforth termed *resources*, which a communicator has available for use in the communication process. These resources are acquired via a dynamic learning process and take the form of interrelated subsets of communication skills (henceforth termed capacities), and strategic knowledge of appropriate communication behavior. The reader will note that we have not included effectiveness (the accomplishment of individual or shared goals) as part of our conceptualization, since we concur with McCroskey (1982) when he argues that effectiveness "is neither a necessary nor sufficient condition for a judgment of competence. One may be effective without being competent and one may be competent without being effective" (p. 3). Thus, it is important to recognize that actual competence and attributions of communication competence are not necessarily the same. Attributions of competence are inferences that are made about an entity's (individual's, group's, or organization's) actual competence based on observation(s) of discrete episodes of communication behavior (performances) which may or may not lead to goal accomplishment. Hence, we conceptualize communication performance as the display of communication behaviors, upon which attributions of competence are based, but which may or may not be related to actual levels of competence. Moreover, as suggested earlier, it appears likely that attributions of competence are closely related to the extent to which a communicator's behavior is above or below consensually defined levels of threshold communication competence (generic communication capacities and knowledge required for work-related tasks).

A general model of the communication process, which is applicable at multiple levels of analysis, and pictorially depicts many of the distinctions drawn among the concepts discussed above, is presented in Figure 6.1. The model is focused at examining attributes of communication within specific interaction episodes. The first components of the model are the parties in the interaction. "Party" is used to designate the unit of analysis in the interaction. Since the model applies to various levels of analysis, party is used to designate the individual, group, or organization participating in the interaction. Each party is assumed to possess some form of threshold-level communication competence (i.e., a threshold level of communication resources). Generally speaking, the greater the amount of resources (capacities and strategic knowledge), the greater will be the party's competence. However, it is essential to recognize that while a party may possess many capacities and considerable knowledge of communication, linkages between knowledge and capacities may not be sufficient or consistent enough to establish an above-threshold level of competence. Parties may not link capacities and knowledge together for a variety of reasons, including ignorance of their own resources and/ or lack of motivation to develop such linkages (Hayes, 1984). Hence, for a party to obtain an above-threshold level of competence, the entity must not only possess abundant amounts of capacities and strategic knowledge, but also the ability to integrate these resources together in various ways.

The model also depicts the process by which each party selects a communication act/acts from its resources to enact within an interaction episode. As indicated in Figure 6.1, this process may be active, conscious, and goal-directed, or lack conscious thought and occur in a mindless manner. Whether or not the selection process is mindful or mindless (or a combination of the two) will be highly dependent on "moderators" present in the interaction setting, and the extent to which these moderators "cue" the party to any unique characteristics in the communication context. Moderators can be categorized into two basic types: (a) situational variables (e.g., job demands, task uncertainty, work environment), and (b) cumulative variables (e.g., relational history, communication norms, group/organizational culture and values). The situational and cumulative factors are interdependent; each influences the other during an interaction.

Figure 6.1 also shows that subsequent to the selection of communication behaviors, some form of behavioral enactment, or performance will occur. These performances allow each party to make attributions about the other party's communication competence, the relative effectiveness (perceived goal accomplishment) of the interaction episode, the extent to which meaning is being shared and uncertainty reduced, etc. Additionally, attributions about one's own communicative performance, as well as that of the other party, serve as forms of feedback that allow learning to occur; they provide each party with information that can be used to reformulate knowledge about the application and use of communication behavior with the other party, and how to communicate in similar interaction settings.

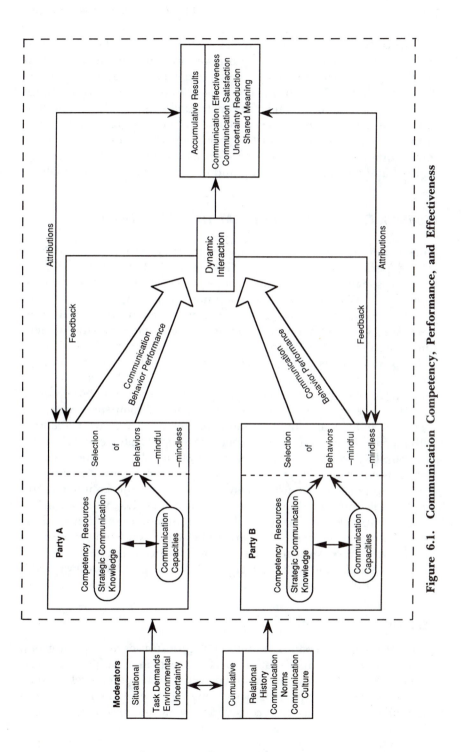

Figure 6.1. Communication Competency, Performance, and Effectiveness

Summary. In the preceding pages we have attempted to review and critique extant research exploring communication competence in organizations. In particular, we have argued that extant research has primarily focused on the individual/dyadic level of communication competence in organizations, and has failed to conceptualize and explore communicative competence at higher levels of analysis (i.e., the group and organizational levels). In order to clarify our position, the next section provides some examples of how communication competence might be conceptualized and studied at the group and organizational levels of analysis.

COMMUNICATION COMPETENCE AT THE GROUP LEVEL

Since communication has been shown to affect group processes and related performance levels (e.g., Gladstein, 1984; Leathers, 1972), it seems reasonable to suggest that groups possess levels of communication competence. While the notion of communication competency in groups is not new, the idea that groups as entities can be conceived of as possessing a group-level competence is somewhat novel. To this point in time, when group-level competence has been conceptualized it's been typically defined as an aggregate of individual-level communication competence (e.g., Anderson, 1984). However, consistent with open systems approaches, communication competence at the group level is more than the mere aggregation of individual members' competencies. Group members' individual communication competence levels are embedded within group communication competence, much like the embeddedness of group-level competence within organizational-level competence.

Consistent with our earlier definition of competence, group-level communication competence is comprised of strategic knowledge and tactical skill (capacities) components. Unfortunately, extant organizational group research has focused limited attention on either of these dimensions of competence. Rather, studies have examined communication-related processes associated with group levels of effectiveness or members' satisfaction with their groups (e.g., Barge & Hirokawa, 1989; Gladstein, 1984).

Strategic Knowledge

Much of the group communication literature focuses on explicit group interaction (i.e., communication performance in groups). However, group-level communication competence, like that at other levels of analysis, cannot be fully explained by focusing on the enactment of communication skills. We must also consider the strategic knowledge component of competence. Knowledge of a group's communication rules may be represented in group rituals and culture (e.g., Schall, 1983). Schein (1985, p. 149) suggests that all definitions of culture imply "shared solutions, shared understandings, and consensus." The culture, or shared-knowledge structures of a group, are outcomes of group learning (Schein, 1985, p. 183) and may serve as standards by which communication competence within the group is evaluated.

Communication competence at the group level can also be conceptualized in terms of communication synergy and group mentality (Bion, 1959). Communication synergy can be conceived of as the group's communication energy that is available for communication activities (Cattell, 1948). Group mentality represents the basic assumptions that are shared among members of the group. Citing the work of Bion (1959), Schein (1985) outlines the process by which basic assumptions become established in groups. He suggests that assumptions first develop as a consequence of the common language used by group members and their sharing of similar experiences. As communication produces more shared assumptions and multiple layers of meaning, a group may then develop more interaction flexibility and adaptiveness, which would seem to enhance its communicative competence. At the same time, however, it is important to recognize that a "strong" group culture may develop which can become problematic for the group, in that it may lead to a competency trap often experienced in the form of "groupthink" (Janis, 1972).

Research exploring the characteristics of "zero history" and "history" groups (e.g., Sorensen & McCroskey, 1977) also supports the notion that groups with histories possess more complex cultures, or knowledge and value structures, which may facilitate communication competence (e.g., Cragan & Wright, 1990; Putnam & Stohl, 1990). Groups with complex sets of shared language and knowledge structures possess the ability for more flexible communication behaviors. In other words, as group situations develop, competent groups can use their sets of shared assumptions to evaluate situations, and have more flexibility to display the necessary synergy in response to the situations they encounter.

Another way in which one might explore the knowledge dimension of competence in groups is with respect to the fantasy themes that "spin out" in groups (Bormann, Pratt, & Putnam, 1978). Through the analysis of fantasy themes, cultural assumptions of groups can be revealed. Moreover, fantasy themes may not only reflect shared social realities (consensually shared knowledge) within groups, but may also affect communication processes within groups (e.g., Bormann et al., 1978).

In summary, any conceptualization of group-level communication competence must include a component concerned with the group's knowledge of appropriate communication behavior. Existing literature related to group communication knowledge centers around group cultures. Group synergy, mentality, and fantasy themes are all related to the development of group culture. Cultures guide the strategic communication activities performed by groups, and hence, may potentially reflect the knowledge dimension of group-level communication competence.

Communication Capacities

The communication capacities of a group include the ability to gather, transmit, and accurately interpret information. One way of conceptualizing these capacities is in terms of information processing theory. For example, Tushman and Nadler (1979) suggest that if groups are to be successful they must be capable of matching their information processing capacities with the information processing requirements of their tasks. Along these lines, Tushman (1978) provides evidence indicating that high-performing project groups are "able to match their communication networks to meet the information processing demands of their work" (p. 642). Similarly, it seems apparent that groups that possess internal feedback structures and procedures may be more competent than those that do not contain such mechanisms, since feedback can cue group members to necessary changes in performance strategies (e.g., Nadler, 1979). In brief, many of the sorts of variables that frequently are explored in studies of group process (e.g., Jablin & Sussman, 1983) can be reconceptualized in terms of the functions they serve in providing groups with the capability of responding to the information requirements of their information environments.

In addition, capacities such as those described earlier can be considered with respect to inter- as well as intragroup communication competence. For example, groups require forms of intergroup communication networks and coordination modes in order to integrate their activities with those of other groups within the organization with which they are interdependent (e.g., Hage, 1974; Hage, Aiken, & Marrett, 1971; Van de Ven, Delbecq, & Koenig, 1976). Such capacities not only serve instrumental functions with respect to group tasks, but also provide groups with opportunities to develop coalitions with other groups which may enhance capabilities of obtaining resources through quid pro quo arrangements (e.g., McCann & Galbraith, 1981).

Finally, it is important to note that the types of communication capacities required of a workgroup are likely to change as the group develops over time. Research has demonstrated that group process requirements with respect to task and social issues vary according to phases of task-oriented interaction (e.g., Gladstein, 1984; Tuckman & Jensen, 1977). Accordingly, Anderson (1984) suggests that an essential dimension of group competency is knowledge of the types of communication behaviors which are appropriate for given phases of group development. Thus, part of a group's communication competence may involve the selection and enactment of communication skills which are congruent (appropriate) with the group's phase of development.

COMMUNICATION COMPETENCE AT THE ORGANIZATIONAL LEVEL

While some research has been directed at exploring the effectiveness of communication systems at the organizational level of analysis (e.g., Farace, Taylor, & Stewart, 1978), we know of no studies that have directly explored the notion of communication competence at the organizational level of analysis. In part, lack of attention to organizational-level competence is due to problems associated with the defining this level of analysis. In particular, while we can define "actual" communication competence in terms of the resources of the organization (e.g., management information systems, available communication media, organizational histories), organizational members who are responsible for representing the organization to its external and internal audiences are frequently perceived of as *the* organization by these groups. Thus, for example, organizational members may perceive the house organ as communication from the organization as an entity, since most of the messages in such periodicals are devoid of information concerning the authorship of articles. The author is *the* organization. Similarly, in conducting external communication activities, such as press conferences, stockholders meetings, and the like, the representatives of the organization are typically identified as *the* organization by their audiences (e.g., Eisenberg et al., 1985). Thus, when we conceptualize and explore organizational-level communication competence we must recognize that attributions of competence may occur in any context in which communicators are perceived of by an audience as representing the organization.

In light of the above issues, threshold communication competence at the organizational level can be conceptualized as the possession of strategic communication knowledge and the tactical communication abilities (capacities) that are necessary for basic survival in the environment(s) in which an organization is embedded. While threshold levels of knowledge and communicative skills are required for an organization to merely survive, resources which allow flexibility in both communication knowledge and skill provide an organization with capabilities above the threshold level. Possession of such competencies often provides the organization with competitive advantages.

Strategic Knowledge

As Johnston and Carrico (1988) argue, "knowledge bases" are critical to organizational competitiveness. Knowledge bases or organizational memories (e.g., Hedberg, 1981; Walsh & Ungson, 1991) are both the collective knowledge of groups and individuals within an organization and the strategies which guide the interpretation of situational and environmental cues. Thus, while individuals come and go "organizations preserve knowledge, behaviors, mental maps, norms and values over time," and it is these cognitive systems and memories which enable members of organizations to "interpret as a system" (Daft & Weick, 1984, p. 285).

Organizations must have basic threshold levels of knowledge to survive in their environments, but flexible and changing knowledge bases are necessary to move beyond the threshold level. In other words, an organization's ability to learn about its internal and external environments is a key determinant of its likelihood of achieving above-threshold-level competence. Generally speaking, organization learning is a by-product of environmental scanning and information gathering, the ability of organizational members to translate information into shared forms of meaning, and the capacity of the organization to interpret feedback associated with its actions (Argyris & Schon, 1978; Daft & Weick, 1984). As a consequence of their learning posture, organizations which possess strategic knowledge above the threshold level have the capability to assign multiple meanings to information gathered from the environment. Hence, the more complex an organization's strategic knowledge, the more value is attached or added to internal and external information as it relates to strategies to achieve competitive advantage.

To some extent, the number and variety of "semantic networks" (configurations of organizational members who share similar interpretations of organizational symbols, environments, actions, goals, and the like, e.g., Monge & Eisenberg, 1987) that exist in an organization may be indicative of the organization's strategic communication competence. However, an organization with above-threshold-level competence must not only possess many and varied semantic networks, but also the ability to integrate meanings across disparate networks. In essence, in order for an organization to make use of its semantic knowledge bases/networks it must have the capacity to relabel/translate meaning across networks so that all organizational subsystems understand (though not necessarily agree with) alternative interpretations of organizational symbols, environments, and the like (which is also a necessity for organizational learning to occur, e.g., Huber, 1991).

Communication Capacities

As stated earlier, tactical competencies are the communication capacities of the organization. At the organizational level, communication capacities (encoding and decoding skills) refer to the communication structures and programs which allow for the production, reception, and basic interpretation of messages exchanged with external and internal audiences. Capacities to exchange messages with external audiences include (a) interorganizational communication networks, (b) public, governmental, and community relations functions, (c) advertising campaigns, (d) sales and marketing functions, and (4) company recruiting efforts, and so forth. On the other hand, capacities to exchange messages with internal audiences are exemplified by an organization's employee relations programs (including corporate communication, e.g., house organs) and human resource functions. Thus, an organization's repertoire of skills (capacities) include the mechanisms which allow it to process and exchange information with its environments and its capacities to promote among organizational members understanding of alternative interpretations of available information.

If an organization's communication capacity is adequate (at the threshold level), it will possess the necessary mechanisms to process and interpret information without causing the system to overload. On the other hand, in an organization with above-threshold competence the communication/information processing system will not only meet current needs, but will be capable of meeting future needs, that is, the system will be capable of anticipating future requirements (e.g., Huber, 1991). For example, if an organization's communication capacity is at the threshold level, it will be capable of storing information in the "interpretive" classification and form in which it was originally acquired and subsequently processed. In contrast, an organization with above-threshold capabilities will not only store information in its current interpretive scheme/form but also anticipate future interpretive schemes/forms in which the information may be required. Hence, the information will be stored in a manner that allows it to be easily retrieved using conceptualizations (interpretive schemes) other than those with which it was originally classified and stored. In sum, organizations with competence above the threshold level will possess encoding and decoding capacities that are long-term versus short-term in focus, thus, allowing for information to be processed, stored, retrieved, and so on, via multiple interpretive schemes (consistent with the principle of equifinality).

Potential Research Directions

Several lines of recent research suggest possible ways of studying communication competence at the organizational level of analysis. For example, research by Daft and his colleagues (e.g., Daft & Lengel, 1984, 1986; Trevino, Lengel, & Daft, 1987), exploring information richness in organizations, might be adapted to examine communication competence in organizations. Trevino et al. suggest that communication media have varying capacities for reducing ambiguity, transmitting data, and meeting interpretation needs. In particular, they argue that communication media (face-to-face, memos, electronic mail, etc.) can be characterized as "lean" or "rich" based on their capacity to provide instant feedback, multiple cues, and natural language. Moreover, while they posit that choice of media for exchanging messages should vary depending upon such factors as environmental uncertainty, organizational technology, and organizational structural characteristics, Trevino et al. (1987) also note that "corporate culture may define which medium is appropriate for many communications. Organizational values may indicate which matters are put into writing and which matters are handled face-to-face" (p. 570). In other words, the value structures of organizations may represent a form of strategic knowledge about appropriate ways of communicating to internal and external audiences, while the communication media that an organization has available for use are elements of the organization's communication capacity.

Seemingly, the more media available, the greater an organization's ability to adapt to communication situations in a manner congruent with information richness requirements. However, as suggested above, an organization's communication competence with respect to media use may also be closely related to an understanding of the symbolic cues that target audiences associate with particular media (e.g., formality, sensitivity, openness, rationality). Along these lines, an interesting case study of communication competence might be an examination of Exxon's efforts in communicating to the American public about the 1989 Alaska oil spill. (This might also be examined in terms of the impression/issue management capabilities of the company with respect to key audiences/ stakeholders such as shareholders, e.g., Bettman & Weitz, 1983; Crable & Vibbert, 1983; Salancik & Meindl, 1984.)

Another avenue for research exploring organizational-level communication competence might be in terms of the types of interorganizational linkages/networks that organizations maintain directly and indirectly (through third parties such as public relations firms, e.g., Danowski, Barnett, & Friedland, 1987) with one another. The number, variety, quality, and so on, of institutional, representative, and personal linkages (Eisenberg et al., 1985) an organization (and its members) maintains with other organizations might be conceptualized as organizational communication resources. As Ewusi-Mensah (1981) suggests, organizational adaptiveness and flexibility cannot occur without access to adequate knowledge of underlying environmental conditions. At the same time, however, it is important to realize that an organization must not only be competent in acquiring information via interorganizational networks, but also possess the capability to disseminate the information among organizational units and interpret the frequently equivocal forms of information they have gathered.

Relatedly, research might also be directed at exploring how organizations use information technologies and computerized information systems to enhance their information gathering, processing and interpreting capabilities (e.g., Huber, 1990). In particular, it would be useful to study how organizations use information technologies to build strategic knowledge bases (for instance, through the development of expert systems, e.g., Leonard-Barton & Sviokla, 1988), and how interorganizational information systems augment the strategic and tactical communication competence of organizations (e.g., Johnston & Vitale, 1988).

SUMMARY AND CONCLUSION

In this chapter we have argued for a broader view of communication competence in organizations than is currently in vogue in the literature. More specifically, we have suggested that rather than focus only on the individual/dyadic (interpersonal) level of analysis, conceptualizations of communication competence in organizations must also consider competence at higher levels of analysis—the group and organizational levels. At the same time, however, we have also stressed that communication competence at the group and organizational levels are not simply aggregations of individual competencies, but are forms of competence that constitute more than the sum of their parts. In order to facilitate research exploring communication competence at multiple levels of analysis, a general model of communication competence applicable at the individual/dyadic group, and organizational levels of analysis was proposed. Finally, in the latter sections of the chapter we suggested specific ways of conceptualizing and operationalizing communication competence at the group and organizational levels of analysis. While in these sections we tried to present a wide variety of examples, the approaches offered represent just a handful of the many ways in which workgroup and organizational communication competence might be investigated. In conclusion, we hope that our review of extant research exploring communication competence in organizations, coupled with our critique of that literature, proposed model of communication competence, and ideas for conceptualizing and operationalizing competence at the group and organizational levels of analysis, will stimulate and provide direction for additional research exploring these issues.

REFERENCES

Anderson, J. (1984). Communication competency in the small group. In R. S. Cathcart & L. A. Samovar (Eds.), *Small group communication: A reader* (4th ed., pp. 357–365). Dubuque, IA: Wm. C. Brown.

Argyris, C., & Schon, D. A. (1978). *Organizational learning: A theory of action perspective.* Reading, MA: Addison-Wesley.

Arrington, C. B., & Sawaya, R. N. (1984). Managing public affairs: Issues management in an uncertain environment. *California Management Review, 26,* 148–160.

Barge, J. K., & Hirokawa, R. Y. (1989). Toward a communication competency model of group leadership. *Small Group Behavior, 20,* 167–189.

Bennett, J. C., & Olney, R. J. (1986). Executive priorities for effective communication in an information society. *Journal of Business Communication, 23*(2), 13–22.

Berryman-Fink, C. (1985). Male and female managers' views of the communication skills and training needs of women in management. *Public Personnel Management, 14,* 307–313.

Bettman, J. R., & Weitz, B. A. (1983). Attributions in the board room—causal reasoning in corporate annual reports. *Administrative Science Quarterly, 28,* 165–183.

Bion, W. R. (1959). *Experiences in groups.* London: Tavistock.

Bormann, E. G., Pratt, J., & Putnam, L. (1978). Power, authority, and sex: Male response to female leadership. *Communication Monographs, 45,* 119–155.

Boyatzis, R. E. (1982). *The competent manager: A model for effective performance.* New York: Wiley.

Brush, D., & Schoenfeldt, L. (1980). Identifying managerial potential: An alternative to assessment centers. *Personnel, 57,* 68–76.

Burns, T. (1954). The direction of activity and communications in a department executive group. *Human Relations, 7,* 73–97.

Byham, W. C. (1971). The assessment center as an aid in management development. *Training and Development Journal, 25*(12), 10–22.

Cattell, R. (1948). Concepts and methods in the measurement of group syntality. *Psychological Review, 55,* 48–63.

Clark, H. B., Wood, R., Kuehnel, T., Flanagan, S., Mosk, M., & Northrup, J. (1985). Preliminary validation and training of supervisory interactional skills. *Journal of Organizational Behavior Management, 7,* 95–115.

Crable, R. E., & Vibbert, S. L. (1983). Managing issues and influencing public policy. *PR Review, 11,* 3–16.

Cragan, J. F., & Wright, D. W. (1990). Small group communication research of the 1980s: A synthesis and critique. *Communication Studies, 41,* 212–236.

Cushman, D., & Whiting, G. C. (1972). An approach to communication theory: Toward a consensus on rules. *Journal of Communication, 22,* 217–238.

Daft, R. L., & Lengel, R. H. (1984). Information richness: A new approach to managerial behavior and organizational design. In B. Staw & L. L. Cummings (Eds.), *Research in organizational behavior* (Vol. 6, pp. 191–233). Greenwich, CT: JAI Press.

Daft, R. L., & Lengel, R. H. (1986). Organizational information requirements, media richness and structural design. *Management Science, 32,* 554–571.

Daft, R. L., & Weick, K. E. (1984). Toward a model of organizations as interpretation systems. *Academy of Management Review, 9,* 284–295.

Danowski, J. A., Barnett, G. A., & Friedland, M. H. (1987). Interorganizational networks via shared public relations firms' centrality, diversification, media coverage and public images. In M. L. McLaughlin (Ed.), *Communication yearbook 10* (pp. 808–830). Newbury Park, CA: Sage.

Dansereau, R., & Markham, S. E. (1987). Superior-subordinate communication: Multiple levels of analysis. In F. Jablin, L. Putnam, K. Roberts, & L. Porter (Eds.), *Handbook of organizational communication: An interdisciplinary perspective* (pp. 343–388). Newbury Park, CA: Sage.

DiSalvo, V. S. (1980). A summary of current research identifying communication skills in various organizational contexts. *Communication Education, 29,* 283–290.

DiSalvo, V. S., Larsen, D., & Seiler, W. (1976). Communication skills needed by persons in business organizations. *Communication Education, 25,* 269–275.

DiSalvo, V. S., & Larsen, J. K. (1987). A contingency approach to communication skill importance: The impact of occupation, direction, and position. *Journal of Business Communication, 24,* 3–22.

Downs, C., & Conrad, C. (1982). Effective subordinancy. *Journal of Business Communication, 19,* 27–37.

Eisenberg, E., Farace, R., Monge, P., Bettinghaus, E., Kurchner-Hawkins, R., Miller, K., & Rothman, L. (1985). Communication linkages in interorganizational systems: Review and synthesis. In B. Dervin & M. Voigt (Eds.), *Progress in communication sciences* (Vol. 6, pp. 231–262). Norwood, NJ: Ablex.

Ewusi-Mensah, K. (1981). The external organizational environment and its impact on management information systems. *Accounting, Organizations, and Society, 6,* 301–316.

Farace, R. V., & MacDonald, D. (1974). New directions in the study of organizational communication. *Personnel Psychology, 27,* 1–15.

Farace, R. V., Taylor, J. A., & Stewart, J. P. (1978). Criteria for evaluation of organizational communication effectiveness: Review and synthesis. In B. Ruben (Ed.), *Communication yearbook 2* (pp. 271–291). New Brunswick, NJ: Transaction Press.

Giacalone, R. A., & Rosenfeld, P. (Eds.). (1991). *Impression management in the organization.* Hillsdale, NJ: Erlbaum.

Gioia, D. A. (1986). Symbols, scripts, and sensemaking: Creating meaning in the organizational experience. In H. Sims, D. Gioia, & Assoc. (Eds.), *The thinking organization: Dynamics of organizational social cognition* (pp. 49–74). San Francisco: Jossey-Bass.

Gladstein, D. L. (1984). Groups in context: A model of task group effectiveness. *Administrative Science Quarterly, 29,* 499–517.

Habermas, J. (1970). Toward a theory of communicative competence. In H. P. Dreitzel (Ed.), *Recent Sociology, 2,* 115–148.

Hage, J. (1974). *Communication and organizational control.* New York: Wiley.

Hage, J., Aiken, M., & Marrett, C. (1971). Organization structure and communication. *American Sociological Review, 36,* 860–871.

Hanna, M. S. (1978). Speech communication training needs in the business community. *Central States Speech Journal, 29,* 163–172.

Harris, L., & Cronen, V. E. (1979). A rules-based model for the analysis and evaluation of organizational communication. *Communication Quarterly, 27,* 12–28.

Hayes, J. (1984). The politically competent manager. *Journal of General Management, 10,* 24–33.

Hedberg, B. (1981). How organizations learn and unlearn. In P. Nystrom & W. Starbuck (Eds.), *Handbook of organizational design* (Vol. 1, pp. 3–27). New York: Oxford University Press.

Huber, G. P. (1990). A theory of the effects of advanced information technologies on organizational design, intelligence and decision making. *Academy of Management Review, 15,* 47–71.

Huber, G. P. (1991). Organizational learning: The contributing processes and the literatures. *Organization Science, 2,* 88–115.

Jablin, F. M., & Krone, K. J. (1987). Organizational assimilation. In C. R. Berger & S. M. Chaffee (Eds.), *Handbook of communication science* (pp. 711–746). Newbury Park, CA: Sage.

Jablin, F. M., & Sussman, L. (1983). Organizational group communication: A review of the literature and model of the process. In H. H. Greenbaum, R. L. Falcione, & S. A. Hellweg (Eds.), *Organizational communication: Abstracts, analysis and overview* (Vol. 8, pp. 11–50). Newbury Park, CA: Sage.

Janis, I. L. (1972). *Victims of group think*. Boston: Houghton-Mifflin.

Johnston, H. R., & Carrico, S. R. (1988). Developing capabilities to use information strategically. *MIS Quarterly, 12*, 37–48.

Johnston, H. R., & Vitale, M. R. (1988). Creating competitive advantage with interorganizational information systems. *MIS Quarterly, 12*, 153–165.

Katz, D., & Kahn, R. (1966). *The social psychology of organizations*. New York: Wiley.

Kolb, D., Lublin, S., Spoth, J., & Baker, R. (1986). Strategic management development: Using experiential learning theory to assess and develop managerial competencies. *Journal of Management Development, 5*, 13–24.

Kotter, J. P. (1982). *The general managers*. New York: Free Press.

Langer, E. (1978). Rethinking the role of thought in social interaction. In J. H. Harvey, W. J. Ickes, & R. F. Kidd (Eds.), *New direction in attribution research* (Vol. 2, pp. 35–58). Hillsdale, NJ: Erlbaum.

Larson, C., Backlund, P., Redmond, M., & Barbour, A. (1978). *Assessing functional communication*. Falls Church, VA: ERIC/SCA.

Leary, M. R., & Kowalski, R. M. (1990). Impression management: A literature review and two-component model. *Psychological Bulletin, 107*, 34–47.

Leathers, D. G. (1972). Quality of group communication as a determinant of group product. *Speech Monographs, 39*, 166–173.

Leonard-Barton, D., & Sviokla, J. J. (1988). Putting experts systems to work. *Harvard Business Review, 64*, 91–98.

Lorenzo, R. (1984). Effects of assessorship on managers' proficiency in acquiring, evaluating, and communicating information about people. *Personnel Psychology, 37*, 617–634.

Luthans, F., & Larsen, J. K. (1986). How managers really communicate: An empirical investigation of the relationship between communication behavior and managerial activities. *Human Relations, 39*, 161–178.

Luthans, F., Rosenkrantz, S. A., & Hennessey, H. W. (1985). What do successful managers really do? An observational study of managerial activities. *Journal of Applied Behavioral Science, 21*, 255–270.

March, J. G. (1988, April). *Learning and taking risks*. Keynote address at the annual Texas Conference on Organizations, Lago Vista, TX.

McCann, J., & Galbraith, J. R. (1981). Interdepartmental relations. In P. Nystrom & W. Starbuck (Eds.), *Handbook of organizational design* (Vol. 2, pp. 60–84). London: Oxford University Press.

McCroskey, J. C. (1982). Communication competence and performance: A pedagogical perspective. *Communication Education, 31*, 1–8.

McCroskey, J. C. (1984). Communication competence: The elusive construct. In R. N. Bostrom (Ed.), *Competence in communication*. Newbury Park, CA: Sage.

Meister, J., & Reinsch, N. L. (1978). Communication training needs in manufacturing firms. *Communication Education, 27*, 235–244.

Mintzberg, H. (1973). *The nature of managerial work*. New York: Harper & Row.

Monge, P. R., Bachman, S. G., Dillard, J. P., & Eisenberg, E. M. (1982). Communicator competence in the workplace: Model testing and scale development. In M. Burgoon (Ed.), *Communication yearbook 5* (pp. 505–527). Newbury Park, CA: Sage.

Monge, P. R., & Eisenberg, E. (1987). Emergent communication networks. In F. Jablin, L. Putnam, K. Roberts, & L. Porter (Eds.), *Handbook of organizational communication: An interdisciplinary perspective* (pp. 304–342). Newbury Park, CA: Sage.

Morse, B. W., & Piland, R. N. (1981). An assessment of communication competencies needed by intermediate-level health care providers: A study of nurse-patient, nurse-doctor, nurse-nurse communication relationships. *Journal of Applied Communication Research, 9,* 30–41.

Moses, J., & Byham, W. (1977). *Applying the assessment center method.* New York: Pergamon Press.

Nadler, D. A. (1979). The effects of feedback on task group behavior: A review of the experimental research. *Organizational Behavior and Human Performance, 23,* 309–338.

Parks, M. (1977). *Issues in the explication of communicative competency.* Paper presented to the Western Speech Communication Association convention, Phoenix, AZ.

Parks, M. (1985). Interpersonal communication and the quest for personal competence. In M. Knapp & G. Miller (Eds.), *Handbook of interpersonal communication* (pp. 171–201). Newbury Park, CA: Sage.

Pavitt, C., & Haight, L. (1985). The "competent communicator" as a cognitive prototype. *Human Communication Research, 12,* 203–224.

Pearson, J. C., & Daniels, T. A. (1988). "Oh, what tangled webs we weave": Concerns about current conceptions of communication competence. *Communication Reports, 1,* 95–100.

Putnam, L. L., & Stohl, C. (1990). Bona Fide groups: A reconceptualization of groups in contexts. *Communication Studies, 41,* 248–265.

Powers, E. (1987). Enhancing managerial competence: The American Management Association Competency Programme. *Journal of Management Development, 6,* 7–18.

Rader, M., & Wunsch, A. (1980). A survey of communication practices of business school graduates by job category and undergraduate major. *Journal of Business Communication, 17*(4), 33–41.

Ranson, S., Hinings, B., & Greenwood, R. (1980). The structuring of organizational structures. *Administrative Science Quarterly, 25,* 1–17.

Rousseau, D. M. (1985). Issues of levels in organizational research: Multi-level and cross-level perspectives. In B. Staw & L. Cummings (Eds.), *Research in organizational behavior* (Vol. 7, pp. 1–37). Greenwich, CT: JAI Press.

Salancik, G. R., & Meindl, J. R. (1984). Corporate attributes as strategic illusions of management control. *Administrative Science Quarterly, 29,* 238–254.

Schall, M. S. (1983). A communication-rules approach to organizational culture. *Administrative Science Quarterly, 28,* 557–581.

Schein, E. H. (1985). *Organizational culture and leadership.* San Francisco: Jossey-Bass.

Shimanoff, S. B. (1980). *Communication rules: Theory and research.* Newbury Park, CA: Sage.

Snavely, W. B., & Walters, E. V. (1983). Differences in the communication competence among administrator social styles. *Journal of Applied Communication Research, 11*(2), 120–135.

Sorensen, G., & McCroskey, J. C. (1977). The prediction of interaction behavior in small groups. *Communication Monographs, 44,* 73–80.

Spitzberg, B. (1983, February). *Recasting the competency construct.* Paper presented at the annual meeting of the Western Speech Communication Association, Albuquerque, NM.

Staley, C. C., & Shockley-Zalabak, P. (1986). Communication proficiency and future training needs of the female professional: Self-assessment vs. supervisors' evaluations. *Human Relations, 39,* 891–902.

Stewart, R. (1976). *Contrasts in management.* Maidenhead, England: McGraw-Hill.

Sypher, B. D. (1984). The importance of social cognitive abilities in organizations. In R. N. Bostrom (Ed.), *Competence in communication* (pp. 103–127). Newbury Park, CA: Sage.

Sypher, B. D., & Sypher, H. E. (1983). Perceptions of communication ability: Self-monitoring in an organizational setting. *Personality and Social Psychology Bulletin, 9,* 297–304.

Sypher, B. D., & Zorn, T. (1986). Communication-related abilities and upward mobility: A longitudinal investigation. *Human Communication Research, 12*, 420–431.

Trevino, L. K., Lengel, R. H., & Daft, R. L. (1987). Media symbolism, media richness, and media choice in organizations: A symbolic interactionist perspective. *Communication Research, 14*, 553–574.

Tuckman, B. N., & Jensen, M. A. C. (1977). Stages of small-group development revisited. *Group and Organization Studies, 2*, 419–427.

Tushman, M. L. (1978). Technical communication in research and developmental laboratories: The impact of task characteristics. *Academy of Management Journal, 21*, 642–645.

Tushman, M. L., & Nadler, D. A. (1979). Information processing as an integrating concept in organizational design. In D. A. Nadler & M. L. Tushman (Eds.), *Managerial Behavior* (4th ed., pp. 157–190). New York: Columbia University Press.

Van de Ven, A. H., Delbecq, A. L., & Koenig, R. (1976). Determinants of coordination modes within organizations. *American Sociological Review, 41*, 332–338.

Van Hoeven, S. A. (1985). What we know about the development of communication competence. *Central States Speech Journal, 36*, 33–38.

Walsh, J. P., & Ungson, G. R. (1991). Organizational memory. *Academy of Management Review, 16*, 57–91.

Weick, K. E. (1969). *The social psychology of organizing*. Reading, MA: Addison-Wesley.

Wellmon, T. (1988). Conceptualizing organizational communication competence: A rules-based perspective. *Management Communication Quarterly, 1*, 515–534.

Wexley, M. N. (1986). Impression management and the new competence: Conjecture for seekers. *Et cetera, 43*, 247–258.

Wheeless, V. E., & Berryman-Fink, C. (1985). Perceptions of women managers and their communicator competencies. *Communication Quarterly, 33*, 137–148.

Whitely, W. (1984). An exploratory study of managers' reactions to properties of verbal communication. *Personnel Psychology, 37*, 41–59.

Whitely, W. (1985). Managerial work behavior: An integration of results from two major approaches. *Academy of Management Journal, 28*, 344–362.

7

An Emerging Macrolevel Theory of Organizational Communication: Organizations as Virtual Reality Management Systems

James A. Danowski

BACKGROUND

Organizations as Media Systems: An Emerging Perspective

If one were to ask students of communication, "what is a 'media organization'?," their answer would probably be similar to this: "It is a large corporation owing television stations, radio stations, magazines, newspapers, and other media." A less typical answer would be: "All large organizations are media organizations." This chapter perceives the latter perspective as defining an emerging perspective on organizational communication. Consider that no matter what organizations produce—from widgets to wishes—they rely on media systems for their internal management and for their external relations. Many forms of media are used in some combination by nearly all organizations above a small size: corporate video, employee newspapers, information kiosks, elevator music, electronic mail, voice mail, audio and video teleconferencing, databases, fax, and many other forms of media.

Moreover, organizations manage the content of messages they distribute through their media. Organizations are not simply common carriers of some others' messages. Rather, a great deal of corporate attention is given to what messages the organization itself should communicate, with what participants, in what style, through what media, to what ends, and how it should evaluate and tune these communication functions over time. Just one example is the attention given to corporate annual reports. The typical organization spends the better part of a year preparing the annual report, with the involvement of the most senior management, and often with costs in the hundreds of thousands of dollars.

From this perspective, all large organizations are media organizations. They manufacturer and manage virtual realities. The concept of virtual reality will be treated in more detail later. This section, however, is a brief overview. Virtual realities are mediated representations of nonmediated processes and content. The more virtual the reality, the closer it comes to the real thing. In the extreme, virtual realities involve all the human senses: touch, sight, sound, taste, smell and movement. These enable people to experience the mix of sensory inputs as closely as possible to the nonmediated reality. Less virtual realties range down to the simplest and least complicated technologies, such as printed texts and pictures. No matter how virtual, media systems strive to enable users to move closer to an "as if" experience, as if they were experiencing the reality of others who are the subjects or the producers of the media content and processes. Only recently are theoretical frameworks emerging that can treat organizations in these terms. These offer promise for integrating organizational and mass communication theory.

Chapter Goal

This chapter builds a stronger bridge between the fields of mass communication and organizational communication. The underlying image comes from an early spring backpacking trip in the Porcupine Mountains wilderness of Michigan's Upper Peninsula. After an uneventful, calming trek through virgin timber stands, two friends and I came to the bank of a rushing river. The long, broad log that had served as a bridge in years past was now washed away by the swollen, snow-melt, spring waters. Only fallen trees provided a tangled, slippery path across the torrent below. After studying the situation, we searched far up and down the bank for a better crossing, but found none. So, resolving to strike forward, we inched across the twisted trunks, suppressing fears of falling, and being swept away, and snagged precipitously on branches downstream.

Charting this chapter brought me metaphorically back to this episode. The large, well-traveled woods from which we came is like the organizational communication field: safe, soothing, and serene. The river separates the mass communication territory to the north. Earlier travelers had built a simple bridge linking the two sides through the work on media such as employee publications. Then, the technological torrent unleashed by the computer revolution washed wildly through. New bridges now needed to be built to enable easier travel between the organizational and media sides.

It is clear to see from studies of citation patterns across communication journals (Rice, Borgman, & Reeves, 1988) that the fields of mass and organizational communication, have been only weakly linked. Analysis of communication researchers' divisional affiliations in the International Communication Association finds mass communication and organizational communication in two separate blocks or groups (Barnett & Danowski, 1992). Mass communication together with political communication forms one group. Constituting a different group, organizational communication links with information systems, communication and technology, and public relations.

Paralleling these citation and affiliation patterns are differences in conceptual focus. Historically, and still today, mass communication research has mainly studied the individual audience member. Most research takes as given the content available, media organizations' structure and processes, and relationships with their information suppliers and their clients.

Organizational communication has also centered on individual communicators. Research has examined individuals' perceptions of climate, interpersonal communication, and communication network structures (Farace, Monge, & Russell, 1977; Jablin, 1980; Redding, 1972). Theorists assumed that the content of what communicators said was much more important than the form in which it was delivered. This "media transparency" bias fits well with the traditional message-oriented perspectives in communication studies (Knapp & Miller, 1985; Miller, 1966). Until recently (Fulk & Boyd, 1991; Steinfeld & Fulk, 1990), media in organizations have been ignored, except during a period of atheoretical work on employee publications in the 1950s and 1960s (Jablin, 1980).

Currently, the forbidding torrent between the mass and organizational communication fields is narrowing. On the one side, mass communication research is increasingly concerned with questions that move it in the organizational direction. An example is investigation of boundary-spanning interactions among reporters and public information officers, as journalists select and shape content obtained through organizations' public relations activities (Dunwoody & Ryan, 1983, 1987).

From the organization side, there is intensifying interest in understanding individual managers' choices of media in organizations, and what effects these have. The recent "media richness" research (Daft & Lengel, 1986; Danowski, 1988a; Steinfeld & Fulk, 1987; Trevino, Lengel, & Daft, 1987) has been triggered by the proliferation of new media associated with computers Danowski, 1988b; Rice & Associates, 1984).

"Media richness" (Daft & Lengel, 1986; Trevino, Lengel, & Daft, 1988) research builds from earlier work on the "social presence" of various media (Short, Williams, & Christy, 1976). Organizational members are thought to choose media based on their ability to transport information that reduces equivocality, which is uncertainty or variability in potential meanings (Weick, 1979). As well, situational variables associated with task characteristics have been explored (Steinfield & Fulk, 1990). Media richness research provides an abutment for building the mediation bridge. Let's critically examine its composition.

In the media richness literature, media are primarily defined in terms of material hardware/software/messageware features, instead of their social location and functions. Although sociotechnical systems perspectives have argued for moving the locus of conceptualization to social construction (Ellul 1964,1980), communication technology research generally defines media by their concrete product features, not by their social features. This concretization limits abstract theorizing.

Media richness and media effects are conceptualized mainly at the individual level, although media systems fundamentally are organized social systems, not individual creations. Nevertheless, media are defined as individual sense extensions (McLuhan, 1964; Williams, 1982). Moreover, the "social presence" concept is based on sensory information about people. Though Daft and Lengel (1986) move media richness toward more symbolic constructs, such as meaning and equivocality, they still center its definition on media capacity to provide feedback and cues. These are process and signaling functions closer to the sensory recognition domain than to the symbol/referent relational domain. The latter would focus on how people construct linguistic information within the media, or how they attach meanings to media (Hiemstra, 1983). This enables social-level theory development about media, not limiting it to individual differences in sensory-based variables. It avoids the more narrow psychological-level theory.

Media are studied uniplexicly instead of multiplexicly. Many studies focus on a single technology, such as computer-mediated communication. Less common are studies that treat a set of communication technologies in an interrelated fashion. These studies look at various substitutions of one communication technology for another (Dormois, Fioux, & Gensollen, 1978; Picot, Klingensberg, & Kranzel, 1982). They also examine how individuals use clusters of technologies, and how these clusters change with the introduction of newer media (Danowski, 1983; Rice & Bair, 1984). Even when researchers have conceived of channels in multiplex ways, they have tended to conceptualize them on only a single dimension like social presence or media richness. Theoretical progress may be accelerated through conceptualizing media in a multidimensional matrix of attributes. Moreover, viewing media from an organizational-level perspective appears fruitful.

ORGANIZATIONS AS A USEFUL UNIT FOR MEDIA THEORY

In developing an organizational theory of media processes and effects, our focus is on organizations as a key unit of observation and analysis. Media institutions are seen as networks of organizations shaping media content according to various regularities (Anderson & Meyer, 1988; Shoemaker & Reese, 1991). We can conceptualize "institutions" as patterns of interorganizational and intraorganizational relationships. As we define institutions in organizational relations terms, it is analytically valuable to pitch theorizing at the organizational level. As a result, there is an isomorphism between the locus of action theorized and the level at which we unitize the social relations context.

Moreover, "mediation" is fundamentally an organizational activity. The creation and maintenance of the means of information gathering, message creation, packaging, and dissemination require organized social processes (Shoemaker & Reese, 1991). There are social agreements on task differentiation, integration, standards for workmanship or performance, and technical standards for the interfacing of hardware and software for the information processing involved in mediation (Anderson & Meyer, 1988).

Furthermore, at merely the methodological level, there is value in framing organizational-level units of analysis, of sampling, and of observation. Taking a systems view of mediation, theories of mediation would apply to social systems generally, and to their subsystems. By studying organizations as social systems, we have more diverse elements to sample than if we studied whole societies as elements. Moreover, a system view of organizations is consistent with a large body of organizational theorizing over the last three decades (Katz & Kahn, 1978).

ORGANIZATIONS' ATTEMPTS TO CONTROL MEANINGS

Strategic Shifts

A historical look at organizations' strategic orientations provides a backdrop for theorizing about organizations and mediation. In the 1950s, extraordinary economic growth fostered a strategic focus on production. Demand was such that many organizations simply had to produce sufficient quantities of products and their marketing would almost take care of itself. Organizational media were treated as tools to aid production, if treated at all.

Then, increasing competition in the 1960s pushed strategic activity into a marketing perspective through the 1970s and into the 1980s (Hax

& Majluf, 1984; Scherer, 1980). Mediation became more important as an aid to the marketing function.

More recently, observers perceived a shift out of a marketing framework toward a public opinion and public relations framework. This move characterized organizations as moving out of the "share of market" strategic view that accelerated in the 1960s into a "share of mind" view of the 1980s (Cutlip & Center, 1984). Public opinion and public images became the primary target of some large organizations, instead of the by-product of striving for other goals. Strategic business management involves strategic media management through public relations and advertising. The perceived roles of media in organizations evolved from tactical tools toward key strategic components of the business plan.

As this conceptual evolution about media continues, we are moved to characterize organizations in terms of their management of meanings (Eisenberg, 1984, 1986), rather than in terms of market share or of mind shares. Consider how organizations may seek to control how the environment values the organization for its signification processes. Signification is the process of creating signs and symbols. It is the formation of information that is intentionally prepared to refer to something else. In the broadest sense, signification includes producing any sort of message, in whatever medium, including face-to-face. The form and the content of the message is chosen to elicit some intended references in audiences. The aim is to help the receiver create a virtual reality. Mediated signification is any such message production and distribution that delivers messages in other than a face-to-face mode, with no interposed technological device.

MEANINGS AND RESOURCE VALUATION: EFFICIENT MEANING-DRIVEN MARKETS

Organizations seek control over the meanings that interlocking networks of individuals interpret about the organization. As Osgood, Suci, and Tannenbaum (1957) have demonstrated, meaning includes an "evaluative" component. This involves a valuation of a concept. As we place this into a contemporary content, we see individuals as exchanging information about their valuations. As these exchange processes are more organized they form explicit markets in which valuations drive the buying and selling of shares of ownership in organizations.

In a fundamental sense these are "meaning markets." The meanings that individuals create specify a time/space value for the organization. Individuals can exchange money, goods, or services based on these meanings. Individuals generally appear to move their money where their meaning is. Differences in meanings drive the movement of shares among individuals in social or economic markets.

At any point in time, an economic value is set through individuals' interpretations as to the meaning of an organization's signification. The organization signifies X, individuals interpret the meanings of X, and can trade on differences in their meanings. Stock, in this sense, can be considered a share of signification production potential. In purchasing stock, an investor buys into an organization's signification potential. The investor assumes that in the future the organization will manage the means of its signification, to sufficiently control the meanings that individuals interpret so that they place higher economic value on the organization. Accordingly, the organization's resources will increase.

Trading on signification shares is in effect trading on expectations of the transactional value of future meanings. Finance scholars widely accept that expectations of future performance are key determinants of stock prices (Modigliani & Cohn, 1979), instead of only a product of the past financial performance of the organization. Moreover, the ubiquitous "efficient markets" hypotheses (Fama, Fisher, Jenson, & Roll, 1969) suggests that a stock's price reflects all available information about a firm. Much of this information pertains to the risk of the return on the investment in the stock. It is useful to view expectations as meanings that evolve as individuals interpret information from the environment, and value it.

Evidence for this view of valuation is that many investment analysts talk about a stock being "undervalued" or "overvalued." This means that the stock price is either lower than or higher than the fundamental financial data alone would warrant. Variations in meaning can be considered to account for under and over valuation of an organization's common stock.

Efficient market proponents argue that a stock is always just valued given all available information, whether about financial performance or estimated risk. Some even use daily price changes as an indicator of new information having been available (Arbel & Jaggi, 1982). Explicating these efficient market notions in information terms, Pearce and Roley (1985) posit that "security prices should respond only to the unexpected part of any announcement—that part that is truly news—since the expected part of the announcement should already be embedded in stock prices" (p. 49). They find evidence that reports of aggregate-level economic indicators related to monetary policy whose values deviate from the expectations of money managers significantly effect prices, while expected announcements have no effect.

As well, traditionally conceptualized "hard news" from a journalistic perspective has seen limited investigation. Niederhoffer (1971) analyzed newspaper headlines about world events and detected a response in stock prices. "True news" need not be considered "hard" factual information only. Davies and Caves (1978) demonstrate that stock analysts' recommendations reported in the "Heard on the Street" column of the *Wall Street Journal* significantly affect daily stock prices upon publication.

Note that while not all organizations are publicly owned and traded in organized financial markets, the theory in its broader expression can account for valuation of any sort of organization. Yet, it is useful to conceptualize meaning valuation in financial terms because publicly owned and traded organizations dominate within the broader network of all organizations. If we accept the assumptions of the efficient market hypothesis, we have available a good measure of an organization's value—its stock price. Such an operationalization of value is a reliable, precise, reproducible, isomorphic with the conceptualization of value, available at low cost, and valid for most the largest world organizations.

Organizations seek to control their economic resources necessary to reach their other goals, whether the organization is privately or publicly held, profit or nonprofit, a socialist state agency or an entrepreneurial venture in a freer-market society. The particular ways it measures economic resources will vary by cultural level and by local organizational factors. Nevertheless, an organization usually tries to optimize its resource control to achieve its other goals.

LOCAL SPACE CONTROL AND INTERPERSONAL INTERACTION

In their most primitive states, organizations try to control meanings that people have for their signification at the most local levels possible. They control what people can do in concrete physical space. They restrict people's behaviors according to physical locations. Certain behaviors are disallowed in certain areas. Movement across spatial boundaries is restricted. As organizations control local physical space, they limit the time width of signification that individuals can connect to space as they interpret it. Narrower opportunities for spatial movement narrow the possible linkage of mediated information to the past and to the future. More spatial control by organizations fosters, among individuals subjected to it, a focus on the present. The less control individuals have over their locations in space, the more present-oriented their interpretations of signification.

Supporting this general point, research has found that individuals with more interlocking personal networks have more restricted spatial locations for their social contacts. In contrast, radial network individuals talk with people who are located over a wider geographic area

(Danowski, 1986). As networks become more interlocking, individuals use the present tense for verbs more as they create messages in an interpersonal context (Danowski, 1987).

In short, the more restricted the space for interpersonal interaction, the more present-oriented the interpretations for signification. If an organization wants a higher degree of control over individuals' interpretations of the meanings of its signification, it first seeks to establish more control over the physical space within which the individuals can interact.

EFFICIENCY LIMITS ON LOCAL CONTROL

While more local space control may be effective, it may not be efficient. Attempted local control of meaning takes intensive resources. Control of space generally requires a high degree of physical control over the movement of people. Whether this control is automated through physical access systems, through rules restricting movement, or through presence of security force personnel, movement control requires intensive local surveillance, enforcement, and costs, as was witnessed in the Soviet bloc for several post-World War II decades. Control must be monolithic because competing social frameworks and contexts erode the ability to maintain meaning control. So, in short, local control of space is costly, and limits the optimality of space control as an efficient means of meaning control.

SIZE LIMITS ON LOCAL CONTROL LEAD TO MEDIATION

Size of the social system is another factor limiting local control. As systems become larger beyond some small level, limits on interpersonally managed meanings quickly reach threshold. These are a result of individual communicators' personal information processing capacities (Miller, 1956). There are well-recognized "span of control" limits on direct interpersonal management. Moreover, as information moves from one interpersonal control agent or manager to another, we know that distortions occur (Allport & Postman, 1947). The longer the interpersonal chain of communication, the more the distortion of the original message due to information leveling, sharpening, and assimilation. So, span of control and distortion problems limit the interpersonal control of signification and interpretation at the local levels.

The system, therefore, is moved to create signification systems that are mediated. This is so more people can be exposed over time to the same signification. The tradeoff for more direct actual control of interpretation is wider distribution of signification. They move the locus of control from the physical social space to the virtual social space.

So, with increasing system size comes more control over signification, but more apparent diversity in social meanings at local levels. Because size directly relates to ability to obtain, transform, and distribute resources, organizations are moved to become larger. Yet, they are constrained by their ability to control signification so that the local meanings maintain the collective identification with the system. This is an upper limit on signification in terms of how macro it can become.

Organizations are driven to control meanings because these include valuation of its resources. These enable its goal accomplishment. System size limits optimal local control of meanings, which is the control of individual's interactions in space. Increasing size exceeds the limits of span of control and of distortion for effective interpersonal management of meaning. Accordingly, nearly all organizations above a small size must manage mediated signification to sufficiently control identification with the system. As organization size increases, therefore increasing the importance of signification management, we should observe an increase in the status and resources of their communication functions.

COMMUNICATION STATUS

As signification control becomes more important, organizations give communication functions higher intrasystem status. Organizations generally operationalize status according to how close to the top of the organization a unit reports. So, the more important signification control is to the organization, the higher the reporting levels of the communication departments. They more strongly influence attempted meaning control.

Supporting this point, Cook (1983) found that public relations practitioners who report higher in the organization are more involved in decision making, and have higher usage of and preference for mediated communication, and a lower preference for face-to-face interaction. Taking a more departmental unit of analysis, another study found across a sample of 33 organizations that larger organizations had communication departments that report more closely to the top (Danowski, 1988a). This supports the reasoning that the larger the organizational size, the greater its limits for direct space control to manage meanings. So, as size increases, the organization moves the locus of control to mediation. As this signification control is more important, the communication management functions have higher status in the organization.

COMMUNICATION RESOURCES

Another measure of the importance of the communication function is budget amount. As size increases, communication functions have higher relative capitalization. Across the 33 organizations, controlling for effects of communication department size, the larger the organization, the more money in the total communication budget. Expenditures per communication worker increased with organization size. This is consistent with our reasoning that larger organizations place more value on signification for meaning control.

INFLUENCES ON SIGNIFICATION OTHER THAN SIZE

Besides size, there are other limits on local space control that move organizations toward mediated signification control. One is diversification. Although it is related to size, there may also be independent relationships between diversification and attempted meaning control. A key driver of diversification is environmental uncertainty.

Environmental Uncertainty

Management science observers have suggested (Hax & Majluf, 1984; Scherer, 1980) that there have been widespread increases in environmental uncertainty beginning several decades ago. The extraordinary economic growth of the 1950s started to slow in the 1960s, driving up competition in some key American industries. As a result, managers switched primary attention from production to marketing.

Also, sociopolitical forces increased environmental uncertainty. The period of the late 1960s into the 1970s saw environmental, consumer, and social activist groups mobilize and attack some organizations in their sociopolitical environments. In the late 1970s and in the 1980s economic factors again dominated, as global production and marketing competition intensified. This compressed production time frames, and increased volatility in consumers' price-brand purchase decisions. These factors added environmental uncertainty for competing organizations.

In response to environmental uncertainty changes, organizations are thought to change their external and/or internal relationships (Pfeffer, 1972). Some scholars have suggested that increases in environmental uncertainty force organizations to develop and maintain contacts with other organizations. Through such linking, organizations can coordinate action, exchange resources, and/or share information; thereby reducing uncertainty about their relevant environments (Burt, 1983;

Eisenberg et al, 1985; Pennings, 1981). Paralleling the change in relations between organization and environment is the possibility of changing internal structure to deal more effectively with a dynamic environment (Katz & Kahn, 1978; Thompson, 1967), such as segmenting the organization into autonomous "strategic business units (SBUs)" (Rothschild, 1980).

RESPONSE TO ENVIRONMENTAL UNCERTAINTY: DIVERSIFICATION AND MEDIATED SIGNIFICATION

Organizations seek to reduce their environmental uncertainty to maintain stability in their internal structures and in environmental conditions affecting them (Katz & Kahn, 1978; Thompson, 1967). As a strategy for dealing with this uncertainty, long-range planning is less effective as competitive time frames become shorter. To get around this planning problem, one way large organizations attempt to manage environmental uncertainty is to diversify. This enables faster planning and shorter time horizons in each of the diversified units. In contrast, more monolithic organizations require longer time horizons. This can be explained by the notion that their greater control of space requires more intensive energy. It requires longer lead times for its acquisition.

Diversification is a time compressor. While it shortens time horizons, it shrinks the basic social time unit. For example, a yearly time unit reduces to quarterly, monthly, weekly, daily, and so on. Diversification also allows for more polychronic activities (Hall, 1966, 1976) across organizational units, replacing the monochronic activity in the monolithic organizational structure. In other words, multiple time frames can coexist more effectively as diversification increases. This would be possible as some central unit would function as the "master time-base corrector," translating different social times to some standard or mean organizational time to enable synchronization with environmental time.

To diversify, an organization often segments the monolithic structure into a series of autonomous "strategic business units" (Rothschild, 1980). An intermediate option is backward or forward integration of other suppliers' or customers' operations through acquisition or merger. This is like Thompson's (1967) more abstract notion of the organization creating input and output buffers to maintain the certainty needs of its core technology.

More extreme, the organization acquires firms in diverse sectors. It forms a conglomerate of unrelated businesses. The organization then becomes a holding company, monitoring divisions' performance, balancing cash flow, and allocating resources to competing business activities.

In any of these cases, as economic and other market conditions differentially impact on these diverse businesses, the organization can buffer fluctuations and maintain a more steady state. Planning time horizons and response times are shortened for the organization substructures compared to the long-term planning possible with the monolithic organizational structure. So, this is a strategy of optimizing risk by lowering it at the aggregate level (Cyert, Feigenbaum, & March, 1959; Pfeffer & Salancik, 1978).

As organizations diversify in any of these ways, we hypothesize that they become more central between other nodes in information flow networks. Centrality is an inverse function of the average-minimum path distance for a node to reach all other nodes in the network through direct or indirect links. Why do more diversified nodes become more central? Nodes become more similar to one another through the exchange of more common information (Danowski, 1974; Rogers & Kincaid, 1981). Conversely, as nodes exchange more diverse information they become increasingly different from one another. Given the "strength of weak ties" aspects of networks (Granovetter, 1973), nodes in more central positions are linked with more diverse nodes and, hence, process more diverse information. To encode and decode more diverse information requires a more structurally diverse internal system (Ashby, 1956; Galbraith, 1977; Lawrence & Lorsch, 1967; Mintzberg, 1983).

Another reason for the link between diversity and centrality may be that more central organizations are able, if they choose, to control their communication environments more. Research has found more structurally independent organizations engage in more boundary-spanning activity (Kapp & Barnett, 1983). As a particular type of boundary spanning, organizations or their agents may be more able to influence media organizations to cover them.

There are more grounded reasons why diversification may be associated with greater centrality in information-flow networks. One is that with increased market competition (driving diversification), the organization requires more competitive intelligence information, both in terms of richness and timeliness. Public relations, advertising, and market research firms, among others, gather information about the environment and input it to organizations.

With greater market competitiveness, organizations try to differentiate their products more from competitors'. If customers identify unique benefits they are less price sensitive in choosing a product. Public relations product promotion coupled with advertising is the main way in which the organization attempts to position the product in the customers' minds.

An additional reason for diversification being linked to centrality in information networks is the attempt of the parent organization to influence the investment communities' perceptions of the organization, through investor relations communication. More diversified organizations depend more on valuation of their signification, and on short-term changes in them to influence stock prices. Less diversified, more monolithic organizations not only have longer time horizons. Analysts tie their prices more to economic performance, such as more conservative interpretation of the price/earnings ratio (Rockart, 1979).

A study of the Fortune 100 organizations found support for the hypothesis that the greater the organization's centrality in interorganizational networks, the greater the organizational diversification (Danowski, Barnett, & Friedland, 1987a). Diversification is a key factor that limits organizations' local space control in managing meanings. Greater diversification moves the organization away from local space control and toward more mediated signification control.

ORGANIZATIONAL MEDIA RICHNESS, SPACE, AND TIME SHIFTING

Organizational-level media richness is the extent to which media reduce the equivocality of organizational identity symbols. Media's effectiveness at this equivocality reduction process is a function of their decontextualizing of communication. This is the loosening of space and time binding of the message to the encoding/decoding process. Space and time can be shifted. The less social time is bound to space by the media, the greater their reduction of equivocality about the meanings of organizational signification. Meanings become less locally diverse and more globally unified.

As communication moves from unmediated interpersonal to mediated, both space and time are loosened, but in different magnitudes depending on the type of media. The most concrete loosening is of space. This enables people to communicate who are located in different places. Nevertheless, they still need to be synchronized in time, such as is true for normal telephone communication, or for audio or video teleconferencing. Such communication technologies enable more distance transcendence. They tradeoff synchronous telecommunication for transportation of humans to shared locations (Nilles, Nilles, Carlson, Gray, & Hanneman, 1977).

The work of Innis (1952, 1964, 1972) was an interesting prelude to intensive attention to space and time manipulation that newer media brought. Although Innis confounded space and time aspects in terms of mass media at societal levels, his work heralded a later era in which space and time would be more differentially impacted by newer media, and in which the links between social organization, space, time, and meaning would become clearer.

The trends toward distributed organization, toward virtual reality and virtual organizations, have called into question physical propinquity as a primary predictor of organizational communication network activity (Kriste & Monge, 1974). Pointedly, Korzenny (1978) has suggested "electronic propinquity" as a substitute for physical propinquity when people use communication technologies. So, for these media, the loosening of space binding (i.e., space shifting) is significant.

The other kind of decontextualizing is of a higher order. To space shifting it adds time shifting. The concept most often used to refer to the time binding attribute of media is "synchronous/asynchronous." As media are more asynchronous, they increase the distance in time between the encoding and decoding of messages. Examples of asynchronous organizational media would include: database information systems, electronic mail, voice mail, and traditional print information such as memos, newsletters, newspapers, reports, and so on. Media between the extremes of space- and time-shifting media would include normal video and traditional audiovisual media.

Note that it is conceivable that time shifting need not include space shifting, but normally it does. For example, two people sharing the same office could communicate asynchronously with each other by voice mail, while in the same space during the day. Yet, this is not likely, for the individuals would generally talk face to face if exchange was needed, unless they were trying not to bother one another while working on individual tasks. Normally, time shifting entails space shifting.

In freeing participants from the needs to share space and time for communication, asynchronous communication technologies most fully decontextualize communication processes. As communication processes are decontextualized, people depend less on physical contexts for the framing of their signification and meanings. They depend more on sharing increasingly abstract conceptual frames and symbol/referent systems.

This abstract subtextualization, as it becomes more shared, reduces the need for the observer trying to analyze communication to contextualize it in physical space and time. Rather, he must account more for the signification and meaning networks of communicators. Accordingly, it may be more than coincidental that the use of new media in organizations roughly parallels contemporary attention to organizational culture.

SOCIAL TIME SHIFTING

Asynchronicity is fundamentally a social time variable. It calls into focus the relationships of time, message form, message content, media, and participants, and their differential access to and distribution of messages over time. Asynchronous media are ones that enable communication between senders and receivers that encode and decode messages at different time frames. So, asynchronous media are time-shifting media. There are at least eight ways in which the concept of time links with the communication process:

1. Time distancing between message encoding and decoding, which ranges from large distances to zero distances, when the encoders and decoders are synchronously communicating.
2. Time marking of the message, made prominent to the decoder, and the inclusion of time in the framing of the message, such as by putting date and/or time codes on message headers (e.g., occurs for newspapers, electronic mail, fax, databases, etc).
3. Tensing of content, the extent to which the text orients to the past, present and future.
4. Time awareness of the decoders.
5. Time unitizing, the size of the social/organizational system interval used for management.
6. Time periodicity versus linearity, whether the system views time as cyclical or moving only forward.
7. Time coding the accessing of messages by social units, making it possible to tell who got messages at what times, and enabling the tracing of diffusion networks over time.
8. Time float compression in interpersonal relations, the normative amount of time people expect between communication initiation and response.

These eight social time variables are not independent. The greater the time distance between encoding and decoding, the greater the time marking of the message itself. As this time-marking increases, tensing of message content becomes both more past and more future oriented, and less oriented to the present. Time awareness of decoders during the communication activity increases with greater time marking of messages. Further externalizing time from the communication experience, time marking and monitoring the time access of social units to messages leaves visible the trace of message movement through the system. Time shifting leads to smaller social time units and to reduced social time float.

Conversely, as communication becomes more synchronous (encoding/decoding time distance approaches zero), and messages are unframed by marking time, and as content is more present tensed, communicators become less time aware and are more subjectively immersed in a process. They "space out" more. There is also an action inversion. Action in the content is increasingly important, while active processing of participants declines.

Because with synchronous media, social units are more likely to simultaneously get the same messages, time coding of the diffusion processes is less relevant. Without reliable time traces, diffusion is difficult for observers to reconstruct.

Time-shifting media "freeze" time for the framing of the message. Time is coded explicitly into the message format, whether in newspapers, electronic mail, voice mail, databases, or like media. As time is fixed in the format of the message, it more freely varies in the content. The past and the future can be addressed in such messages to a greater extent than for messages in which time varies with the framing of the message. These non-time-shifting media, in which time varies in message framing, include telephone, teleconferencing, video, and face-to-face media. Because time varies in the message framing, the process becomes more important relative to the content, compared to freeze-frame media.

Freeze-frame media, more content oriented, foster a wider time horizon in message content. The past and the future take on greater significance relative to the present. There is lower present action orientation. As well, the shifting of content from the present and from action, fosters more abstractness in message content. Abstraction is generalization, and as such, imparts time transcendence to concepts.

In contrast, packaging is important for action. People who take a more passive posture in processing information need to be more stimulated by message form to be aroused to action. Those already activated place more attention on content; slick form turns them away from content or leads them to discount its value (Grunig, 1982; Grunig & Hunt, 1984).

To shift time in these ways requires externalizing it from the communication experiences of participants. Shifting time requires a linear perception of time. A more periodic perception of time, of natural cycles embedded in experiences, would not fit as well with the requirements of managing time: distancing encoding and decoding, marking time frames, tensing content, and monitoring access.

Interestingly, Szamosi (1986) characterizes the classic Greek civilization as having a periodic model of time. This is thought to have lead to the heightened importance that that civilization placed on space and touch, on geometry and sculpture. In contrast, the Judeo-Christian concept of time has been linear. In this civilization, abstract concepts have appeared of more interest than space and touch.

In organizations, higher use of space-shifting media than time-shifting media would be associated with periodicity and seasonality of organizational time perceptions. The system would represent itself as cyclic, ebbing and flowing, changing management activities to fit the season, in touch with its surroundings, waiting till the time is right, farming, and

Table 7.1. Media Time-Structure Correlates

Time-Shifting Media	Space-Shifting Media
• Decontexualized	• Contextualized
• Content important	• Process important
• Packaging aesthetics less valued	• Packaging style high value
• Future and past tensed	• Present tensed
• Linear time perception	• Cyclical time perception
• Longer time horizon	• Shorter time horizons
• Analytically oriented content	• Action-oriented content
• Abstract content	• Concrete content
• Relational content	• Orgocentric content
• Active decoding	• Passive decoding
• Formal environment	• Informal environment
• Stable system functions	• Volatile
• Static visuals	• Motion visuals
• Textual coding	• Oral coding
• Communicators autonomous	• Communicators interdependent
• Status task-based	• Status socioemotionally based
• Acceptance of dominance	• Conflict over domination
• Openness to boundary spanning	• Boundary guarding
• Radial network structure	• Interlocking networks

harvesting markets. On the other hand, high use of time-shifting media should link to more linear perceptions of time. The system would represent itself as progressing, evolving, moving forward, projecting itself, guided by a vision more mechanistic or computer-based than agricultural. Table 7.1 lists some summary distinctions among synchronous and asynchronous media in terms of form, content, and participants.

TIME-SHIFTING AND NETWORK ROUTE DEPENDENCY

Social-time information is route dependent. The more that time is altered in the ways noted, the more that the mediation system is network-dependent for its message distribution. Messages are less likely to be broadcast uniformly to social elements and more likely differentially directed through constrained networks of elements. The distinguishing characteristics of nodes' positions in message distribution networks become more varied as these networks become more differentiated.

On the other hand, the most space-shifting media "glow" information like a light bulb uniformly "fills" an unobstructed space with light. They radiate content uniformly in all directions. In contrast, time-shift media "beam" information like a laser-carried light, switched through a fiber-optic network. Each beam has a specific path it follows in delivering information to the addresses of the intended recipients. The paths are selective and constrained. Only some small proportion of possible paths in the social matrix are activated by particular messages as they beam through it.

Thought of in another way, messages that are broadcast, rather than routed through specific interpersonal networks, have less interpersonal relational quality. People are less likely to talk about the meanings of broadcasted signification than routed signification because space-shifting signification is less equivocal than time-shifting signification. Space is central to the content. It is directly represented in it.

Space may be shifted from physical location anchors, but it is still quite intact in mediated representations of the space-shifted sort. There is a sense of space and place that people can identify as they process these messages. Physical space itself is often visually presented in visual space-shift media. Physical space is implicit in audio space-shift media like normal telephone conversations. As they communicate, the participants are embedded in their own spaces and are aware that the other party is not in the same space, but another. In short, space-shift media convey a sense of space and place. They shift it in modular ways, instead of radically restructuring and transforming its underlying dimensionality.

In time-shifting media there is more complete decontextualization of space. Messages are differentially available and processed by people in the mediated network. So, they need to interact more to arrive at shared meanings. Time-shifting media give individuals more control over content, interpretations, and the negotiation of meanings.

In short, time-shifting media externalize time from the communication experience, as they explicitly manage this social time. This is seen in the time distancing of encoding and decoding, in marking time in the message frame, in tensing content, in compressing time units, and in monitoring the accessing of messages over time. This externalization and manipulation of social time may point to perhaps the one most important feature of time-shifting media. They enable organizations to reestablish control over a special kind of space for interpersonal communication. This space is not physical. The time-altered space is mediated social space. It is a virtual space, a virtual social reality. It is defined not by proximity of people in physical locations, but by proximity in terms of processing mediated, time-shifting information. It is a shared meaning space. It is a virtual, networked space. It is a virtual reality overlaid onto physical reality.

Social status in the time-shifting system is based on more central positioning within the information flow network over time. This is a virtual spatial positioning. In contrast, in the space-shifting system, social status is based more on individuals' positions within the physical space control system. There, a territorial dominance hierarchy is more important. Here, power is the control of physical space, signified in securing the corner office. In contrast, in the time-shifting environment, power is securing an earlier time window in information distribution networks.

In more classic terms, space-shifting systems define power in "position." Time-shifting systems define power in "merit." In physics terms, space-shifting systems define power by the location of a social particle (a person). Time-shifting systems define power by the shape of a wave, the nature of the wave envelope passing through the person as information flow cuts paths through the social matrix over time. Individuals' absorption, transformation, and radiation of valued waves at optimal social times defines power there.

COMMUNICATION CENTRALIZATION AND USES OF TIME-SHIFTED MEDIA

Organizations with more centralized communication structures find the freeze-frame/asynchronous/time-shifting media more useful. Consider that a centralized communication structure has communication departments linking with departments that do not link much with one another. In other words, the communication department is radially positioned in the interdepartmental network.

When communication departments are centrally positioned and other departments do not communicate much with one another, each of these departments has more autonomy. They are likely to develop increasingly different orientations. The departments become more internally homogeneous in intradepartmental identification of members (Danowski, 1980). At the same time, the various departments become more heterogeneous relative to one another in their intradepartmental identification.

As this intradepartmental concentration of identity increases, identification with the organization becomes more tenuous. Equivocality about organizational signification increases. Increased communication is required to reduce this equivocality and to build and maintain identification with the organization. The central communication department is positioned to efficiently manage this organizational identity information through controlling mediated signification.

As centralization of communication and the use of more time-shifting media increases, the semantic networks for organization signification become less differentiated and more integrated. The missing direct links among departments in the present are replaced by the linkages of ideas. The information/energy moves to the more abstract time-transcendent domain of meanings for organizational signification. It is the idea that substitutes for direct action. The idea of linkage provides coordinated identity. Organizational identity is less formed by direct contact among departments, and more by the contact with compact organizational signification.

So, the organizational structure is inversely related to the structure of meanings for organizational signification. There is a structure/meaning inversion. The greater the centralization of communication departments, the more integrated the meaning network. There is a kind of "conservation of information." It is as if the information contained in the semantic activation networks about organizational signification and the information from the paths of communication traffic among departments come from a common and relatively closed pool of information. As one becomes more structured, the other must become less structured. Communication energy is conserved between the domain of meaning and the domain of message movement. As message traffic networks are more centralized, meanings for organizational signification become more integrated. Concepts are more interlinked.

In other words, meaning is network-route dependent. The more structured the distribution networks for signification, the more intensive the meanings that individuals interpret as they process. In contrast, the more widely and synchronously signification is broadcast through a social system, the less intensive and weaker the meanings. Meaning is a function of differential distribution. The more uniform the distribution of signification, such as with space-shifted media, the less they mean. They are less abstract and more particular to space and time locations in the social matrix.

The communication departments centrally positioned in organizations use the information energy that would have flowed among departments in a process-action present. Central communication departments concentrate this energy and project it into the future. The signification is the lens. As it is more integrated, it enables a tighter beam. Intentionality in controlling resources determines the intensity. It illuminates a path of shared meaning further into the future.

Effective management of organizational identity is enhanced to the extent that message content is more abstract, reaches further into the past, projects further into the future, is actively processed, and stabilizes activity with respect to the organization as an entity. The departments themselves, being more interlocking internally and using more synchronous, space-shifting media, act in the present. What is missing is the past and the future. The central communication department provides the links to these. It couples history and a vision of the future and links them to present action. Time-shifting media are particularly effective at this content tensing. Their decontextualization, the loosening of communication encoding and decoding from time and space bounds, enables the stretching or warping of message content into the past and the future.

Moreover, the time marking of message form in asynchronous media enables central communication departments to be the "timekeepers" of the organization. In marking time, the communication departments are the system clock, the master time-base corrector, the synchronizer, the manager of virtual reality.

STRUCTURAL AND CULTURAL CHANGE

Major changes in organizational structure present challenges for organizations to control meanings through mediated signification control. The uses of media after merger or acquisition in relation to cultural convergence reveal which media are most effective at changing meanings after major structural discontinuities. In a study (Bell, 1989) of Chicago organizations ($n = 56$) which had experienced merger and acquisition employee newspaper and photo use were the only strong correlates of cultural convergence.

SPACE-SHIFTING MEDIA AND FALSE CONSENSUS

A notion of critical theories of organizations and of media is the idea that they promote a false consensus to maintain a system of domination of oppressed minorities by hegemonically inclined capitalist elites. Space-shifting media may foster an illusion of shared meanings among organizational members. Consider space-shifting media like video.

Video and related media present visual images that people take as "real." The idea is "what you see is what you get." They think everyone else sees the same thing that they see. They project their own view onto others. These processes would result in an illusion of agreement, a false sense of shared meaning. Such equivocality would be useful to social systems in which communication management was not centralized, and in which different groups were competing for dominance, yet there was need to mobilize members around the sense of shared meanings for system-level identification. "False" consenses could drive action, which if properly managed, would contribute to system-level goals.

Nevertheless, over the long run, it seems that false consensus induced by video media would be caught in contradictions. As the media became vehicles for communicating different people's interpretations, the lack of shared meaning would become apparent. So, the longer that these media excluded information on alternative interpretations, the longer that false consensus could survive. It could continue to be useful to system goal attainment when the system has a pluralistic mix of groups with competing agendas and lack of centralized communication management.

Organizational video, and its larger system commercial cousin—broadcast television—do not focus much on showing a diversity of meanings. Mainly at special times when the pressures to control social meaning are greater, such as during system crises, do individual meanings become the content of mediation itself. Here, hyper-meaning management is practiced as an attempt to restabilize a system that is shocked by threats to signification systems themselves (Schramm, 1971). First is coverage of the events, followed by a stage of exploration of the possible causes. Then comes the interpretation stage during which meanings are sought. This interpretation stage leads to reintegration and a return to a normal state. There, interpretations again recede as signification of a more space-shifted content orientation again dominates.

So, individuals usually see only their own meanings as the link between social time and social space. This link becomes the basis for their reflexive view of the signification system. If they look back at the signification system or they try to estimate others' meanings, they tend to project their own. It is usually the only window to look through. Their own process of specifying meaning created a footprint of their local space on social time. This footprint is like a shadow. One cannot see what caused a shadow by looking at the shadow from underneath alone. One needs to know two other things. One is the source of illumination and the other is the object that was illuminated.

This suggests that signification and meaning by themselves are not sufficient to understand mediation. One must also know the source of illumination and the brightness and duration. At the societal level, the source of illumination is organizations seeking resource control. The brightness and duration reflect the strength of their intent as they project their energies through the lens of signification.

At the organizational level, those groups within the organization seeking greater resource control, hence, exhibiting more forceful intentionality, are those illuminating more strongly. The signification system is the lens and image framed. Shared meanings are to some extent like the projected picture illuminated on the social matrix "screen." It reflects some light, depending on its degree of organization and the uniformity of social "surface." Individual meanings are the refracted and absorbed light and the shadows that do not form part of the coherent image of shared meaning.

These processes, then, suggest the possibility of an "illusion of shared meaning." DeLucca (1987) found some evidence for it. In a sample of 56 organizations, use of video and other traditional audio-visual media was associated with higher perceived shared meaning among top, middle, and lower levels in the organization. This relationship was consistent with Beniger's (1983) theory of the effects of television on shared meaning. Yet, paradoxically, the semantic meaning networks were more differentiated and less integrated. False consensus was implicated.

As well, Beniger's theory is questionable. Video media may foster more common recognition of the content of signification, but not more shared meaning for it. Beniger (1983) and Cerulo (1984) measured only the labeling of graphic media content with words. They did not directly measure shared meaning. They only inferred it by a reduction in the use of words to label graphics over time. They observed a correlation between television penetration and reduction in labeling of graphics in the mass media over time, as television diffused in the United States. Instead of inferring shared meaning, we measured it directly.

Meanings can be viewed as networks of referent words evoked by the triggering signification. The system image is represented by a network of word associations constituting perceptions of system identity. Key identity signification is contained in the system logo and slogans. Equivocality of meanings for them is higher as the number of groups in the word association network increases, and as they are less integrated by intergroup linkage by liaison words.

To obtain the texts regarding the meanings of signification, one can ask individuals open-ended questions, such as "when you look at your organization's logo, what comes to mind? When you think of the organization's slogan, what comes to mind?" We can represent the shared meanings embodied in these responses by performing content analysis (Danowski & Harro, 1992).

ORGANIZATIONAL STRUCTURE, MEDIATION, AND NETWORKS OF SHARED MEANINGS

As organizations become larger and more diversified they must foster more uniformity in meanings for system identity through more use of mediated time-control signification than through more local space control. These forces are associated with centralization of communication functions within the system. This enables systems to maintain their social power by reinforcement of simple and appealing signification. To mobilize and maintain uniform behavior with respect to the system as a whole, they must maintain optimal repetition of clear, uniplexic, and unequivocal signification. The opposite pattern—communicating diverse, ambiguous, and varying intensity signification—would lead to system member demobilization, social diversity, heterogeneity, conflict, and intrasystem focus.

Unlike the social psychology theorists that dominate the current definition of media richness, we define it as the extent to which media reduce the equivocality of organizational-level signification. In semantic network terms, media would foster a simpler semantic network for these signification that would be less differentiated and more integrated. Differentiation is the extent to which there are semantic groups in the network. Integration is the extent to which these groups are interlinked.

Two studies of organizations ($n = 33$, $n = 56$) found support for the hypothesis that centralization of communication systems in organizations was associated with more time-shifting media. These media were also associated with less differentiated networks of meaning for system-identity signification. These networks were also more integrated as these time-shifting media were used more.

Media Use and Abstractness of Meaning Networks

As more centralized organizations create more time-shifting signification, the meanings for them become more abstract. To test this notion, words in the networks from the study of 56 organizations described were rated by two coders for abstractness. Results were as expected (Kozlowski, 1988). More centralized interdepartmental structures for communication, which we found in two studies to use more time-shifting media, had more abstract words in their shared-meaning networks.

Centralization and Orgo-Centrism versus Relational Orientation

As more centralized communication systems in organizations generate more time-shifting signification, time-shifting signification is "beamed" in more route-dependent ways than is space-shifting content, which is radiated. Relationships among social units defined by the passing of messages through a network are more important to the centralized system.

While this proposition is explained at the organizational level, we can also see parallel supportive reasoning and evidence at the individual network level. The "strength of weak ties" principle (Granovetter, 1973) suggests that radial-network individuals create more emotionally weak links with others as they search for diverse instrumental information. We can infer that to successfully relate to diverse individuals in the pursuit of instrumental goals, radial-network individuals are more flexible, adaptive, and empathic in orienting to others. Radial individuals may be more "chameleon-like communicators," as they change communication styles to fit the interpersonal surroundings.

In what they said in a computer conference of public relations and marketing professionals, radial individuals had nearly three times higher of a ratio of the word "you" to the word "I" (Danowski, 1987), than did interlocking-network individuals. The latter were more egocentric. Although they said "I" at the same rate as radial individuals, they said "you" much less. As well, interlocking individuals are apparently more suspicious of others. They said the word "trust" 43 times more than did radial individuals. These findings are consistent with the reasoning that radial-network individuals have higher other orientation than interlocking-network individuals. Extending these findings and reasoning to the interdepartmental level, more radial interdepartmental networks were hypothesized to have a more relational orientation, and less orgocentrism in their departmental and organizational image networks.

To test this hypothesis, we took all the words in the semantic network from the study of 56 organizations. Coders rated how much each word in the network was either "relationally oriented" or "node-centric." Node-centric words refer to the node itself and its attributes. Relationally oriented words refer to the links between the node and others, or refer to other nodes themselves. Results showed the expected higher relational orientation for more centralized networks. It was the interlocking, less centralized organization that had more semantic content referring to itself.

In particular, associated with differences in semantic network structures are asynchronous, freeze-frame media with time coding of the message frames, and with abstract and wider tensed content. These media cut across the ages. Old print forms (e.g., newsletters and newspapers), old static visual forms (e.g., slides and photos), and newer computer-based media for electronic mail, computer-based training, and database information management are functionally related tools for the management of shared organizational meanings. Hence, we can conceptualize these media as "orgic" media, as integral to the system-level operation of the organization.

Other media were found unrelated to organizational structure, that is, *aorgic*. Aorgic media included the space-shifting media of telephone, teleconferencing, and video. In a fundamental way these process media, with their present tensing and action orientation, operate largely independently of macrosystem structure and meanings. Structure and process reflect a more basic synchronic and diachronic independence. Synchronicity is action freed from structure and time. Diachronicity is control through the binding of tense and content to message distribution space. In short, systems with more centralized communication management structures appear to exert more control over shared meanings through more use of time-shifting media.

Centralized organizations' themes are more compact, less varied, and more integrated. As we listen to the signification strains of more centralized systems, they more actively project their identity in one voice. They sing solo, not as an ensemble.

The findings suggest that the space-shifting media that involve synchronous interaction do not substitute for direct control of space in the management of meanings. Rather, the time-shifting media appear to do so. This may be because time-shifting media establish direct control over a new kind of space, a social space defined through networks of message distribution. This virtual space reestablishes proximity of individuals in interaction, but through a closeness based on message flow, not on physical nearness.

ORGANIZATIONAL STRUCTURE AND MEDIATION AND MARKETPLACE VALUATION

At the beginning of this chapter, valuation of shares in signification potential was proposed as a good way of thinking about the valuations that individuals interpret for organizations. Then, mainly intraorganizational processes were treated. Is there any relationship between internal organizational communication structure, media used, meaning networks, and valuation of organizations in the marketplace?

Intraorganizational centralization of communication management is associated with centrality in interorganizational networks. Interorganizational network centrality, in turn, is related to stock prices. In a study of Fortune 100 organizations, defining centrality based on network analysis of shared public relations firm use, it was found that greater centrality was associated with higher daily stock price fluctuations (Danowski, Barnett, & Friedland, 1987b). This is consistent with the efficient markets hypothesis that stock prices reflect the net valuation of all available information about a company. More central organizations have more microlevel volatility in valuations. An earlier study (Danowski, Barnett, & Friedland, 1987a) found that more central organizations had more signification observable in the business press.

The next study (Danowski, Barnett, & Friedland, 1987b) looked at the associations between specific stories in the *Wall Street Journal* and changes in the stock prices from the close of the previous day to the close of the day the story appeared. More central organizations had more positive relationships to prices and less negative relationships, compared to peripheral organizations. More central organizations' signification were associated with more of an increase in valuation when the story was positive, and less of a decrease in valuation when the story was negative.

A subsequent study (Danowski, 1988c) addressed the question: Does the environment value companies more that are more internally orientated to signification management? Does the marketplace place a premium on organizations with more time-shifting signification control? A premium valuation was conceptualized to occur as the stock price for a company exceeded its objective measure of shareholder value, as computed by financial indices (Rappaport, 1986). Stock price and shareholder value indices were first standardized. Then the ratio of stock price to shareholder value was computed. A premium occurred to the extent that the relative stock price exceeded relative shareholder value for a firm. We found that higher premiums were associated with:

• more media use, in particular: FAX, computer bulletin boards, employee newspapers, computer-based training, and voice mail.
• less differentiated and more integrated semantic networks for organizational signification.
• less uniform meanings within the lowest levels and between the lowest—middle, and lowest—top.
• greater importance placed on external news.

Metaphoric Messages

This chapter has argued that organizations that use time-shift media more place further attention on meaning management and on symbolism. Evidence supports the proposition that organizations that value communication functions more have more abstract and less orgo-centric images. Nevertheless, there are financial community observers that largely dismiss the importance of what organizations say in their messages, and look only at what they do. For example, behaviors such as stock repurchases are taken as actions about which observers infer the orientations of management. Although evidence presented here has shown that the media that organizations use are related to marketplace valuations, is there any evidence that the content of the messages delivered through media make any difference?

Consider that message abstractness is given relevance and meaning via rhetorical devices such as metaphor. Metaphors provide a linkage across areas of messages that are normally not connected. They link them through narrative constructions. Metaphors are among the most nonliteral, abstract, and figurative of message content features. Metaphors and other nonliteral language provide the interpretive tissue necessary for abstract signification to be assigned meaning and value by receivers. Without metaphor, abstract messages are more like abstract art. There is no socially shared meaning for such signification, except the most global, primitive, and halting recognition that it is "abstract art."

In a study of organizations' annual reports, we found one type among five others that coders rated as: more artistic, more abstract, and containing more ambiguous graphic material that is not obviously linked with the textual content of the report. We found that organizations that produced such reports had communication departments, which although well funded, were more isolated from other departments in the organization. This suggests that abstractness alone, particularly that generated from the periphery of the organization, may not contribute to effective meaning management. It would appear that when the communication department is isolated, yet responsible for producing organizational signification, the resulting messages fail to tell a coherent story of the organization. For abstractness to be cogent, perhaps the storytellers must be communicatively central in the organization. Otherwise, the stories they produce may look good on face, but be analytically incoherent.

Based on the theory in this chapter, organizations that have more centrally positioned communication departments in the organization use more time-shift media, and the messages they produce are more abstract and decontextualized. As such, they use metaphors more, and these metaphors are associated with higher marketplace valuations of the corporations. We empirically examined metaphor use and effects by searching the letters to shareholders contained in the Compact Disclosure database on 11,000+ corporations, using keywords associated with metaphoric communication (Danowski & Harro, 1992). There were 27 such organizations identified. The stock price-earnings ratio was obtained for each and used as a dependent variable. As the stock price is higher relative to earnings, this indicates that the marketplace is assigning a premium value to the corporation. On the other hand, the lower the ratio, the more the marketplace is discounting the value of the corporation. For a comparison group, we extracted price-earnings ratios for a random sample of 27 other organizations using a skip interval method. We found that metaphor using corporations had significantly higher price-earnings ratios than the control group. Moreover, financial services organizations (e.g., banks, investment companies, and the like) were significantly more prevalent in the metaphor group than in the random group.

This can be understood considering the theory in this chapter. Across the range of organizations, those most deeply involved in time shifting are financial services organizations. In a basic sense, they are providing transaction services that shift time for buyers and sellers and for savers and borrowers. For example, a lending institution, on behalf of the buyer, gives a lump sum of money to the seller of a property at one point in time, and, in turn, via a mortgage to the buyer, collects the money owed with interest over many years. Given their basic time-shifting activities between buyers and sellers, one would hypothesize that financial services organizations are heavy users of time-shift media. Dealing with such diverse frames of symbolic reference among its relevant stakeholders, financial institutions could be expected to use more abstract, nonliteral ways of constructing messages, so that these diverse stakeholders could more flexibly project their own frames of reference onto the corporation's imagery and feel they understand it.

On face, it may seem strange to think that banking and financial organizations would exert the greatest control over social imagination. Most people think of such institutions as boring, conservative, and numbers oriented. They are not commonly known for their rhetorical skills and expressive powers. Yet, the theory and the evidence on metaphoric language would suggest otherwise. Banks apparently know how to get more bang for their communication bucks. Perhaps they view their economic roles in society as more oriented to managing meanings and perceptions than most other organizations do. Consider the media treatment of economic recession as primarily a problem of consumer perceptions and expectations. Perhaps consideration of financial institutions as the premier time-shift organizations give new meaning to the old adage, "time is money." Organizations that shift time more, create larger meaning differentials about them in the marketplace. Markets enable investors to trade ownership of organizations based on meaning differences calibrated in monetary terms; therefore, time is money. To accumulate money requires shifting time.

SUMMARY

Organizations are in the business of creating virtual realities and charging people money to experience them. Virtual reality is time shifted, mediated space, in which space is not physical but virtual, in that it is defined by networks of message distribution. Virtual reality is shared symbolic reality. Organizations create it as they use time-shift media to stimulate compact and abstract signification and differentially distribute it through social networks. Network distribution, in contrast to broadcasting, creates a more uneven field of meanings across people. Differences in meanings then provide the basis for trading shares of ownership in the organizations that produce the signification.

The most effective messages are metaphoric. These are created by organizations who position their communication functions centrally in the intraorganizational network. When the communicators are at the center, they are more able to spin out stories that capture social imagination. The content is interesting, and the timing is right.

This emerging theory of organizations, as managers of virtual reality explains, links among internal organizational communication structure and processes, media, messages, meanings, markets, and money. While we can still honor the adage that "time is money," we see more clearly that between time and money is a virtual world of media, messages, meanings, and markets. It is a world where nearly all large organizations are media organizations. In a remote region of this world, we walk on this bridge between the banks of organizational and mass communication, a bridge now more firmly based and broad of beam. We can stop in the center, calmly look into the torrent below, and enjoy its refreshing spray.

REFERENCES

Allport, G., & Postman, L. (1947). *The psychology of rumor.* New York: H. Holt & Company.

Anderson, J. A., & Meyer, T. P. (1988). *Mediated communication: A social action perspective.* Newbury Park, CA: Sage.

Arbel, A., & Jaggi, B. (1982). Market information assimilation related to extreme daily price jumps. *Financial Analysts Journal, 38,* 60–66.

Ashby, H. R. (1956). Variety, constraint, and the law of requisite variety. *An introduction to cybernetics* (pp. 202–209). London: Chapman & Hall.

Barnett, G., & Danowski, J. (1992). The structure of communication: A network analysis of the International Communication Association. *Human Communication Research, 19,* 264–285.

Bell, S. (1989). *Media use and cultural convergence after organizational restructuring.* Unpublished master's thesis, University of Illinois at Chicago.

Beniger, J. (1983). Does television enhance the shared symbolic environment? Trends in labeling of editorial cartoons, 1948–1980. *American Sociological Review, 48,* 103–111.

Burt, R. S. (1983). *Corporate profits and cooptation: Networks of market constraints and directorate ties in the American economy.* New York: Academic Press.

Cerulo, K. (1984). Television, magazine covers, and the shared symbolic environment: 1948–1970. *American Sociological Review, 49,* 566–570.

Cook, J. (1983). *Public relations executives' organizational communication behaviors.* Unpublished master's thesis, University of Wisconsin, Madison.

Cutlip, S. M., & Center, A. H. (1984). *Effective public relations* (rev. 5th ed.). Englewood Cliffs, NJ: Prentice-Hall.

Cyert, R. M., Feigenbaum, E. A., & March, J. G. (1959). Models in a behavioral theory of the firm. *Behavioral Science, 4,* 82–83.

Daft, R. L., & Lengel, R. H. (1986). Organizational information requirements, media richness and structural design. *Management Science, 32,* 554–571.

Danowski, J. A. (1974, April). *An information processing model of organizations: A focus on environmental uncertainty and communication network structuring.* Paper presented to the International Communication Association, New Orleans.

Danowski, J. A. (1980). Group attitude-belief uniformity and connectivity of organizational communication networks for production, innovation, and maintenance content. *Human Communication Research, 6,* 299–308.

Danowski, J. A. (1983, May). *Perceived effects of computer-communication media on other organizational communication modes.* Paper presented to the International Communication Association, Minneapolis.

Danowski, J. A. (1986). Interpersonal network radiality and non-mass media use. In G. Gumpert & R. Cathcart (Eds.), *Intermedia* (3rd ed.). New York: Oxford University Press.

Danowski, J. A. (1987, February). *Who-to-whom communication network structures and semantic activation networks.* Paper presented to the Seventh Annual Sunbelt Social Networks Conference, Clearwater Beach, FL.

Danowski, J. A. (1988a, May). *Media richness: Decontextualizing communication and changing the semantics of organizational symbols.* Paper presented to the International Communication Association, New Orleans.

Danowski, J. A. (1988b). Organizational infographics and automated auditing: Using computers to unobtrusively gather as well as analyze communication. In G. Goldhaber & G. Barnett (Eds.), *Handbook of organizational communication* (pp. 335–384). Norwood, NJ: Ablex.

Danowski, J. A. (1988c, June). *Measuring the effects of investor communication variables.* Paper presented to the Executive Seminar, Education Foundation, National Investor Relations Institute, Phoenix.

Danowski, J. A., Barnett, G. A., & Friedland, M. (1987a). Interorganizational diversification, media coverage, and publics' images. In M. L. McLaughlin (Ed.), *Communication Yearbook 10.* Beverly Hills, CA: Sage.

Danowski, J. A., Barnett, G. A., & Friedland, M. (1987b, May). *A theory of media dependency: Interorganizational network position, media coverage, and daily stock price volatility.* Paper presented to the International Communication Association.

Danowski, J. A., & Harro, T. (1992). *Metaphor use in corporate annual reports and stock/price earnings ratios* (Monograph). University of Illinois at Chicago.

Davies, P. L., & Caves, M. (1978). Stock prices and the publication of second-hand information. *Journal of Business, 51,* 43–56.

DeLucca, C. (1987). *Audio-visual media use and shared meaning for organizational symbols.* Unpublished master's thesis, University of Illinois at Chicago.

Dormois, M., Fioux, F., & Gensollen, M. (1978). Evaluation of the potential market for various future communication modes. In M. Elton, W. Lucas, & D. Conrath (Eds.), *Evaluating new telecommunications services* (pp. 367–384). New York: Plenum.

Dunwoody, S., & Ryan, M. (1983). Public information persons as mediators between scientists and journalists. *Journalism Quarterly, 60,* 647–656.

Dunwoody, S., & Ryan, M. (1987). The credible scientific source. *Journalism Quarterly, 64,* 21–27.

Eisenberg, E. M. (1984). Ambiguity as strategy in organizational communication. *Communication Monographs, 51,* 227–242.

Eisenberg, E. M. (1986). Meaning and interpretation in organizations. *Quarterly Journal of Speech, 72,* 88–97.

Eisenberg, E. M., Farace, R. V., Monge, P. R., Bettinghaus, E. P., Kurchner-Hawkins, R., Miller, K. I., & Rothman, R. (1985). Communication linkages in inter-organizational systems: review and synthesis. In B. Dervin (Ed.), *Advances in communication science* (pp. 231–261). Norwood, NJ: Ablex.

Ellul, J. (1964). *The technological society.* New York: Vintage Books.

Ellul, J. (1980). *The technological system.* New York: Continuum.

Fama, E. F., Fisher, L., Jensen, M., & Roll, R. (1969). The adjustment of stock prices to new information. *International Economic Review, 10*, 1–21.

Farace, R. V., Monge, P. R., & Russell, H. (1977). *Communicating and organizing.* Reading, MA: Addison-Wesley.

Fulk, J., & Boyd, B. (1991). Emerging theories of communication in organizations (technology). *Journal of Management, 17*, 407–446.

Galbraith, J. (1977). *Organization design.* Reading, MA: Addison-Wesley.

Granovetter, M. S. (1973). The strength of weak ties. *American Journal of Sociology, 73*, 1361–1380.

Grunig, J. E. (1982). The message-attitude-behavior relationship: communication behaviors of organizations. *Communication Research, 9*, 163–200.

Grunig, J. E., & Hunt, T. (1984). *Managing public relations.* New York: Holt, Rinehart, & Winston.

Hall, E. T. (1966). *The hidden dimension.* Garden City, NY: Doubleday.

Hall, E. T. (1976). *Beyond culture.* Garden City, NY: Anchor Press.

Hax, A. C., & Majluf, N. S. (1984). *Strategic management: An integrative perspective.* Englewood Cliffs, NJ: Prentice-Hall.

Hiemstra, G. (1983). You say you want a revolution? Information technology in organizations. *Communication Yearbook, 7*, 802–827.

Innis, H. A. (1952). *Changing concepts of time.* Toronto: University of Toronto Press.

Innis, H. A. (1964). *The bias of communication.* Toronto: University of Toronto Press.

Innis, H. A. (1972). *Empire and communications.* Toronto: University of Toronto Press.

Jablin, F. (1980). Organizational communication theory and research: An overview of communication climate and network research. In D. Nimmo (Ed.), *Communication yearbook 4.* New Brunswick, NJ: International Communication Association.

Kapp, J. E., & Barnett, G. A. (1983). Predicting organizational effectiveness from communication activities: A multiple indicator model. *Human Communication Research, 9*, 239–254.

Katz, D., & Kahn, R. (1978). *The social psychology of organizations.* New York: Wiley.

Knapp, M. L., & Miller, G. R. (1985). *Handbook of interpersonal communication.* Beverly Hills, CA: Sage.

Korzenny, F. (1978). A theory of electronic propinquity: Mediated communication in organizations. *Communication Research, 5*, 3–23.

Kozlowski, K. (1988). *Radiality and semantic network structure.* Unpublished master's thesis, University of Illinois at Chicago.

Lawrence, P. R., & Lorsch, J. W. (1967). *Organization and environment: Managing differentiation and integration.* Boston: Division of Research, Graduate School of Business Administration, Harvard University.

Kirste, K., & Monge, P. (1974, November). *Proximity: Location, time, and opportunity to communicate.* Paper presented at the Annual Meeting of the Western Speech Communication Association, Newport Beach, CA.

McLuhan, M. (1964). *Understanding media: The extensions of man.* New York: McGraw-Hill.

Miller, G. A. (1956). The magic number seven plus or minus two: Some limits on our capacity for processing information. *Psychological Review, 63*, 81–97.

Miller, G. R. (1966). *Speech communication: A behavioral approach.* New York: Bobbs-Merrill.

Mintzberg, H. (1983). *Power in and around organizations.* Englewood Cliffs, NJ: Prentice-Hall.

Modigliani, F., & Cohn, R. (1979). Inflation, rational valuation, and the market. *Financial Analysts Journal, 35*, 3–23.

Niederhoffer, V. (1971). The analysis of world events and stock prices. *Journal of Business, 44*, 193–219.

Nilles, J., Nilles, J., Carlson, F., Gray, P., & Hanneman, G. (1977). *Telecommunication transportation tradeoffs.* Reading, MA: Addison-Wesley.

Osgood, C. E., Suci, G. J., & Tannenbaum, P. H. (1957). *The measurement of meaning.* Urbana: University of Illinois Press.

Pearce, D. K., & Roley, V. V. (1985). Stock prices and economic news. *Journal of Business, 58*, 49–67.

Pennings, J. M. (1981). Strategically interdependent organizations. In P. C. Nystrom & W. H. Starbuck (Eds.), *Handbook of organizational design* (pp. 433–455). London: Oxford University Press.

Picot, A., Klingensberg, H., & Kranzel, H-P. (1982). Office technology: A report on attitudes and channel selection from field studies in Germany. In M. Burgoon (Ed.), *Communication yearbook 6* (pp. 674–692). Beverly Hills, CA: Sage.

Pfeffer, J. (1972). Size and composition of corporate boards of directors. *Administrative Science Quarterly, 17*, 218–228.

Pfeffer, J., & Salancik, G. R. (1978). *The external control of organizations.* New York: Harper & Row.

Rappaport, A. (1986). *Creating shareholder value: The new standard for business performance.* New York: Free Press; London: Collier Macmillan.

Redding, C. A. (1972). *Communication within the organization: An interpretive review of theory and research.* New York: Industrial Communication Council.

Rice, R. E., & Associates. (1984). *The new media: Communication, research and technology.* Beverly Hills, CA: Sage.

Rice, R. E., & Bair, J. (1984). New organizational media and productivity. In R. E. Rice (Ed.), *The new media: Communication, research, and technology* (pp. 185–215). Beverly Hills, CA: Sage.

Rice, R. E., Borgman, C., & Reeves, B. (1988). Citation networks of communication journals, 1977–1985: Cliques and positions, citations made and citations received. *Human Communication Research, 15*(2), 256–263.

Rockart, J. F. (1979). Chief executives define their own data needs. *Harvard Business Review, 57*(2), 81–92.

Rogers, E. M., & Kincaid, D. L. (1981). *Communication networks: Toward a new paradigm for research.* New York: Free Press; London: Collier Macmillan.

Rothschild, W. E. (1980). How to insure the continuous growth of strategic planning. *Journal of Business Strategy, 1*(1), 11–18.

Scherer, F. M. (1980). *Industrial market structure and economic performance.* Chicago: Rand McNally.

Schramm, W. (1971). Communication in crisis. In W. Schramm & D. F. Roberts (Eds.), *The process and effects of mass communication* (pp. 525–553). Urbana: University of Illinois Press.

Shoemaker, P., & Reese, S. (1991). *Mediating the message.* New York: Longman.

Short, J., Williams, E., & Christy, B. (1976). *The social psychology of telecommunications.* London: Wiley.

Steinfield, C., & Fulk, J. (1987). On the role of theory in research on information technologies in organizations: An introduction to the special issue. *Communication Research, 14*(5), 479–490.

Steinfield, C., & Fulk, J. (1990). *Organizations and communication technology.* Newbury Park, CA: Sage.

Szamosi, G. (1986). *The twin dimensions: Inventing time and space.* New York: McGraw-Hill.

Thompson, J. (1967). *Organizations in action.* New York: McGraw-Hill.

Trevino, L., Lengel, R., & Daft, R. (1987). Media symbolism, media richness and media choice in organizations: A symbolic interactionist perspective. *Communication Research, 14*(5), 553–575.

Weick, K. E. (1979). *The social psychology of organizing* (2nd ed.). Reading, MA: Addison-Wesley.

Williams, F. (1982). *The communications revolution.* Beverly Hills, CA: Sage.

8

Electronic Mail and Democratization of Organizational Communication

Susan H. Komsky

INTRODUCTION AND LITERATURE REVIEW

If we ask people why they have implemented a new communication technology in the workplace, their answers usually focus on improvement or enhancement of one or more organizational factors: improved productivity, enhanced jobs and tasks, improved efficiency, enhanced organizational status, improved work environment, and/or enhanced organizational image. These technologies appear to promise a future that overcomes perceived problems in today's workplace. As Laudon (1977) describes it, "in the United States the messiah is technology" (p. 1). Certainly the managerial point of view revolves around using technology to facilitate organizational goal achievement.

At the same time, communication technologies affect the social and political contexts within which they are embedded (Hiemstra, 1986; Slack, 1984; Taylor, 1986). New communication technologies are expected to "usher in a new era of democratic participation and decentralization" in the workplace (Singer, 1986, p. 221). This perspective on the future suggests that organizational barriers derived from difference in status, achievement, charisma, and power will disappear and universal access will translate into communication equality where everyone's voice will be equal (Kochen, 1981). Increased interaction among organizational members is expected to produce increased organizational cohesion and identification with organizational goals (Albertson, 1977). In short, the general line of reasoning suggests that electronic communication technologies will facilitate direct individual access to the communication process with less delegation of authority (Holt, 1969), which will empower all members of the organization. The social structure of the organization will be democratized.

Two basic research questions immediately emerge. First, in what manner will communication technologies accomplish this task of democratization? Second, will communication technologies succeed as catalysts for democratization? Some research studies have attempted to address the first of these questions and will be reviewed later. The purpose of the present report is to address the second question, using an exploratory qualitative study of perceived democratization by users of electronic mail in an organizational setting.

Effects on Authority Structures in Organizations

Laudon (1977) examined the use of telephone conferencing by the League of Women Voters as a means of decreasing inequality between the state leadership and local chapters. Impacts of geographical size and time constraints on access to League decision making were ameliorated by using the technology and "did have the effect of weakening the power of the state leadership vis-a-vis local chapters" (p. 100). However, problems arising from demographic size and inequality among individual members could not be solved with the available technology. Leduc (1979) found that computer conferencing by-passed traditional barriers and led to a greater number of interorganizational messages compared to intraorganizational messages. Thus, electronic groups could function to erode borders between organizations or between separate units within organizations. Johansen and DeGrasse (1979) found that computer conferencing likewise led to increased frequency of interaction, especially between distantly located colleagues who would not otherwise communicate, and computer conferencing was judged more productive than telephone and traditional mail. However, the effects of access on working relationships could not be predicted systematically.

Guillaume (1980) examined the effects of computer conferencing on communication patterns in groups and concluded that it contributed to a breakdown in group cohesiveness as users perceived less influence by the group on the members. Albertson (1977) found that teleconferencing contributed to decreasing the saliency of the group as such. One interpretation of these results suggests a breakdown in group processes, but an alternative interpretation suggests that changing the configuration of communication channels will change patterns of authority and power (Boulding, 1971; Duncan, 1967).

Rice and Case (1983) examined the introduction of electronic mail into a university organization and reported some evidence that administrators began communicating with lower level personnel, but these contacts were not necessarily desired. These new contacts may have been initiated because of the limited diffusion of the technology within the university.

The general trend of these findings suggests that communication technologies exert some changes on authority structures in organizations. By circumventing hierarchical filtering structures, the existing social order is mediated. By permitting open communication that bypasses hierarchical channels, the nature of information changes, which can change the symbols used to express and maintain the social order (Singer, 1986).

Effects on Social Cues

Other research findings suggest that communication technologies impact interpretation of organizational messages because fewer contextual cues are carried over mediated channels (Grande, 1980). Kiesler, Siegel, and McGuire (1984) found that social context cues that reinforce status, prestige, and authority relationships were missing in computer-mediated communication situations and that a new interaction etiquette had to be developed to coordinate interaction. Similarly, Hiemstra (1986) reported that communication rules were altered in mediated communication situations and new rules emerged. For example, voice-activated media tended to favor the loudest speaker, so shouting and speaking loud became appropriate behaviors for requesting a turn to participate. Computer-based media required controlling both listening and participation roles, so users who could assimilate written text and jump in quickly got a chance to participate. Hiltz (1976) found it was easy for users to ignore some questions that never got answered. Steklasa (1977) suggested that communication style over electronic mail became "very informal and to the point" (p. 4) and replaced the more formal etiquette of face-to-face, written, and telephonic interaction. Messages on electronic media tended to be shorter and less formal, and cues signaling status differences were downplayed (Taylor, 1981, p. 10).

Sproull and Kiesler (1986) suggested that when social context cues were weak or missing, communicators were more anonymous and thus engaged in more self-centered and unregulated behavior. In an experimental study of electronic mail users, Siegel, Dubrovsky, Kiesler, and McGuire (1986) found that electronic mail was perceived as carrying fewer social context cues, and reduced-cues situations were associated with more antisocial behavior and more extreme decisions. Sproull and Kiesler (1986) found that the decrease in social context cues on electronic mail substantially deregulated communication. Specifically, messages from subordinates were no different from messages from superiors, there was a greater willingness to communicate bad news, and users tended to flout social conventions. However, electronic mail tended to be preferred for upward communication over downward communication, suggesting that superiors tended to desire status cues when communicating with subordinates while subordinates tended to take advantage of the absence of cues when communicating with superiors.

The general trend of these findings suggests that users of electronic mail perceived the elimination of many social context cues usually associated with status and power differences between communicators. To the extent these cues are associated with real or perceived barriers to democratic participation in organizational communication, elimination of these cues should democratize the communication process.

Though much has been written about the democratizing potential of communication technologies (see e.g., Becker, Hedebro, & Paldan, 1986, and others), little research has been performed to assess it. Laudon's (1977) study of the League of Women Voters directly addressed the issue of democratic participation but focused on a technology that was limited and rudimentary and the technological possibilities have expanded greatly in the last fifteen years. The Rice and Case (1983) study of a pilot implementation of electronic mail in a university addressed democratization as a side issue of system use. Thus, the present study focuses on users across all hierarchical levels and directly examines users' perceptions of the potential and the use of electronic mail as a democratizing medium, and attempts to answer two basic research questions:

1. To what extent do users of electronic mail agree with the potential of the medium to democratize the communication process in their organization?
2. In what ways do they perceive that this medium can contribute to democratization and/or will inhibit democratization?

METHODOLOGY

Participants

Following a quantitative survey of electronic mail users at a western university, 42 users were asked to participate in intensive interviews regarding their use of electronic mail. At the time of data collection all participants were regular users of the mail system. All participants held positions within the administrative-staff hierarchy in the university organization, including vice-presidents, middle-level administrative management directly reporting to the vice-presidents, school deans, department chairs, administrative staff, and clerical and technical staff. Fifteen of the participants were female (2 from middle-level administrative management, 5 from administrative staff, 1 from school-level administration, 1 department chair, and 6 from clerical staff) and 27 participants were male. Tenure in the present job ranged from less than 1 year to greater than 7 years (the length of implementation of electronic mail in the organization).

Data Collection

Based on prior literature, an interview questionnaire was designed to examine factors associated with electronic mail use. There was little resistance to the interview: Heavy users were enthusiastic to talk about electronic mail and light users usually were willing to cooperate with the research effort. Even those who disliked electronic mail wanted an opportunity to explain why. Forty-two interviews were conducted between March 1988 and July 1988. All interviews were audiotaped, with participants' permission, and professional transcription yielded a verbatim text for each interview.

Data Analysis

Data were analyzed using pattern coding techniques to reduce large amount of text into analyzable units and to build a cognitive map for understanding what was happening (Miles & Huberman, 1984). Domain definitions for content categories were produced. A priori categories were based on the specific question topics contained in the interview. As additional categories emerged from the data, these domain definitions were added.

Each transcript was carefully read and portions of text were assigned to the category codes. The unit of analysis was defined as a single theme or subtheme, based on content and linguistic markers. While this yielded analytical units that ranged from one sentence to several "paragraphs," it was deemed most consistent with the operationalizations. No attempt was made to restrict analytical units to mutually exclusive category codes and units were coded into as many categories as seemed appropriate. At this level of analysis, it was deemed better to err on the side of underdiscrimination with multiple codes than to lose the richness of the text from overdiscrimination. Also, categories probably are correlated to some degree since they all focus on patterns of electronic mail usage and the reasons underlying those patterns; thus, there seemed to be no benefit to mutual exclusivity. Text was coded exactly as it had been transcribed from the tape except in those situations in which obvious redundancies (e.g., "perhaps maybe" or "but however") could be eliminated. Occasionally, a word or phrase was inserted in brackets to clarify the text; these insertions usually indicated the question to which the participant was responding.

For the present analysis, responses to the specific interview question regarding democratization were analyzed. The interviewer generally provided expanded explanation of the question when presenting it to participants. After examining the transcripts it was determined that the question was presented to respondents in the following manner:

> Many people in my field suggest that electronic mail is at least potentially what they are calling a democratizing medium. They usually mean one of two things; the most common meaning is the idea of access: that once people have access to the system, they also have access to everybody else who is on the system, so that gives them greater access, at least potentially, to the communication process. The other thing that they sometimes mean, though somewhat less frequently, is that electronic mail is also kind of a flat medium in that it blends out a lot of status differences: you wouldn't necessarily put your title down as you would in a written memo; because it's only first initial, last name, it really eliminates biological sex, at least as an identifier, if you don't know the person. So, I'm asking people to give me a reaction to this idea, whether they agree, disagree or some combination and why that is their reaction.

Coded data were arranged in summarizing matrices based on the research questions. These matrices permitted reduction of complex textual data and organization of data and analysis in a compact, simultaneous, and ordered manner (Miles & Huberman, 1984) to facilitate interpretation. Participants were assigned to one of five hierarchical categories depending on their job titles at the time of the interview: (a) *Department Chairs*, regular faculty performing administrative-leadership tasks for academic departments (*n* = 6); (b) *Deans and Associate Deans*, individual performing administrative-management tasks at the school (college) level, with faculty retreat rights to academic departments (*n* = 8); (c) *administrators*, individuals performing administrative-management at the University level (*n* = 9); (d) *administrative staff*, individuals performing administrative support activities at either the school or university level (*n* = 9) and (e) *clerical and technical staff*, individuals performing clerical and/or technical support activities at all levels (*n* = 10).

RESULTS AND DISCUSSION

Potential Democratization from Electronic Mail

The first research question focused on the extent to which users of electronic mail agree with the potential of the medium to democratize the communication process in their organization. Tables 8.1a–8.1e display matrices of comments separated into two categories: "electronic mail is a democratizing medium," which includes participants' comments that agree with the premise that electronic mail is, at least potentially, a democratizing medium for organizational communication, and "electronic mail is *not* a democratizing medium," which includes participants' comments that disagree with the premise. The matrices separate comments by hierarchical categories.

Table 8.1a examines responses made by Department Chairs. Most responses indicate that these participants disagree with the premise that electronic mail democratizes the communication process in the university organization, and most responses focus on personal experiences and/or experiences of colleagues. These participants do not believe that they have either increased access to the communication process or any perceived hierarchical leveling and most do not believe that their colleagues have either. For example,

I don't think that has happened to any great degree. I may get annoyed with a Dean in another school but I don't feel that I've got any more access to that person through electronic mail than I do through the telephone or the memo.

I think I probably have the same level of anxiety about receiving an electronic mail message from [the Vice President] as I do receiving a written memo from him. So I don't think the democratizing scenario has put itself in place.

Well, since I see email as simply a quicker form of memos, then it doesn't seem to [democratize]. It seems to me that if one of our faculty members wants to communicate with the Dean, he could either write out a memo or use e-mail and it's the same thing. I don't see people as more accessible or less accessible.

In general, Department Chairs use electronic mail to communicate with their Deans, Associate Deans, and other school-level personnel. For them, the medium is almost exclusively for upward vertical communication, with little utility for downward vertical communication because the medium is poorly diffused among individual faculty. Likewise, Department Chairs receive little or no electronic mail from individual faculty and there seems to be little or no horizontal use of electronic mail among Department Chairs.

Table 8.1b summarizes responses made by Deans and Associate Deans. This group of participants tends to be more ambivalent about the issue of democratization, with approximately the same number of responses indicating agreement with the premise that electronic mail is democratizing as responses indicating disagreement with the premise. The members of this group tend to perceive themselves as more accessible because they receive an increased amount of electronic mail from

Table 8.1a. Perceptions of Democratization from Electronic Mail Department Chairs

"Electronic mail is a democratizing medium"	"Electronic mail is *not* a democratizing medium"
I suppose in terms of style, yes.	I don't think that that has happened to any great degree. I may get annoyed with a Dean in another school but I don't feel that I've got any more access to that person through electronic mail than I do through the telephone or the memo.
Certainly in terms of the way people address each other, I think there is probably a more equalizing kind of thing, because the person who sends the message has the power at that particular point in time. And so as a result, there is not as much difference on electronic mail as there is in person or on the telephone.	I don't believe that there is much history of the chairs [in my school] sending increased numbers of messages to the President or the Vice Presidents.
You can feel free—but I would feel free to make a telephone call in that case too.	I think that may be a function of the relatively small number of faculty who actually have easy access to electronic mail. I'm not at all certain just what would happen if all 1000 of them had terminals in their offices and then had access to Deans and Chairs and each other.
Once in a while I'll get a message from [the Vice President] and a person looking at that message can't tell anything about the relative importance of him versus me. It just says [VPRES] and it is [DEPTCHAIR] on plain white paper. Whereas with memos: you're right; that's interesting. If you get something from [the President], it has gold letterhead, embossed seals and all of that. . . . When you send a memo, you are very conscious of differences in status.	I think we're just too politically sensitive about putting our concerns out in the open through electronic mail.
	I think I probably have the same level of anxiety about receiving an electronic mail message from [the Vice President] as I do receiving a written memo from him. So I don't think the democratizing scenario has put itself in place.

182

In terms of access, no, not really. I would not send an electronic mail message to someone who was of a higher status than I was unless I knew that they were willing to receive the message . . . that they would be receptive.

When . . . was Vice President for . . ., he was an enthusiastic user of electronic mail. And occasionally I would send him messages—it was more an experiment kind of thing: will he respond to this? Well, I either wouldn't get a response or I got a response that was nice but indicated that he really didn't appreciate receiving electronic mail from people two levels below him, that he would really appreciate it if I went through my Dean instead.

No . . . there are just people who I know use it who I would never send a message to unless I was invited to do so. I would always use another medium to reach those people.

No. I don't see too much difference between using electronic mail and working with [other media]. I have not experienced that at all.

By hooking in cc:'s or copies or broadcasting it to a variety of people who may be on the list, it would communicate information to those people I want to get it to, but I don't see it as democratization . . . I would be selective who I would send it to.

It would not be, from the point of view of the department, necessarily politically expedient to let everybody know what's going on in a particular area. Not that we have a lot of stuff to hide, but I could envision where it would be a problem.

Well since I see email as simply a quicker form of memos, then it doesn't seem to. It seems to me that if one of our faculty members wants to communicate with the Dean he could either write out a memo or use email and it's the same thing. I don't see people as more accessible or less accessible.

Table 8.1b. Perceptions of Democratization from Electronic Mail Deans and Associate Deans

"Electronic mail is a democratizing medium"	"Electronic mail is *not* a democratizing medium"
When you send a message on email, you are sending to a particular handle. There are no titles. Whereas, when you write a memo which is formally typed, you always put in the person's title and you always put in your title. So, from what you are saying, that to me is a potential form of democratization, just in the vanishing of the titles.	I don't go along with that. First of all, if there is a significant difference in status between two people, one of them won't feel all that free to send an email to the other. If the person does, there probably will be involved in that email all the formalities necessary to maintain the distance that does, in fact, exist.
I get messages from secretaries that I probably wouldn't get before and there are even individual faculty who are on email who I get messages from that I might not get otherwise. Some of them might have taken the time to call me and try to reach me by phone or what have you, but I think they find it easier to reach me in this particular fashion. They don't have to go through people to get to me. They know they can get me directly this way.	[The Dean] asked me recently to do something for him and it involved sending a message to [the Vice President]. What I noticed is that I didn't do it through email. There is no reason I couldn't email [the Vice President] but I found myself doing a memo on it. It just somehow rather seemed more appropriate. I'm sure that [the Dean] would have emailed him and [the Vice President] emails all the time.
I am dealing with more people as a result [of email].	I would not send an email message to [the Vice President], for example, except under extraordinary circumstances . . .
But if we look at the other side, if you had occasion to write me two or three more times, I think that our communicating in this way may produce somewhat friendlier feelings than if you had written me memos three or four times.	I have the same feelings when I use email as I do with a phone call. I would no more call up [the President] on the telephone than probably send him an email. . . . So I still keep that same set of distances.

But I think it makes friends. I think perhaps my department secretaries feel a little closer to me because I send them messages from time to time. Sometimes amusing, sometimes to encourage them or whatever.

I think it would help communication and understanding.

I think it might be good, because a lot of people hear rumors and they're not likely to phone and say that. But if they could just hit it out on the email and say "I heard such-and-such, is it true?"—they're a little bit more anonymous when they do it. They're not anonymous because they have an account, but it's a little different than phoning a person and hearing "Why are you bothering me with that?" They're worried about getting that kind of thing. I think they might do it with electronic mail.

There aren't any titles, but you still know who people are.

So, in all my communications, I worry about the level of bothering them and making sure I'm communicating with the right person in sort of the right form. So, I don't think it has democratized much of what I do, particularly.

I guess my immediate reaction would be to say no. It might appear to hide status differences but I couldn't imagine a departmental secretary addressing [the President] or [the Vice President]. I also think that if they did, they would get some static from the other end. I don't think the medium diminishes real status differences that exist.

If we need electronic mail to democratize the communication system, then maybe we ought to look at ourselves as how we react to others. Do we go in with a preconceived idea that "this is a female, so she is less qualified than I because I am a male" or the female will say, "this is a male, he's going to look down his nose at me." I think we have to look to ourselves and I don't think the electronic media or any media are going to get rid of that.

Table 8.2c. Perceptions of Democratization from Electronic Mail Administrators

"Electronic mail is a democratizing medium"	"Electronic mail is *not* a democratizing medium"
I certainly get electronic mail from people I would not normally either get a phone call from—and this is on the subordinate level—or certainly not get a letter from. So they feel much freer to communicate with me electronically, I guess, because it is less intrusive.	I don't agree with either of those notions of [democratization]. Communication, by its very nature, is a prejudicial action and it is both given and received as prejudice. If you don't know the sender or the sender's position, then the prejudice is involved in how you read the words that are being sent. I don't see anything that is democratizing about it. Email automatically attaches an author to a message sent, so there is no anonymity to your ability to reach somebody . . . whatever democratization there may be in it I think is very superficial and very shortlived.
But, yes, I would write [the Vice President]. I wouldn't write the President, although I have written the President [but] I know his secretary picks it up.	It's democratic in principle, but in practice, not everyone shares the resource.
As I think about it, I think there is some element of truth to that because I get messages from people at all levels and I communicate with them. Whereas, if I didn't have electronic mail, I think a lot of those communications would not occur directly; they would be going through other people.	Another nondemocratic aspect of it is [regular] users . . . have an inside track. The users who know that such-and-such administrators use email can reach that individual with messages that the [nonuser] has to go and meet with them and get an appointment. And it may be that the issue goes away or whatever by the time that appointment comes along or they can't get an audience on a timely basis.
I would state that this is true, because the protocol is for addressing the individual—it doesn't necessarily require [titling] the individual . . . it doesn't have to say "President . . ." on it and with a formal heading that you have in a memo. All the formality is stripped away and it's just "XXXXXXX".	It does not bring people down to one common level. It does not democratize, no.
It's hard to believe that something electronic can be humanizing but I think it strips away the formalities of the person's position and you're now focusing on communication with the	Mail that I receive—people know who they're sending it to.

individual for the purpose that you have in mind. It is not unlike the same kind of thing that would happen if you know them personally and you were good friends and you were talking over the fence, except that it is a written communication.

I received a mail message from a higher-up administrator on the campus, the first mail message I had ever received from this individual. And because there is no spelling checker, there were three or four spelling errors, and there were three or four syntax errors which would not have been acceptable to that administrator under any circumstances . . . it's okay. That was the only case that I can ever think of where it democratized.

I think that it is indeed true, that it flattens out the different levels, and I think that's good.

I think it creates a more informal, relaxed feeling about communication and it opens up channels that never were opened up before. If you feel free to sit down and send a mail message to every employee saying "Here's an idea," and those people feel free, regardless of their level, to say, "It stinks."

I wonder if [she] had written a formal memo or if she had written this other person a formal memo with traditional cc:'s on it, if she would have felt as comfortable copying me without copying her immediate supervisor.

I don't think access would change because you still have the means of communicating in writing. In fact, I have more confidence that a written memo to someone in the administration from the faculty would maybe have a better chance of eliciting a response than I would from an electronic mail message. It might be more convenient to send an email message than a memo and maybe more informal, but again, I think you have to look at who it is you're supposedly wanting to communicate with.

I would see there being less access if this was the only way to communicate [because it's too informal for certain types of contacts]. That's not my experience. Generally, I have found that people that are communicating with me are the same people who might otherwise have called me and we might have played telephone tag for half a day. Instead the message comes through, I get it, read it, and answer it. And then it's over with.

I have not experienced people using it to get to me that the chain of command wouldn't allow them otherwise to talk to me, for example. I haven't had that happen.

I guess my first reaction would be that there would be the normal kind of restraint about sitting down and having a thought and putting it to [the President] as opposed to some of the Deans or someone. You would still be restrained by not wanting to take up the President's time unless you thought it was a somewhat more important matter, than you might to somebody else.

Table 8.1d. Perceptions of Democratization from Electronic Mail Administrative Staff

"Electronic mail is a democratizing medium"	"Electronic mail is *not* a democratizing medium"
I think it would (democratize). I think that a lot of the problems that we have on this campus stem from miscommunication just because of time. You don't have time to get out or to call someone . . . if they could see some of the development and some of the logic, I think it would make a big difference.	It depends on the individual . . . I do think there are individuals who like the idea that they are inaccessible except via some screening process. Those people wouldn't use electronic mail so you couldn't get to them.
I think it does do that. I mean, when you're communicating with a Vice President or someone at a much higher level, it does tend to put you on a more equal footing. I don't know how to account for it psychologically. I think there is an element of that in electronic mail; I think it does have that democratizing tendency.	There are some people who become accessible through email and are a little uncomfortable with it. That is, they like to use it as a means to communicate outward to others, but they really don't want to feel that those individuals can then communicate back to them. There are certain little signals that I think are the result of that. And whether or not those are perceived by the users of email probably depends a great deal on how sensitive the individual is.
It allows you an access you might not have if you used the phone. If you use the phone, you might get a protective secretary who asks who you are and what it is you want, etc. So I think there is a certain element of that.	I think the barriers that exist about someone at a middle level calling up a high level person are just about the same when you're sending the electronic mail.
On the whole I think it at least gives you a feeling that you may be ignored but at least you were able to do it, to say it in ways that you might not have been able to.	I think that's an overstatement . . . when you talk about democracy, you're talking about the value of the input someone makes. Just because you get somebody a forum to talk doesn't mean anybody listens to them, doesn't mean they're

involved in the decision process. They're not casting a vote . . . I mean, a lot of people have a forum per se, giving their opinions, but the decision process has become so sophisticated in adapting to the communication channels which are available to us now, it doesn't necessarily mean that these people have any influence.

Just because somebody says something doesn't mean they have influence or doesn't mean that they have any effect on the outcome. The only thing that happens is that the people who are in the decision making roles at the top fine tune their process to tune out those people . . . so they adjust the decision process. I wouldn't say it democratizes it at all.

It's not that simple because like any form of communication, there are forms of protocols and conventions . . . the premise behind your question is that they no longer exist with electronic mail. Of course they exist; it's just harder to find them out.

The fact that you know the President's "handle" and you can send a memo to the President, doesn't mean it's a good idea. It doesn't mean that it would be wise to start sending [messages] out to the President . . . there are other cases where it opens up new possibilities, but there are lots of pitfalls and lots of limitations and lots of conventions and matters that get established that the unwary can be trapped by.

I find it hard to believe that people would not know who it was they were dealing with, at least in this institution. I read articles that indicate that so-and-so, some low level, is able to get somehow up to a vice president with some ideas that way and I suppose it's someone really more frustrated than bold who figures "why not give it a try."

Then you've got the issue of . . . there are all those levels in between that you have to confront if word gets out that you've not followed the normal process.

Table 8.1e. Perceptions of Democratization from Electronic Mail Clerical and Technical Staff

"Electronic mail is a democratizing medium"	"Electronic mail is *not* a democratizing medium"
The first thought that comes to mind is when these systems are initially set up, I think that is very true as far as bringing everybody onto the same level. Vice presidents go down and clerical assistants come up and they're all people at least initially. And then after the fun wears off, then it seems to go back to where it used to be. Because now the vice presidents are . . . going to have their secretaries do it. I think in that respect the democratization you're talking about may be temporary.	I don't think anybody's empowered by it.
Yes, that's true. I've had cc:'s from people about personal things to the Dean, just because somewhere they had seen my name and I am sure they don't know who I am. "He cc:'d her so it must be important."	I don't know if they're opening up channels.
It's a way to have access to certain people in a less threatening kind of way.	I think we have a problem that's in our society with people who can't afford any kind of computer access being able to communicate in this fashion. So, you have this typical situation of the "haves" and the "have-nots" and if the gap is widened—
I think in some ways it has bridged a gap. Because there are some people by virtue of their rank or whatever you want to call it who would never be approached. Now they are approached and . . . are initially resistant. Now I feel that [they] very much appreciate that and so I think, in some ways, it's very useful in terms of making information flow more easily from stratum to stratum.	I still think you just go through the proper channels, no matter what, even though you could just directly send a memo. I'm thinking of it more in a complaining type of way.
I think it's easier to approach someone you don't know and have no relationship with through electronic mail than through the phone.	I have found, on this campus, that the people are very class concious and my feeling is that "No, it has not." I find that a phone call, if I'm speaking to a Dean as a secretary, I can convey more through a phone call that I can through electronic mail. This university is very class conscious.

I guess in that sense, it breaks down a little bit of a barrier.

I guess when I receive information from the Dean it works: it's like he's sending something directly to me and it's kind of . . . an opening of communication because he's sending it to "K . . ," and not just to "the" department secretary. I would feel more comfortable doing it by email than by calling.

I've always thought that computers, especially microcomputers in general, are democratizing just because they are a powerful form of communication. Pretty much everyone has access to them. I tend to see word processing even more important along those lines because it's a literacy scale of the future.

I'm aware that my written materials, in general, including electronic mail, look more high status than I do in person, but that's partly because my technical skills have always given me the luxury of not caring too much about the impression that my clothing and grooming make.

It has the same democratizing influence that good communication always has. You can be dressed in rags, but if you stand up and address people intelligently, after a while they forget the way you look. Whereas if you stand up in a $400 suit and act like an idiot, people will say "There's an idiot in a $400 suit."

It's democratizing in the effect that it has in situations where I'm at the top of the heap because I do respond to all electronic mail. I could think of specific instances where students, undergrads, who have seen my name on a list of mail users, have sent me messages and in some cases have asked me technical questions and I have responded to those questions because I appreciate getting those questions by mail rather than having somebody grab my sleeve while I'm going through the hall and I suppose for those users, it is then democratizing, in that if a freshman started asking me technical questions in the hallway, I would say "I'm sorry; I don't really have time to deal with it." Whereas, if that freshman is smart enough to send me an electronic mail message, it's partly an intelligence test.

I think it is pretty much true. It is a lot easier to address a mail message to [the President] perhaps and not stand in quite so much awe . . .

unexpected sources. At the same time, they tend to describe their own reluctance to send electronic mail to "unexpected" receivers. Responses tended to be based on personal experience. For example,

> I get messages from secretaries that I probably wouldn't get before and there are even individual faculty who are on e-mail who I get messages from that I might not get otherwise. Some of them might have taken the time to call me and try to reach me by phone or what have you, but I think they find it easier to reach me in this particular fashion. They don't have to go through people to get to me. They know they can get me directly this way.

> I am dealing with more people as a result [of e-mail].

> [The Dean] asked me recently to do something for him and it involved sending a message to [the Vice President]. What I noticed is that I didn't do it through e-mail. There is no reason I couldn't e-mail [the Vice President] but I found myself doing a memo on it. It just somehow rather seemed more appropriate.

In a similar manner, comments for this group respond to the issue of hierarchical level due to the absence of social context cues. Again the results tend to be mixed, with about an equal number of responses indicating perceptions of leveling and responses indicating a lack of perceived leveling. In general, this group tends to perceive democratization as affecting their receiving patterns rather than their sending patterns.

Table 8.1c summarizes responses provided by administrators who participated in this study. These responses also tend to be ambivalent. Administrators tend to base their agreement with the democratization premise on their own personal experiences and usually tend to base their disagreement with the premise on philosophical argument. For example,

> I get electronic mail from people I would not normally get a phone call or letter from on the subordinate level. So they feel much freer to communicate with me electronically, I guess, because it is less intrusive.

> As I think about it, there is some element of truth to that because I get messages from people at all levels and I communicate with them. Whereas, If I didn't have electronic mail, I think a lot of those communications would not occur directly; they would be going through other people.

> I don't agree with either of those notions [of democratization]. Communication, by its very nature, is a prejudicial action and it is both given and received as prejudice. If you don't know the sender or the sender's position, then the prejudice is involved in how you read the words that are being sent. I don't see anything that is democratizing about it. E-mail

automatically attaches an author to the message sent, so there is no anonymity to your ability to reach somebody.

As with the Deans and Associate Deans, administrators tend to perceive
democratization in receiving patterns more than sending patterns.

Table 8.1d summarizes responses made by administrative staff and
most of these comments indicate that these participants do not see
electronic mail as a democratizing medium. For members of this group,
there is much less personalization in their responses, talking about
"democracy" in more abstract terms and talking about others in the
university organization in generalized, collective terms. For example,

> I think it does do that. I mean, when you're communicating with a Vice
> President or someone at a much higher level, it does tend to put you on a
> more equal footing. I don't know how to account for it psychologi-
> cally. . . .

> I think the barriers that exist about someone at a middle level calling up a
> high-level person are just about the same when you're sending electronic
> mail.

> It's not that simple, because like any form of communication, there are
> forms of protocols and conventions . . . the premise behind your question
> is that they no longer exist with electronic mail. Of course they exist; it's
> just harder to find them.

Finally, Table 8.1e summarizes the responses for clerical and technical staff. Most of these responses indicate that these participants do see
electronic mail as democratizing for both receiving patterns and sending
patterns. These participants tend to use both personalized experiences
and general discussions of the concept of democratization as the bases
for their responses.

> Yes, that's true. I've had cc:'s from people about personal things to the
> dean, just because somewhere they had seen my name and I am sure they
> don't know who I am. "He cc:'d her, so it must be important."

> I think it's easier to approach someone you don't know and have no
> relationship with through electronic mail than through the phone.

> I have found, on this campus, that the people are very class conscious and
> my feeling is that, "No, it is not." I find that a phone call, if I'm speaking to
> a dean as a secretary, can convey more than electronic mail. This university
> is very class conscious.

The data analyses presented in Tables 8.1a-1e suggests that perceptions of democratization differ according to participants' positions in the
organizational hierarchy. The only group that consistently indicates

agreement with the democratization premise is clerical and technical staff. Department chairs and administrative staff tend to indicate disagreement with the democratization premise. And the remaining groups indicate both agreement and disagreement with the premise. In general, Deans and Associate Deans and administrators perceive democratization operating on who sends messages to them rather than on to whom they send messages. Clerical and technical staff tend to perceive democratization primarily operating on to whom they send messages with a secondary effect on who sends messages to them. Thus, to whatever extent electronic mail is perceived by users to democratize communication in this university organization, democratization occurs primarily in upward communication. This is consistent with Sproull and Kiesler (1986), who found that electronic mail is described in terms of upward communication rather than downward communication.

The overall perceptions across participants demonstrate ambivalence. To summarize, Deans, Associate Deans, and administrators perceive more effect on receiving than on sending behaviors; clerical and technical staff perceive effect on both receiving and sending behaviors; and Department Chairs and administrative staff perceive little or no effect on both receiving and sending behaviors. Only clerical and technical staff initiate new communication actions with electronic mail, but they do not indicate much empowerment as a result of these actions. Individuals at higher levels of the hierarchy indicate resistance to behaviors consistent with democratization and they do not establish new communication relationships with lower level staff. As one Department Chair stated,

> When . . . was Vice President for . . ., he was an enthusiastic user of electronic mail. And occasionally I would send him messages—it was more an experiment kind of thing: will he respond to this? Well, I either wouldn't get a response or I got a response that was nice but indicated that he really didn't appreciate receiving electronic mail from people two levels below him, that he would really appreciate it if I went through my dean instead.

The general trend suggests that electronic mail has not democratized much of the vertical communication process in this organization.

How Electronic Mail Produces or Inhibits Democratization

The second research question examines the ways participants perceive the medium contributing to or inhibiting democratization. Comments were coded into two major categories that are consistent with the literature reviewed for this study: (a) access, which includes comments that describe the ability or inability to reach another person using electronic mail and/or other media, comments that specifically refer to "*access*," and comments that describe the ability or inability to be reached by other people using electronic mail and/or other media (see Table 8.2a); and (b) *cues*, which includes comments that describe the presence or absence of cues indicating status, authority, or hierarchical relationships between communicators, comments that specifically refer to "status" cues, and comments that describe stylistic differences when using electronic mail compared to other media that participants believed indicated elimination or retention of status, authority, or hierarchical relationships between communicators (see Table 8.2b). Participants' comments were divided into positive and negative positions for each of the two content categories.

For Department Chairs, the majority of comments focus on access, with all but one comment on the negative position. For example,

> I may get annoyed with a Dean in another school but I don't feel that I've got any more access to that person through electronic mail than I do through the telephone or the memo.

> In terms of access, no, not really. I would not send an electronic mail message to someone who was of a higher status than I was unless I knew that they were willing to receive the message . . . that they would be receptive.

> I would be selective who I would send it to.

> if one of our faculty members wants to communicate with the Dean he could either write out a memo or use e-mail and it's the same thing. I don't see people as more accessible or less accessible.

Located at the bottom of the administrative hierarchy for academic functions in the university, electronic mail has not increased their access to the communication process. Based on the principles of democratization, the medium should encourage circumvention of hierarchical filtering structures (Singer, 1986), but electronic mail does not increase diagonal communication (e.g., between a Chair in one school and a Dean in another school) as we might expect. Only three comments focus on social context cues. With such limited data, it is difficult to draw general conclusions about the perceptions of this group regarding hierarchical leveling due to reduced cues. However, users tend to perceive that status and authority cues are reduced with electronic mail, and two participants believe this tends to reduce inequality between communicators.

Deans and Associate Deans also tend to focus on access, and most of their comments reflect increased access due to electronic mail. For example,

Table 8.2a. How Electronic Mail can Contribute to Democratization: Effect of Access to Communication

Hierarchical Level	"Electronic mail is a democratizing medium"	"Electronic mail is *not* a democratizing medium"
Department Chairs	You can feel free—but I would feel free to make a telephone call in that case too.	I don't think that has happened to any great degree. I may get annoyed with a Dean in another school but I don't feel that I've got any more access to that person through electronic mail than I do through the telephone or the memo.
		I don't believe that there is much history of the chairs [in my school] sending increased numbers of messages to the President or the Vice Presidents.
		I think that may be a function of the relatively small number of faculty who actually have easy access to electronic mail. I'm not at all certain just what would happen if all 1000 of them had terminals in their offices and then had access to Deans and Chairs and each other.
		In terms of access, no, not really. I would not send an electronic mail message to someone who was of a higher status than I was unless I knew that they were willing to receive the message . . . that they would be receptive.
		By hooking in cc:'s or copies or broadcasting it to a variety of people who may be on the list, it would communicate information to those poeple I want to get it to, but I don't see it as democratization . . . I would be selective who I would send it to.
		Well since I see email as simply a quicker form of memos, then it doesn't seem to. It seems to me that if one of our faculty members wants to communicate with the Dean he could either write out a memo or use email and it's the same thing. I don't see people as more accessible or less accessible.

Deans and Associate Deans	I get messages from secretaries that I probably wouldn't get before and there are even individual faculty who are on email who I get messages from that I might not get otherwise. Some of them might have taken the time to call me and try to reach me by phone or what have you, but I think they find it easier to reach me in this particular fashion. They don't have to go through people to get to me. They know they can get me directly this way. But I think it makes friends. I think perhaps my department secretaries feel a little closer to me because I send them messages from time to time. Sometimes amusing, sometimes to encourage them or whatever. I think it might be good, because a lot of people hear rumors and they're not likely to phone and say that. But if they could just hit it out on the email and say "I heard such-and-such, is it true?"—they're a little bit more anonymous when they do it. They're not anonymous because they have an account, but it's a little different than phoning a person and hearing "Why are you bothering me with that?" They're worried about getting that kind of thing. I think they might do it with electronic mail.	I would not send an email message to [the Vice President], for example, except under extraordinary circumstances . . . So, in all my communications, I worry about the level of bothering them and making sure I'm communicating with the right person in sort of the right form. So, I don't think it has democratized much of what I do, particularly.
Administrators	I certainly get electronic mail from people I would not normally either get a phone call from—and this is on a subordinate level—or certainly not get a letter from. So they feel much freer to communicate with me electronically, I guess, because it is less intrusive. But yes, I would write [the Vice President]. I wouldn't write the President, although I have written the President [but] I know his secretary picks it up.	It's democratic in principle, but in practice, not everyone shares the resources.

Table 8.2a. Continued

Hierarchical Level	"Electronic mail is a democratizing medium"	"Electronic mail is *not* a democratizing medium"
		Another nondemocratic aspect of it is [regular] users . . . have an inside track. The users who know that such-and-such administrators who use email can reach that individual with messages that the [nomuser] has to go and meet with them and get an appointment. And it may be that the issue goes away or whatever by the time that appointment comes along or they can't get an audience on a timely basis.
		I don't think access would change because you still have the means of communicating in writing. In fact, I have more confidence that a written memo to someone in the administration from the faculty would maybe have a better chance of eliciting a response than I would from an electronic mail message.
		I would see there being less access if this was the only way to communicate [because it's too informal for certain types of contacts].
	As I think about it, I think there is some element of truth to that because I get messages from people at all levels and I communicate with them. Whereas, if I didn't have electronic mail, I think a lot of those communications would not occur directly; they would be going through other people.	
	I think it creates a more informal, relaxed feeling about communication and it opens up channels that never were opened up before. If you feel free to sit down and send out a mail message to every employee saying "Here's an idea," and those people feel free, regardless of their level, to say, "It stinks."	
		That's not my experience. Generally, I have found that people are communicating with me are the same people who might otherwise have called me and we might have played telephone tag for half a day. Instead the message comes through, I get it, read it, and answer it. And then it's over with.
		I guess my first reaction would be that there would be the normal kind of restraint about sitting down and having a thought and putting it to [the President] as

opposed to some of the Deans or someone. You would still be restrained by not wanting to take up the President's time unless you thought it was a somewhat more important matter, than you might to somebody else.

It depends on the individual . . . I do think there are individuals who like the idea that they are inaccessible except via some screening process. Those people wouldn't use electronic mail so you couldn't get to them.

There are some people who become accessible through email and are a little uncomfortable with it. That is, they like to use it as a means to communicate outward to others, but they really don't want to feel that those individuals can then communicate back to them. There are certain little signals that I think are the result of that. And whether or not those are perceived by the users of email probably depends a great deal on how sensitive the individual is.

I think that's an overstatement . . . when you talk about democracy, you're talking about the value of the input someone makes. Just because you get somebody a forum to talk doesn't mean anybody listens to them, doesn't mean they're involved in the decision process. They're not casting a vote . . . I mean, a lot of people have a forum per se, giving their opinions, but the decision process has become so sophistiated in adapting to the communication channels which are available to us now, it doesn't necessarily mean that these people have any influence.

Administrative Staff

I think it would [democratize]. I think that a lot of the problems that we have on this campus stem from miscommunication just because of time. You don't have time to get out or to call someone . . . if they could see some of the development and some of the logic, I think it would make a big difference.

It allows you an access you might not have if you used the phone. If you use the phone, you might get a protective secretary who asks you who you are and what it is you want, etc. So I think there is a certain element of that.

On the whole I think it at least gives you a feeling that you may be ignored but at least you were able to do it, to say it in ways that you might not have been able to.

Table 8.2a. Continued

Hierarchical Level	"Electronic mail is a democratizing medium"	"Electronic mail is *not* a democratizing medium"
		Just because somebody says something doesn't mean they have influence or doesn't mean that they have any effect on the outcome. The only thing that happens is that the people who are in the decision making roles at the top fine tune their process to tune out those people . . . so they adjust the decision process. I wouldn't say it democratizes it at all.
		I read articles that indicate that so-and-so, some low level, is able to get somehow up to a vice president with some ideas that way and I suppose it's someone really more frustrated than bold who figures "why not give it a try."
Clerical and Technical Staff	The first thought that comes to mind is when these systems are initially set up, I think that is very true as far as bringing everybody onto the same level. Vice presidents go down and clerical assistants come up and they're all people at least initially. And then after the fun wears off, then it seems to go back to where it used to be. Because now the vice presidents are . . . going to have their secretaries do it. I think in that respect the democratization you talk about may be temporary.	I don't know if they're opening up channels.
	Yes, that's true. I've had cc:'s from people about personal things to the Dean, just because somewhere they had seen my name and I am sure they don't know who I am. "He cc:'d her so it must be important."	I think we have a problem that's in our society with people who can't afford any kind of computer access being able to communicate in this fashion. So, if you have this typical situation of the "haves" and the "have-nots" and if the gap is widened—
	It's a way to have access to certain people in a less threatening kind of way.	

I think in some ways it has bridged a gap. Because there are some people by virtue of their rank or whatever you want to call it who would never be approached. Now they are approached and . . . are initially resistant. Now I feel that [they] very much appreciate that and so I think, in some ways, it's very useful in terms of making information flow more easily from stratum to stratum.

I think it's easier to approach someone you don't know and have no relationship with through electronic mail than through the phone.

I guess in that sense, it breaks down a little bit of a barrier.

I've always thought that computers, especially microcomputers in general, are democratizing just because they are a powerful form of communication. Pretty much everyone has access to them. I tend to see word processing even more important along those lines because it's a literacy scale of the future.

It's democratizing in the effect that it has in situations where I'm at the top of the heap because I do respond to all electronic mail. I could think of specific instances where students, undergrads, who have seen my name on a list of mail users, have sent me messages and in some cases have asked me technical questions and I have responded to those questions because I appreciate getting those questions by mail rather than having somebody grab my sleeve while I'm going through the hall and I suppose for those users, it is then democratizing, in that if a freshman started asking me technical questions in the hallway, I would say "I'm sorry; I don't really have time to deal with it." Whereas, if that freshman is smart enough to send me an electronic mail message, it's partly an intelligence test.

Table 8.2b. How Electronic Mail can Contribute to Democratization: Effects of Reduced Social Cues

Hierarchical Level	"Electronic mail is a democratizing medium"	"Electronic mail is *not* a democratizing medium"
Department Chairs	Certainly in terms of the way people address each other, I think there is probably a more equalizing kind of thing, because the person who sends the message has the power at that particular point in time. And so as a result, there is not as much difference on electronic mail as there is in person or on the telephone. Once in a while I'll get a message from [the Vice President] and a person looking at that message can't tell anything about the relative importance of him versus me. It just says [VPRES] and it is [DEPTCHAIR] on plain white paper. Whereas with memos: you're right; that's interesting. If you get something from [the President], it has gold letterhead, embossed seals and all of that. . . . When you send a memo, you are very conscious of differences in status.	I think I probably have the same level of anxiety about receiving an electronic mail message from [the Vice President] as I do receiving a written memo from him. So I don't think the democratizing scenario has put itself in place.
Deans and Associate Deans	When you send a message on email, you are sending to a particular handle. There are no titles. Whereas, when you write a memo which is formally typed, you always put in the person's title and you always put in your title. So, from what you are saying, that to me is a potential form of democratization, just in the vanishing of the titles.	I don't go along with that. First of all, if there is a significant difference in status between two people, one of them won't feel all that free to send an email to the other. If the person does, there probably will be involved in that email the formalities necessary to maintain the distance that does, in fact, exist. There aren't any titles, but you still know who people are. I guess my immediate reaction would be to say no. It might appear to hide status differences but I couldn't imagine a departmental secretary addressing [the President] or [the Vice President]. I also think that if

202

they did, they would get some static from the other end. I don't think the medium diminishes real status differences that exist.

Email automatically attaches an author to a message sent, so there is no anonymity to your ability to reach somebody . . . whatever democratization there may be in it I think is very superficial and very shortlived.

Mail that I receive—people know who they're sending it to.

Administrators

I would state that that is true, because the protocol is for addressing the individual—it doesn't necessarily require [titling] the individual . . . it doesn't have to say "President . . ." on it and with a formal heading that you have in a memo. All the formality is stripped away and it's just "XXXXXXX".

It's hard to believe that something electronic can be humanizing but I think it strips away the formalities of the person's position and you're now focusing on communication with the individual for the purpose that you have in mind. It is not unlike the same kind of thing that would happen if you know them personally and you were good friends and you were talking over the fence, except that it is a written communication.

I received a mail message from a higher-up administrator on the campus, the first mail message I had ever received from this individual. And because there is no spelling checker, there were three or four spelling errors, and there were three or four syntax errors which would not have been acceptable to that administrator under any circumstances . . . it's okay. That was the only case that I can ever think of where it democratized.

I wonder if [she] had written a formal memo or if she had written this other person a formal memo with traditional cc:'s on it, if she would have felt as comfortable copying me without copying her immediate supervisor.

Table 8.2b. Continued

Hierarchical Level	"Electronic mail is a democratizing medium"	"Electronic mail is *not* a democratizing medium"
Administrative Staff	I think it does do that. I mean, when you're communicating with a Vice President or someone at a much higher level, it does tend to put you on a more equal footing. I don't know how to account for it psychologically. I think there is an element of that in electronic mail; I think it does have that democratizing tendency.	It's not that simple because like any form of communication, there are forms of protocol and conventions . . . the premise behind your question is that they no longer exist with electronic mail. Of course they exist; it's just harder to find them out. I find it hard to believe that people would not know who it was they were dealing with, at least in this institution.
Clerical and Technical Staff	I guess when I receive information from the Dean it works: it's like he's sending something directly to me and it's kind of . . . an opening of communication because he is sending it to "K . . ." and not just to "the" department secretary. I'm aware that my written materials, in general, including electronic mail, look more high status than I do in person, but that's partly because my technical skills have always given me the luxury of not caring too much about the impression that my clothing and grooming make. It has the same democratizing influence that good communication always has. You can be dressed in rags, but if you stand up and address people intelligently, after a while they forget the way you look. Whereas if you stand up in a $400 suit and act like an idiot, people will say "There's an idiot in a $400 suit."	

I get messages from secretaries that I probably wouldn't get before and there are even individual faculty who are on email who get messages from that I might not get otherwise. . . . They don't have to go through people to get to me.

I am dealing with more people as a result [of e-mail].

I think it might be good, because a lot of people hear rumors and they're not likely to phone and say that . . . I think they might do it with electronic mail.

Hierarchically located between individual academic departments reporting to them and upper administration to whom they report and with whom they negotiate on behalf of their departments, they tend to depend on access to communication to perform their jobs. In general, middle-management positions in this university tend to be very sensitive to hierarchical differentiations, so we would not expect this group to perceive much leveling. The comments about reduced cues from this group tend to support this premise.

Comments regarding access from the administrators group tend to argue against democratization. For example,

Generally, I have found that people that are communicating with me are the same people who might otherwise have called me and we might have played telephone tag for half a day. Instead the message comes through, I get it, read it, and answer it. And then it's over.

It's democratic in principle, but in practice, not everyone shares the resource. On the other hand, comments regarding cues tend to argue in favor of democratization. Though perceiving some degree of hierarchical leveling from reduced social cues, this group is concerned that such leveling may be problematic. For example,

I wonder if [she] had written . . . this other person a formal memo with traditional cc:'s on it, if she would have felt as comfortable copying me without copying her immediate supervisor.

Administrative staff also tend to focus their comments on access and to argue against democratization from this position. They take issue with "access to communication" as compared to "access to decision making." For example,

Just because you get somebody a forum to talk doesn't mean anybody listens to them, doesn't mean they're involved in the decision process . . .

Just because somebody says something doesn't mean they have influence or doesn't mean that they have any effect on the outcome . . .

Even one comment that argues in favor of democratization through increased access presents the same point:

> On the whole, I think it gives you a feeling that you may be ignored but at least you were able to do it, to say it in ways that you might not have been able to.

Like Deans and Associate Deans, administrative staff are hierarchically located in the middle but on the staff side, between their own subordinates and the administrators to whom they report. For this group, democratization tends to be defined more in terms of vertical access than horizontal access and little or no democratization is perceived.

Clerical and technical staff comment most frequently on the increased access they derive from using electronic mail:

> It's a way to have access to certain people in a less threatening kind of way.

> I think in some ways it has bridged a gap. Because there are some people by virtue of their rank, or whatever you want to call it, who would never be approached. Now they are approached . . . it's very useful in terms of making information flow more easily from stratum to stratum.

> I think it's easier to approach someone you don't know and have no relationship with through electronic mail than through the phone.

> . . . it breaks down a little bit of a barrier.

Similarly, they suggest that the decreased number of social cues makes them feel more equal to communicators elsewhere in the organization. In fact, all of the comments discussed cues as contributing to democratization:

> . . . . it's like he's sending something directly to me . . . because he's sending it to "K . . . " and not just to "the" department secretary.

> I'm aware that my written materials, in general, including electronic mail, look more high status than I do in person.

When categories of comments are collapsed across hierarchical positions, the majority of the comments emphasize access. Twenty of the access comments support democratization, and 21 do not, so participants are evenly divided on the issue of electronic mail increasing users' access to the communication process. In general, participants agree that certain social cues are eliminated on electronic mail but they tend to disagree on the effect this produces. Examination of comments that could not be categorized as either access or cues may provide some insight on this.

Two general groups of participants' responses could not be classified in terms of access or cues: (a) comments that indicated users do not perceive much difference between electronic mail and other media, and (b) comments that reflected users' concerns with political and/or hierarchical norms. It is this second group of responses that may be more important for understanding participants' perceptions of democratization in this organization. Without reference to hierarchical position, here are the comments reflecting this issue:

> I think we're just too politically sensitive about putting our concerns out in the open through electronic mail.

> It would not be, from the point of view of the department, necessarily politically expedient to let everybody know what's going on in a particular area. Not that we have a lot of stuff to hide, but I could envision where it would be a problem.

> I guess there's a political process no matter where you work in the university.

> I still think you just go through the proper channels, no matter what, even though you could just directly send a memo.

> I have found, on this campus, that the people are very class conscious.

> There are all those levels in between that you have to confront if word gets out that you've not followed the normal process.

> The fact that you know the President's "handle" and you can send a memo to the president doesn't mean it's a good idea . . . There are lots of pitfalls and lots of limitations and lots of conventions and matters that get established that the unwary can be trapped by.

> I think the barriers that exist about someone at a middle level calling on a high-level person are just about the same when you're sending them electronic mail.

> It might be more convenient to send an e-mail message than a memo and maybe more informal, but again, I think you have to look at who it is you're supposedly wanting to communicate with.

> There are just people who I know use it who I would never send a message to unless I was invited to do so. I would always use another medium to reach those people.

> I would no more call up [the President] on the telephone than probably send him an Email. . . . So I still keep that same set of distances.

These comments reflect both a concern for political norms and rules and resistance to violating them. Several additional references to political norms and rules can be gleaned from comments previously coded into Tables 8.2a and 8.2b:

... he really didn't appreciate receiving electronic mail from people two levels below him, that he would really appreciate it if I went through my Dean instead.

I couldn't imagine a department secretary addressing [the President] or [the Vice President]. I also think that if they did, they would get some static from the other end.

I do think there are individuals who like the idea that they are inaccessible except via some screening process.

... they like to use it as a means to communicate outward to others, but they really don't want to feel that those individuals can then communicate back to him.

... there are forms of protocols and conventions ... the premise behind your question is that they no longer exist with electronic mail. Of course they exist; it's just harder to find them.

All of these comments present rationalizations against democratization, both for specific individual user behaviors and for the general premise of democratizing the organizational communication process in general. Approximately one-third of the participants in this study, in all hierarchical categories, specifically mention these norms and rules and reaffirm their importance in the communication process. A few suggest they do not like these norms and rules, a few suggest they favor them, and most suggest a neutral acceptance of them as an element of social structure.

These norms and rules are social constructions that constrain opportunities to communicate in this organization, dictating who can interact with whom and about what they can interact. In general, participants present these norms and rules as if they were natural laws that all of them know and accept as given. The effect of the medium on norms and rules may be mitigated by the organizational culture. Singer (1986) suggested that open communication that bypasses hierarchical channels can change the symbols used to maintain the social order, but others argue that new rules and norms emerge (Hiemstra, 1986; Kiesler, Siegel, & McGuire, 1984). Sproull and Kiesler (1986) suggest that superiors tend to desire status cues when communicating with subordinates and we can expect that they will develop ways to reestablish such cues. Subordinates tend to take advantage of the absence of cues when communicating with superiors, but that may not translate into effective impact on organizational processes.

In order to democratize participation, administrators and organizational members need to consider these social constructions that reinforce hierarchical order (Deetz, 1985). Electronic mail, or any medium of communication, appears to be an ineffective tool for democratization unless the organizational culture is supportive. Participants at all levels tend to describe a culture that counteracts the democratization potential for electronic mail.

CONCLUSION

The general theoretical statements of democratization focus on three major premises. First, new organizational media, such as electronic mail, will change social interaction fundamentally so that social organization as we know it will break down and, in turn, authority structures based on this social organization will dissolve (Singer, 1986). Second, the meaning of social organization is based on the "hierarchical structure of communication and authority" (Boulding, 1971, p. 27), and any change in the configuration of communication channels will change social authority. New organizational media are expected to do precisely that. And third, social stratification (which is important to social organization as we have come to know it) is communicated and maintained by both the content and form of messages (Singer, 1986). Reduced social cues change the meta-information that conveys and reinforces social order. Democratization occurs because traditional social order breaks down, the communication process opens across traditional barriers, and voices become more equal (Kochen, 1981). The results of this study can be examined in relation to these premises.

There is evidence across several hierarchical levels that social interaction has changed with electronic mail: Deans and Associate Deans believe more people and different people have access to them with electronic mail compared to other media; many administrators believe their receiving patterns have changed; clerical and technical staff believe that both sending and receiving patterns have changed with electronic mail. The real question revolves around whether this change is fundamental or superficial. Kochen (1981) predicts fundamental change with the removal of barriers based on status, authority, distance, and power, with improvement in the quality of interaction and equality across organizational members. These results argue to the contrary: one-third of the respondents specifically reiterate traditional norms of status and political power in their comments; most Department Chairs describe personal experiences contradictory to reduce barriers; and administrators, Deans, and Associate Deans describe changes in receiving patterns but not in sending patterns; which argues against equality. These results support predominantly superficial changes in social interaction: Electronic mail is more efficient than telephoning because users avoid "telephone tag"; access can be more direct than other media because some hierarchical filters (e.g., secretaries) may be avoided; the quantity of interaction may increase though not necessarily the quality. In fact, many users describe similar interaction patterns for electronic mail and other media (e.g., memos, telephone).

Albertson (1977) argues that traditional structural barriers and boundaries will dissolve. These results show limited support for his position. Diagonal communication does not appear to increase with electronic mail. Most users describe reluctance to circumvent traditional hierarchical channels. The exception lies with clerical and technical staff who perceive electronic mail as bridging hierarchical gaps and overcoming some traditional barriers; they describe sending messages to people they would not telephone. These appear to be superficial changes that provide staff at the bottom of the hierarchy with perceptions of democratic participation, even if they do not perceive a high degree of empowerment.

There is a little evidence in these results that the addition of electronic mail to the configuration of more traditional communication channels has changed social authority (Singer, 1986). As several respondents suggest, the traditional rules that confirm authority relationships exist with electronic mail, even if they are harder to see. As one respondent says:

> Just because somebody says something doesn't mean they have influence or doesn't mean that they have any effect on the outcome. The only thing that happens is that the people who are in the decision-making roles at the top fine tune their process to tune out those people . . . so they adjust the decision process. I wouldn't say it democratizes at all.

Ultimately, democratization may have more to do with who has what information and the effect of channel usage on which people will have access to that information. This may be fundamentally different from Laudon's (1977) ideas about democratization through participation.

There is considerable evidence that electronic mail reduces social cues that reinforce consensus about social order (Deetz, 1985). Steklasa (1977) describes increased informality in communication style with computer-mediated communication; these respondents perceive increased informality. Kiesler et al. (1984) describe fewer cues reinforcing status and prestige; these respondents describe omitting titles and ranks, elimination of distinctive letterheads, and leveling of individual differences because all electronic mail messages look alike. Sproull and Kiesler (1986) suggest that communication is more anonymous on electronic mail; these respondents specifically deny anonymity because the system automatically attaches the sender's "handle" to each message. Lack of anonymity may mediate other communication behaviors expected to emerge because of reduced social context cues, such as antisocial behavior and ignoring social conventions (Siegel et al., 1984), and more self-centered behavior and less regulated communication behaviors (Sproull & Kiesler, 1986). The present results partially support the premise that changes in meta-information contribute to democratization. However, there is ample evidence that new social cues emerge to replace those lost to the medium and these cues may not fundamentally change the meta-information.

The general theoretical statements of democratization seem to oversimplify the relationship between new organizational media and fundamental change in the social order. This theory assumes extensive change in social structure without describing how that change will occur and how resistance to that change will be overcome. The theory assumes that the communication technology will operate to change the social structure. But the theory ignores the attempts by the social structure to change the technology. Generally, those in power tend to develop mechanisms to reduce the impacts of changes that threaten their interests or to accommodate those changes into the existing structure (Deetz, 1986).

Oversimplification is exacerbated by basic definitional problems. The conceptual definition of democratization is much more complex than the operational definition. To consider access without reference to content and without assessing the impact of content equates "revolutionizing the social structure" with "opportunity to communicate." As social structure evolves out of interactions among organizational members, democratization may not arise until the medium is used to communicate about social structure, until language is used to redefine social reality. There is little evidence that this is occurring.

The results of this study argue strongly for additional research into the relationship between democratic communication processes and communication media. Clearly, the results argue against a simple causal relationship whereby a particular medium can cause democratization to occur. On the other hand, these results do not argue against the potential contribution of this medium to democratization. Finally, these results highlight the complexity of the relationship and provide some indicators of factors that contribute to that complexity.

REFERENCES

Albertson, L. A. (1977). Telecommunications as a travel substitute: Some psychological, organizational and social aspects. *Journal of Communication, 27*(2), 32–43.

Becker, J., Hedebro, G., & Paldan, L. (1986). *Communication and domination.* Norwood, NJ: Ablex.

Boulding, K. E. (1971). *The image.* Ann Arbor: University of Michigan Press.

Deetz, S. (1985). Critical-cultural research: New sensibilities and old reality. *Journal of Management, 11*, 121–136.

Deetz, S. (1986). Metaphors and the discursive production and reproduction of organization. In L. Thayer (Ed.), *Organization-communication: Emerging perspectives* (Vol. I, pp. 168–182). Norwood, NJ: Ablex.

Duncan, H. D. (1967). The search for a social theory of communication. In F. E. X. Dance (Ed.), *Human communication theory*. New York: Holt, Rinehart, & Winston.

Grande, S. (1980). Aspects of pre-literate culture shared by on-line searching and videotext. *The Canadian Journal of Information Science, 5,* 125–131.

Guillaume, J. (1980). Computer conferencing and the development of an electronic journal. *The Canadian Journal of Information Science, 5,* 21–29.

Hiemstra, G. E. (1986). The electronic organization: Communicating and organizing in a new age. In L. Thayer (Ed.), *Organization-communication: Emerging perspectives* (Vol. I, pp. 196–220). Norwood, NJ: Ablex.

Hiltz, S. R. (1976). *Computer conferencing: Assessing the social impact of a new communication medium.* Paper presented to the American Sociological Association, New York.

Holt, J. L. (1969). Cheap communications. *The Futurist, 3,* 25.

Johansen, R., & DeGrasse, R. (1979). Computer-based teleconferencing: Effects on working patterns. *Journal of Communication, 29*(3), 30–41.

Kiesler, S., Siegel, J., & McGuire, T. W. (1984). Social psychological aspects of computer mediated communication. *American Psychologist, 39,* 1123–1234.

Kochen, M. (1981, March). Technology and communication in the future. *Journal of the American Society for Information Science,* pp. 148–157.

Laudon, K. C. (1977). *Communications technology and democratic participation.* New York: Praeger.

Leduc, N. F. (1979). Communication through computers. *Telecommunications Policy, 3,* 235–244.

Miles, M. B., & Huberman, A. M. (1984). *Qualitative data analysis: Sourcebook of new methods,* Beverly Hills, CA: Sage.

Rice, R. E., & Case, D. (1983). Electronic message systems in the university: A description of use and utility. *Journal of Communication, 33,* 131–152.

Siegel, J., Dubrovsky, V., Kiesler, S., & McGuire, T. W. (1986). Group processes in computer-mediated communication. *Organizational Behavior and Human Decision Processes, 37,* 157–187.

Singer, B. D. (1986). Organizational communication and social disassembly: An essay on electronic anomie. In L. Thayer (Ed.), *Organization-communication: Emerging perspectives* (Vol. I, pp. 221–230). Norwood, NJ: Ablex.

Slack, J. D. (1984). *Communication technologies and society: Conceptions of causality and the politics of technological intervention.* Norwood, NJ: Ablex.

Sproull, L., & Kiesler, S. (1986). Reducing social context cues: Electronic mail in organizational communication. *Management Science, 32,* 1492–1512.

Steklasa, R. (1977, Fall). Automation will boost office productivity but what will happen to jobs. *The Financial Post Magazine,* pp. 4–5.

Taylor, J. R. (1981). The office of the future: Weber and Innis revisited. *The Canadian Communications Quarterly, 8,* 4–13.

Taylor, J. R. (1986). New communication technologies and the emergence of distributed organizations: Looking beyond 1984. In L. Thayer (Ed.), *Organization-communication: Emerging perspectives* (Vol. I, pp. 231–273). Norwood, NJ: Ablex.

9

A Model of Mentoring and Other Power-Gaining Communication Strategies and Career Success

Susan E. Kogler Hill
Margaret Hilton Bahniuk
Jean Dobos

INTRODUCTION

Organizational power, politics, and persuasion are increasingly becoming the focus of organizational communication theory and research. Recent texts in the field discuss the political or strategic perspectives of organizational communication (Conrad, 1985; Frank & Brownell, 1989; Frost, 1987). There have been various definitions of organizational power. These definitions include: "the ability to mobilize resources . . . to achieve a person's work goals" (Kanter, 1977, p. 48); "the capacity to effect (or affect) organizational outcomes" (Mintzberg, 1983, p. 4); "the ability to achieve one's goals without interference from others" (Fairhurst & Snavely, 1983, p. 293); and "a neutral force which can yield positive or negative outcomes depending on how it is used" (Frank & Brownell, 1989, p. 409). Communication strategy is one element in obtaining organizational power.

The purpose of this chapter is to develop a model that focuses on communication strategies and how these strategies enhance an individual's power at work and career success. This power-gaining model includes two sets of predisposing factors that might influence a person's career success: individual factors and organizational factors. In addition to these predisposing factors, the model includes two sets of communication strategies: (a) those strategies concerned with connection power, and (b) those communication strategies concerned with information power.

In the model, the predisposing factors plus the communication strategies equal career success. This is the broad outline of the model; the various parts will be discussed in the chapter. The first part of the chapter is devoted to showing the basis on which this model was developed. To understand our model, it is necessary to understand the relationship between communication and power in an organization. If communication strategies facilitate a person's success and these strategies can be learned, then women and men can take more control of their jobs and careers; that is, attain organizational power.

Necessity of Organizational Power

Power and politics are seen as necessary facts of organizational life. Organizational members who become adept at using power effectively are more likely to perform effectively and to attain their own and their work group's goals than members who cannot use power effectively (Frank & Brownell, 1989). Organizations are designed as political structures with power dispersed across levels and roles in a superordinate structure. This formal structure only provides the legitimizing basis for the exercise of power. Farley (1986) suggests that power actually resides in the individuals and their interactions and not in the formal organization. Some individuals avoid the formal organizational rules and lines of authority in seeking power. Politics are necessary to correct the inefficiencies, problems, and inflexibility of the formal systems of influence (Mintzberg, 1983).

Dimensions of Organizational Power

Complete discussions of power in organizations exist elsewhere (Farley, 1986; Frank & Brownell, 1989; Frost, 1987; Goldberg, Cavenaugh, & Larson, 1983; Mintzberg, 1983; Pfeffer, 1981). Most reviews present classifications or topologies indicating the common dimensions, sources, or bases of power. French and Raven (1959) presented a now classical model of social power containing five types of power: reward, coercive, legitimate, referent, and expert. Later, Raven (1965) added a sixth type—information power (the possession of or access to important information). More recently, Hershey, Blanchard, and Natemeyer (1979) added a seventh type of power—connection power (links or ties to important or influential people). These communicative dimensions of power appear in other models of power as well.

Mintzberg (1983) discusses five bases of power: resources, technical skill, knowledge, legal prerogative, and access to those who have the first four. Although the conceptual labels are different, Mintzberg essentially is talking about the same powers as French and Raven. Knowledge is very similar to information power and access is similar to connection power. Both information and connection power are important informal, communicative aspects of organizational power and are the focus of the present model. Other bases of power typically come later in a person's career development, and the power gained from them resides mostly in that person's formal hierarchical position (i.e., because of one's superordinate position one has legitimate power, reward power, and coercive power). One can increase referent power by gaining respect, being visible, and speaking about values and ethics (Frank & Brownell, 1989). One can also increase expert power by increasing visibility and being very selective in tasks and assignments (Conrad, 1985; Kotter, 1979). However, we focus on communication strategies and tactics to gain information and connection power.

An individual needs not only to have a particular power base but to develop and use the base of power. Much of the power literature views an individual's efforts and actions to become an "influencer" as game playing, tactics, or strategies (Frost, 1987; Kanter, 1977; Mintzberg, 1983; Schilit & Locke, 1982). The game-playing literature advocates tactics that can increase an organizational member's influence and power (e.g., mentoring, coalition formation, etc). The literature which focuses on tactics and game playing strongly suggests a relationship between communication and power.

THE RELATIONSHIP OF ORGANIZATIONAL POWER TO COMMUNICATION STRATEGIES

Some organizational members are more likely to want power and to communicate in ways to develop that power. "Those with a need and willingness to use power are likely to use communication more consciously than others as a means to get what they want, to gain control over situations. Their communication behavior will likely emphasize conscious influence strategies" (Frost, 1987, p. 515). The exercise of power requires communication and such communication might well be the most important factor in determining one's power (Richmond, Davis, Saylor, & McCroskey, 1984).

Reviews of organizational game playing, strategies, and tactics exist elsewhere, and some focus more directly than others on communication strategies (Kanter, 1977; Kipnis, Schmidt, & Wilkinson, 1980; Pfeffer, 1981; Schilit & Locke, 1982). Farley (1986) reviews the literature on the power game in organizations and concludes: "All of the game playing and suggestions for the use of tactics or strategies to attain a position of power imply the use of communication. Without communication, there would be no organization and no reason to seek power" (Farley, 1986, p. 57). In Mintzberg's (1985) discussion of political games, he lists three which are related directly to communication strategies: (a) sponsorship —a subordinate or junior professional building a power base with a superior or senior (a type of mentoring relationship), (b) alliance building—line managers building a power base with peers (another mentoring-type relationship), and (c) expertise—staff building a power base with real or feigned knowledge and skills. Frost (1987) provides a classification system of organizational games and game playing. Of particular interest to communication scholars are Frost's individual games. These games are carried out between individuals and groups to gain organizational "context." "Being able to have one's actions viewed in an appropriate context, enables actors to merge self-interests with their organizational work. Absence of such a context reduces their power in the organization" (Frost, 1987, pp. 528–530). The focus of these individual games are sponsorship, mentoring, making it, empire building, lording, and upward influence.

In addition to offering specific strategies for exerting upward, horizontal, and downward power, Frank and Brownell (1989, pp. 423–425) also offer four general strategies for gaining power: (a) rational strategies—logically presenting ideas and gaining access to important information (b) dependency strategies—controlling information or resources that others need (c) assertive strategies—overt strategies to be used only from an established power base, and (d) friendliness strategies —developing warm, supportive relations with others.

Most of these classification systems of strategies focus on the importance of information access and adequacy and relational connections with others in the organization. Our model of power-gaining communication strategies and career success incorporates the communication behaviors used to develop these two bases of social power in the organization. A conceptual elaboration follows.

Information Power

Uncertainty reduction theory asserts that through communication people are able to gain information which allows them to reduce ambiguity and make better predictions and therefore better control their environment (Falcione & Wilson, 1988, p. 156). People who can reduce the most uncertainty are likely to become the most powerful, especially if the information is scarce, essential, and irreplaceable (Frank & Brownell, 1989). "Coping with uncertainty has been shown to confer power and status on organizational units" (Poole, 1978, p. 503).

Two major communication variables have been frequently associated with such information power: (a) information adequacy, and (b) access to the dominant coalition.

Information Adequacy. Employees who send and receive adequate amounts of information can better manage the uncertainty around them. Such individuals are better able to defend and advocate their own points of view, to shape the image others have of them and their ability to perform, to make better decisions, and to avoid making mistakes based on insufficient information.

Employees who receive adequate amounts of information have higher organizational influence and greater satisfaction with organizational relationships (Spiker & Daniels, 1981). Receiving adequacy has also been related to superior–subordinate satisfaction and organizational involvement. Sending and receiving adequate amounts of information have also been found to relate to various indices of academic success—perceptions of success, job satisfaction, increased income and promotions (Hill, Bahniuk, & Dobos, 1989b).

Access to the Dominant Coalition. The dominant coalition of an organization is that group of individuals who occupy the top decision-making level of the organization regardless of status levels. Individuals who have access to this top group will have greater power because they will have access to more information and more key influential people. Moreover, in a recent study comparing the interaction patterns of men and women, Brass (1985) found that men and women formed gender specific informal networks. The women were less central to the men's networks, and women did not have access to the dominant coalition. Those who had access to this dominant coalition were seen as more influential and more promotable. Several mentoring studies have found that having a female mentor does not facilitate career success to the same extent as having a male mentor (Noe, 1988). Perhaps male mentors provide a more direct access or link to the dominant male network of the organization. Access to this dominant coalition is not a personal relationship or connection in the same sense as a peer or a mentor relationship might be. Network position, personal contacts, and direct accessibility all contribute to whether an employee has access to the top power structure and the information held therein.

Connection Power

Relationships have been found to encourage professional socialization, career development, and career success. Such socializing relationships include past agents (parents, teachers), current nonprofessional relationships (spouses and children), and professional relationships (mentors, sponsors, and peers) (Watkins, 1986). Much attention has been focused on professional relationships and how they can aid in career development, offer support, and increase an individual's power base. These relationships provide excellent information for understanding the organization and reducing uncertainty (Falcione & Wilson, 1988, p. 157). These alliances are typically sought out by less powerful organizational members. Since these members do not have power themselves, they increase their chances of accomplishing their goals by aligning with more powerful organizational members (Pfeffer, 1981).

In summary, numerous types of connections are linked to the gaining of organizational power. "Connections as a source of power seem to lie at the core of the political perspective" (Frank & Brownell, 1989, p. 418). Kanter (1977) suggests that political alliances or close contact with powerful others is a source of connection power. Mentoring relationships are one route to establishing close contact with others.

Mentoring-type Connections. Mentors have been frequently seen as the most important organizational connection or relationship, particularly for career success. A mentor is a more senior colleague who takes a paternalistic interest in a more junior colleague's or protege's career development. Mentors enhance the protege's chances of success by bypassing the hierarchy (Willbur, 1987). These mentoring relationships advance the protege's career development by influencing the "power center" in the organization (Daniels & Logan, 1983). Mentors and sponsors increase one's power and have a positive impact on career development and professional success (Watkins, 1986). Mentors and mentoring relationships have been the focus of much research and theoretical speculation (Hall & Sandler, 1983; Hill et al., 1989b; Hunt & Michael, 1983; Merriam, 1983; Noe, 1988). These studies conclude that mentoring facilitates one's career success. Employees who have mentors are more promotable, have stricter adherence to career plans, have increased performance, have greater upward mobility, have higher earnings, have greater job satisfaction, see themselves as successful, and are more likely to become a mentor themselves (Hill et al., 1989b; Hunt & Michael, 1983; Kram, 1980; Missirian, 1980; Roche, 1979; Shelton, 1982; Watkins, 1986).

The lack of mentorships can have negative consequences for the employee, such as poor performance, limited skill development opportunities, fewer promotions, lower self-efficacy, and decreased motivation (Noe, 1988). The number of mentors one has is not as important as the quality and the intensiveness of the mentoring relationship (Willbur, 1987). However, mentoring does not seem to be as available to female employees as it is to male employees (Bowen, 1985; Cook, 1979; Halcomb, 1980; Hunt & Michael, 1983; Rosen & Jerdee, 1974; Siegerdt, 1983). Men in superior positions are less willing or not at all willing to serve as mentors to women (Marcus, 1989). Women are frequently stereotyped as not possessing necessary skills and abilities, not interested in advancement, lacking in achievement orientation, fearful of success, and unwilling to take risks (Noe, 1988). Since males frequently do not select female proteges, another option for females is to be more aggressive in selecting their own mentors. However, women as organizational newcomers do not understand the informal channels, and the rules for forming informal male/female relationships are unclear (Brass, 1985). There are not enough women in top-level positions to mentor other women, and women mentors do not have as wide a base of power nor are they as well networked as their male counterparts (Noe, 1988). Not only is mentoring less available to women, but there simply are not enough powerful mentors, female or male, for the women in today's organization. "Without a mentor, female employees' needs for achievement and power may be stymied, resulting in a lack of motivation to acquire managerial skills and decreased quality of performance in their present positions" (Noe, 1988, p. 70).

Peer Connections. In addition to one's connections and relationships with mentors, much attention has also been given to the relationships one establishes with colleagues and work peers (Missirian, 1980). These connections with work peers can also enhance power. Such connections are extremely important for those excluded from the mentoring-type connections. In this regard Shapiro, Haseltine, and Rowe included peer support in their concept of the patron relationship—a continuum of support ranging from "mentor" to "sponsor" to "guide" to "peer-pal" (1978, pp. 55–56). Kram and Isabella (1985) also incorporated the notion of peer support and distinguished between types of peer relationships at work varying on the level of intensity and intimacy—information peer, collegial peer, and special peer. Until recently, measures of such peer support were not available to assess the influence of peers on career success. Hill, Bahniuk, Dobos, and Rouner (1989a) developed an instrument to measure mentoring support as well as peer or collegial support. Preliminary studies that investigated the facilitative effects of peer connections have had mixed results. Some evidence suggests that collegial relationships of a task nature are facilitative of one's career success, but collegial relationships of a more friendship/social nature can be counterproductive in terms of career success (Hill et al., 1989b).

Supervisor Connections. Kram and Isabella (1985) suggest that in addition to mentor and collegial support, the relationship with one's boss to develop one's career is also important. Lippitt (1982) advocates the importance of influencing upward. The supervisor can, because of frequent interaction, be a role model or socializing agent and provide for increased interpersonal and cultural understanding. A good upward connection can lead to role negotiation as well as positive interaction and feedback (Falcione & Wilson, 1988; Lippitt, 1982). The leader-member exchange model (LMX) advanced by Graen and others emphasizes the role-making process between the employee and his or her immediate supervisor. Employees who actually engage in the role-making process do not merely perform their roles as formally specified but actually negotiate and shape their organizational role (Haga, Graen, & Dansereau, 1974). Supervisors who trust their subordinates agree to give them wider latitude in defining and shaping their role (Dansereau, Graen, & Haga, 1975). This redefining of one's role is viewed as a power-gaining strategy in which the employee negotiates from the supervisor some of his/her own power to define role responsibilities (Zahn & Wolf, 1981). Employees who practice this power-gaining strategy of leader/member exchange have greater job responsibility, higher productivity, and higher performance outcomes (Graen, Liden, & Hoel, 1982; Liden & Graen, 1980). Noe (1988) suggests reasons why women might be excluded from such leader-member exchange. He asserts that women are less likely to be labeled by their superior as an "in-group" member because they are often seen as lacking such characteristics as leadership, assertiveness, competitiveness, and emotional control. These "in-group" members can negotiate a better working environment and can enjoy more challenging work assignments. They can also participate more in decision making and receive more support from their boss.

Connections with Significant Others Outside of Work Environment. In addition to these professional connections at work with mentors, peers, and supervisors, contemporary significant others (e.g., spouses) and historical significant others (e.g., parents) might also be important connections in the development of one's career and the gaining of power (Watkins, 1986). It had been theorized that women do not receive the same levels of job/career support at home as do their male counterparts (Elman & Gilbert, 1984). A recent national poll shows that while men and women agree that women should be able to pursue a career, they both feel that the woman's career should only be supported and pursued as long as it does not hinder or interfere with the man's career path—"a wife should change jobs and defer career advancement in accordance with the unfolding requirements of the husband's career path" (Simon & Landis, 1989, p. 268). It would seem that having career support outside the workplace would facilitate one's career advancement, relocation opportunities, and career shifts. Such support would empower an individual in terms of being mobile, on the managerial fast track, and ultimately more successful. It is important to determine the relative effects of this type of support or lack thereof on career success. It might be that such connections outside the work environment are even more facilitative than the work connections of mentors, peers, and supervisors.

We can organize these relationships between connection and information power-gaining strategies to career success as shown in Figure 9.1. This is a model of the predisposing factors and the power-gaining communication strategies that lead to career success outcomes.

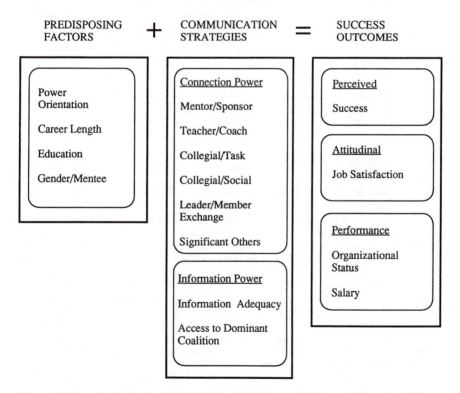

Figure 9.1. A Descriptive Model of Power Gaining Communication Strategies

Description of Model

Predisposing Factors. Several antecedent conditions have emerged as having a predetermining effect on career success. It is important to recognize the relationship of these factors to career success so that their effect can be taken into account when determining the relative effects of various power-gaining communication strategies. Four individual-level variables have been taken into account in the model.

1. *Power orientation,* or one's personal orientation toward power, has been shown to affect various communication behaviors and might predispose one to select or ignore certain power-gaining communication strategies.
2. The longer one's *career length,* the greater the likelihood of achieving higher rank and higher income.
3. Formal *education* also has a positive relationship to success (i.e., more education leads to increased rank and income).
4. *"Gender/mentee" status* has emerged from the mentoring literature as a predisposing factor.[1] Men with mentors are the most successful, followed by men without mentors, followed by women with mentors, and women without mentors (Hill et al., 1989b).

Further development of the model will most likely reveal other predisposing factors and will necessitate revision of the model.[2]

---

[1] As women have entered the workforce, they have found that power is considered a male characteristic (Haslett, 1989). They have also found that women are restricted from organizational participation by negative perceptions of women's work and structural limitations in the organization. If females are more limited in the power strategies which they can use, and if males have over time developed a wide range of acceptable power-gaining behaviors (Johnson, 1976), then it could be argued that it is more difficult for females in the organization to develop power (Farley, 1986). Pilotta (1983) argues that if women understood organizational power, they could empower themselves instead of continuing to use communication patterns of low power and status. Mainiero (1986) suggests that women confirm their own powerlessness by engaging in behaviors that perpetuate female socialization (e.g., acquiescence). Wakefield (1983) discusses in detail the communication patterns of women in relation to organizational power and concludes that women hold lower level positions and salaries; women report lower levels of power, achievement, and performance; women feel more removed from decision making, information, planning, and influence; and women have fewer mentors, fewer network contacts, and less upward confrontation (pp. 216–221).

[2] Early development of the model also included the variable of communication apprehension as a predisposing variable. However, communication apprehension was not significantly related to the communication strategies or success outcomes and was subsequently dropped from the model (Hill et al., 1989b).

Communication Strategies. The model includes those power-gaining communication strategies needed to develop Information Power (Information Adequacy and Access to Dominant Coalition) and Connection Power (Mentor/Sponsor, Teacher/Coach, Collegial/Task, Collegial/Social, Leader-Member Exchange, Significant Others). Future development of the model should also include other bases of power and the strategies to gain them.

Success Outcomes. Downs, Clampitt, and Pfeiffer (1988) advocated studying various organizational outcomes concurrently to determine the relative effects of various communication strategies on these outcomes. Such a multivariate approach seems most appropriate since so much of the power-gaining communication strategy literature has found relationships to so many diverse success outcomes. Three categories of success measures are included in the model. First are the perceived measures of success: perceived success (e.g., I am a successful employee within my present organization), influence (e.g., I influence operations in my area), and fast track (e.g., I feel that I am progressing faster than normal in my career development).[3]

The second category of success outcomes in the model are attitudinal and refer to various aspects of job satisfaction. Is the employee content with various aspects of the job? These perceptual and attitudinal factors are included in the success model so that the employees' views are taken into account in determining what is success. Finally, the third category consists of performance indicators of organizational success: status and income.[4]

Research Supporting Power-Gaining Model

Much research has been conducted establishing many of the individual relationships implied in the model. However, few studies have taken a systematic view to the study of mentoring and other power-gaining communication strategies.

Many previous studies on mentoring simply were case studies of successful individuals. Noe (1988) calls for better operationalizations of

---

[3] Fast trackers once identified are provided different career opportunities (Falcione & Wilson, 1988). Employees who have early successes are usually more assertive, engage in more active communication behaviors, have access to more networks, take more risks, and, subsequently, signal to upper management that they are on the move (Conrad, 1985). Women rarely achieve fast-track status. Sex stereotypes of management may prevent the female from developing this image (Shockley-Zalabak & Staley, 1984). Home demands further restrict mobility and fast track (Borman & Guido-DiBrito, 1986).

[4] Previous study has shown that for academic samples other performance indicators might be more useful, such as number of books and articles published (Hill et al., 1989b).

Hill, Bahniuk, and Dobos

mentoring and rigorous quantitative studies of the antecedents or outcomes of mentoring. Hill et al. (1989a) reviewed the existing instrumentation on mentoring and developed a communication support scale that measured mentoring as well as other types of support including collegial and peer support. In a study of college faculty, Hill et al. (1989b) found three factors of communication support: mentoring support, collegial task support, and collegial social support. In a later study of managers and professionals, a fourth factor emerged, that of teacher/coach support (Bahniuk, Dobos, & Hill, 1990).

The first step in testing this model was the development of a communication support instrument which measured the various dimensions of mentoring and collegial support (Hill et al., 1989a). Results from the academic sample seem to suggest that faculty with high levels of information adequacy, mentoring and collegial support have higher success indicators, especially attitudinal factors of perceived success and job satisfaction. In addition, patterns of communication and success differed for males and females with and without mentors (Hill et al., 1989b). In the study using managers and professionals, the findings were confirmed (Bahniuk, et al., 1990). Dobos, Bahniuk, and Hill (1991) further expanded the model to investigate leader-member exchange and perceptions of fast track among managers. They found that the connection power-gaining communication strategies of leader-member exchanges, mentoring and peer support along with information-adequacy power gaining had effects on the success indicators over and above predisposing factors of career length, education, gender, and "mentee" status.

The results of these studies support the notion that communication interactions in organizations contribute to gaining personal power that enhances career success for individuals in organizations. Currently, our research is investigating the relationship of organizational life cycle, power orientation, access to the dominant coalition, home support connections, and life satisfaction with the other variables in the model.

It is hoped that the continued refinement and testing of the model will lead to a clearer understanding of the relationship of predisposing factors and power-gaining communication strategies and their combined effects on attitudinal, perceptual, and performance indicators of success. Such a comprehensive model should be useful in further theory development as well as useful for employees, both male and female, in developing effective communication strategies for their success.

REFERENCES

Bahniuk, M. H., Dobos, J., & Hill, S. E. K. (1990). The impact of mentoring, collegial support, and information adequacy on career success: A replication. *Journal of Social Behavior and Personality, 5*(4), 431–451.

Borman, C. A., & Guido-DiBrito, F. (1986). The career development of women: Helping Cinderella lose her complex. *Journal of Career Development, 12*, 250–261.

Bowen, D. D. (1985). Were men meant to mentor women? *Training and Development Journal, 24*, 30–34.

Brass, D. J., (1985). Men's and women's networks: A study of interaction patterns and influence in an organization. *Academy of Management Journal, 28*(2), 237–343.

Conrad, C. (1985). Strategic organizational communication: *Cultures, situations, and adaptation*. New York: Holt, Rinehart, & Winston.

Cook, M. F. (1979, November). Is the mentor relationship primarily a male experience? *The Personnel Administrator*, pp. 82–86.

Daniels, T. D., & Logan, L. L. (1983). Communication in women's career development relationships. In R. N. Bostrom (Ed.), *Communication yearbook VII* (pp. 532–552). Beverly Hills, CA: Sage.

Dansereau, F., Graen, G., & Haga, W. J. (1975). A vertical dyad linkage approach to leadership within formal organizations. *Organizational Behavior and Human Performance, 13*, 46–78.

Dobos, J., Bahniuk, M. H., & Hill, S. E. K. (1991). Power-gaining communication strategies and career success. *The Southern Communication Journal, 57*, 35–48.

Downs, C. W., Clampitt, P. G., & Pfeiffer, A. L. (1988). Communication and organizational outcomes. In G. M. Goldhaber & G. A. Barnett (Eds.), *Handbook of organizational communication* (pp. 171–211). Norwood, NJ: Ablex.

Elman, M. R., & Gilbert, L. A. (1984). Coping strategies for role conflict in married professional women with children. *Family Relations, 33*, 317–327.

Falcione, R. L., & Wilson, C. E. (1988). Socialization processes in organizations. In G. M. Goldhaber & G. A. Barnett (Eds.), *Handbook of organizational communication* (pp. 151–169). Norwood, NJ: Ablex.

Farley, M. J. (1986). Communication style and power orientations of managers and non-managers. (Doctoral dissertation, University of Denver, 1986.) *Dissertation Abstracts International, 47*, 1114a.

Fairhurst, G. T., & Snavely, B. K. (1983). Majority and token minority group relationships: Power acquisition and communication. *Academy of Management Review, 8*(2), 292–300.

Frank, A., & Brownell, J. (1989). Communicating to influence others. *Organizational communication and behavior: Communicating to improve performance (2 + 2 = 5)*. New York: Holt, Rinehart, & Winston.

French, J. R. P., & Raven, B. (1959). The basis of social power. In D. Cartwright (Ed.), *Studies in social power*. Ann Arbor: University of Michigan.

Frost, P. J. (1987). Power, politics, and influence. In F. M. Jablin, L. L. Putnam, K. H. Roberts, & L. W. Porter (Eds.), *Handbook of organizational communication: An interdisciplinary perspective*. Newbury Park, CA: Sage.

Goldberg, A. A., Cavenaugh, M. S., & Larson, C. (1983). The meaning of power. *Journal of Applied Communication Research, 11*, 89–108.

Graen, G. B., Liden, R. C., & Hoel, W. (1982). Role of leadership in the employee withdrawal process. *Journal of Applied Psychology, 67*(6), 868–872.

Haga, W. J., Graen, G., & Dansereau, F. (1974). Professionalism and role making in a service organization: A longitudinal investigation. *American Sociological Review, 39*, 122–133.

Halcomb, R. (1980). Mentors and the successful woman. *Across the Board, 17*(2), 13–17.

Hall, R. M., & Sandler, B. R. (1983). Academic mentoring for women students and faculty: A new look at an old way to get ahead. In *Project on the status and education of women*. Washington, DC: Association of American Colleges.

Haslett, B. (1989). *Power, gender, and communication in organizations*. Paper presented at the International Communication Association, San Francisco.

Hershey, P., Blanchard, K. H., & Natemeyer, W. E. (1979). Situational leadership, perception, and the impact of power. *Group and Organization Studies, 4*(4), 418–428.

Hill, S. E. K., Bahniuk, M. H., Dobos, J., & Rouner, D. (1989a). Mentoring and other communication support in the academic setting. *Group and Organization Studies, 14*(3), 355–368.

Hill, S. E. K., Bahniuk, M. H., & Dobos, J., (1989b). The impact of mentoring and collegial support on faculty success: An analysis of support behavior, information adequacy, and communication apprehension. *Communication Education, 38*, 15–33.

Hunt, D. M., & Michael, C. (1983). Mentorship: A career training and development tool. *Academy of Management Review, 8*(3), 475–484.

Johnson, P. (1976). Women and power: Toward a theory of effectiveness. *Journal of Social Issues, 32*(3), 99–110.

Kanter, R. M. (1977). *Men and women of the corporation.* New York: Basic Books.

Kipnis, D., Schmidt, S. M. & Wilkinson, I., (1980). Intraorganizational influence tactics: Explorations in getting one's way. *Journal of Applied Psychology, 65*, 440–452.

Kotter, J. P. (1979). *Power in management: How to understand, acquire, and use it.* New York: Amacom.

Kotter, J. P. (1985). *Power and influence.* New York: The Free Press.

Kram, K. (1980). Mentoring processes at work: Developmental relationships in managerial careers. (Doctoral dissertation, Yale University, 1980). *Dissertation Abstracts International, 41*, 1960B–1961B.

Kram, K. E., & Isabella, L. A. (1985). Mentoring alternatives: The role of peer relationships in career development. *Academy of Management Journal, 28*(1), 110–132.

Liden, R. C., & Graen, G. (1980). Generalizability of the vertical dyad linkage model of leadership. *Academy of Management Journal, 23*(3), 451–465.

Lippitt, R. (1982). The changing leader-follower relationships of the 1980's. *The Journal of Applied Behavioral Science, 18*(3), 395–403.

Mainiero, L. A. (1986). Coping with powerlessness: The relationship of gender and job dependency to empowerment strategy usage. *Administrative Science Quarterly, 31*, 633–653.

Marcus, A. D. (1989, December 4). Successful women lawyers say sex bias has hurt their careers, a survey finds. *The Wall Street Journal*, p. B7.

Merriam, S. (1983). Mentors and proteges: A critical review of the literature. *Adult Education Quarterly, 33*(3), 161–173.

Mintzberg, H. (1983). *Power in and around organizations.* Englewood Cliffs, NJ: Prentice-Hall.

Mintzberg, H. (1985). The organization as a political arena. *Journal of Management Studies, 22*(2), 133–154.

Missirian, A. K. (1980). The process of mentoring in career development of female managers. (Doctoral dissertation, University of Massachusetts, 1980). *Dissertation Abstracts International, 41*, 3654A.

Noe, R. A. (1988). Women and mentoring: A review and research agenda. *Academy of Management Review, 13*, 65–78.

Pfeffer, J. (1981). *Power in organizations.* Marshfield, MA: Pitman.

Pilotta, J. J. (1983). Trust and power in the organization: An overview. In J. J. Pilotta (Ed.), *Women in organizations: Barriers and breakthroughs* (pp. 1–10). Prospect Heights, IL: Waveland Press.

Poole, M. S. (1978). An information-task approach to organizational communication. *Academy of Management Review, 3*, 493–504.

Raven, B. (1965). Social influence and power. In I. D. Steiner & M. Fishbein (Eds.), *Current studies in social psychology* (pp. 371–382). New York: Holt, Rinehart, & Winston.

Richmond, V. P., Davis, L. M., Saylor, K., & McCroskey, J. (1984). Power strategies in organizations. *Human Communication Research, 11*(1), 85–108.

Roche, G. R. (1979, January–February). Much ado about mentors. *Harvard Business Review,* pp. 14–28.

Rosen, B., & Jerdee, T. H. (1974). Sex stereotyping in the executive suite. *Harvard Business Review, 52,* 45–58.

Schilit, W. K., & Loche, E. A. (1982). Methods used to influence superiors. *Administrative Science Quarterly, 27,* 304–316.

Shapiro, E., Haseltine, G., & Rowe, M. (1978). Moving up: Role models, mentors, and the patron system. *Sloan Management Review, 19,* 51–58.

Shelton, C. K. (1982). The relationship of mentoring and behavioral style to selected job success variables. (Doctoral dissertation, Northern Illinois University, 1982). *Dissertation Abstracts International, 43,* 2072A.

Shockley-Zalabak, P., & Staley, C. C. (1984). *The female professional: Communicative proficiencies and predictors of organizational advancement.* Paper funded through a grant from the Research and Creative Works Committee, University of Colorado at Colorado Springs.

Siegerdt, G. A. (1983). Communication profiles for organizational communication behavior: Are men and women different? *Women's Studies in Communication, 6,* 46–57.

Simon, R. J., & Landis, J. M (1989). Women's and men's attitudes about a woman's place and role. *Public Opinion Quarterly, 53,* 265–276.

Spiker, B. K., & Daniels, T. D. (1981). Information adequacy and communication relationships: An empirical examination of 18 organizations. *The Western Journal of Speech Communication, 45,* 342–354.

Wakefield, D. G. (1983). Perceptions of organizational communication and power among female and male administrators. (Doctoral dissertation, East Texas State University, 1983). *Dissertation Abstracts International, 44,* 1626A.

Watkins, H. D. (1986). An analysis of dyadic career developmental relationships in academe. (Doctoral dissertation, University of Georgia, 1986). *Dissertation Abstracts International, 47,* 2057A.

Willbur, J. (1987, November). Does mentoring breed success? *Training and Developmental Journal,* pp. 38–41.

Zahn, G. L., & Wolf, G. (1981). Leadershnip and the art of cycle maintenance: A simulation model of superior-subordinate interaction. *Organizational Behavior and Human Performance, 28,* 26–49.

Author Index

Subject Index